The Highland Regiments
TIGERS IN TARTAN

The Highland Regiments
TIGERS IN TARTAN

W. Pratt Paul

IMPULSE BOOKS

ABERDEEN

First published by Impulse Publications Ltd.
28 Guild Street, Aberdeen
Scotland
1971

© W. Pratt Paul 1971

PRINTED IN SCOTLAND AT
THE UNIVERSITY PRESS
ABERDEEN

Cuimhnichibh na suinn
Nach maireann
Mairidh an cliu beo gu brath

In memory of the heroes
who are no more
May their fame live for ever

Contents

Illustrations

Into battle with the 'Auld Forty-Twa'- odyssey of The Black Watch

There is no word in the Gaelic for 'rustlers',
but there is a phrase for 'vigilantes'. It is
Am Freiceadan Dubh — The Black Watch. Like
the rolling American West in the days of the
pioneers Scotland too had range wars, cattle
and sheep stealers and bandits

CLAN fought clan, clan stole from clan and sometimes they joined forces in plundering forays deep into the Lowlands. Then the Highlanders with their spoils vanished into the steaming mists of the hills and high passes.

Much of the Highlands consisted of mountains, moors and hills, the ground was poor and unproductive though some areas yielded good crops and grazing. The clan chiefs organised 'protection rackets'. They would promise not to steal from a farmer if he paid them an agreed sum of money. It was 'Pay up – or else!' And no doubt a finger was drawn across the throat by way of emphasis.

But should some patrolling Redcoat soldiers appear over the horizon during a raid the opposing clansmen usually joined forces and took on the Government troops. There was no shinty or soccer in these days and a skirmish in the hills was welcomed by the Highlanders. If the Redcoats were in force the clansmen disappeared into the mists and the Sassenachs – probably burdened with some casualties – were hesitant to pursue them in case of ambush.

These affrays provided invaluable battle training for young clansmen and before long they became as skilled as their elders in that popular Highland pastime – baiting the Redcoats. Several of these encounters added to the wonderful 'repertoire' of anecdotes re-told to up and coming generations. Some of the ploys are the themes of poems, songs and stories and are kept evergreen in pipe airs, known as 'rants', and in the music of the *clarsach*, or Highland harp.

Emboldened by their successes some clans took things a logical stage further. They formed alliances and 'non-agression' pacts and the raids were launched more frequently with deeper penetration of the prosperous Lowlands. And the hauls, of course, were larger – good economics!

Possibly tired of early methods of 'buck-passing' – and no doubt under pressure from powerful sources – the authorities raised bands of Highlanders and formed them into Independent Companies to police the turbulent Highlands. The authorities thought they were being clever by so implementing the old adage 'it takes a thief to catch a thief'. But soon these fore-runners of the Civil Service began to have doubts. . . .

Naturally the clans resented such drastic action by gentlemen on the wrong side of the Highland line. It was felt that they were challenging the ancient and acknowledged national sport of the Highlanders. And, as they were employing clansmen against clansmen they regarded this as 'the unkindest cut of all!'

The Independent Companies were raised in 1624 to 'watch upon the braes'. These formations had their pipers – and 'fiddlers' too. For prisoners were sometimes set free on a pay-ment being made and it is on record that there were occasions on which these armed Highland policemen drew more pay than their entitlement.

They moved away from a district on being forewarned of an impending clan clash or raid – provided, of course, they were 'squared'. Understanding, obliging guardians of the law were the Independent Companies, with a flair for 'private enterprise'. Maybe the 'fines' and other payments went into their 'Comforts Fund'!

After the Jacobite Rising of 1715 King George I had troubled dreams – and probably not a few nightmares – about bands of Highlanders under arms and on the rampage. So, in 1717, the Independent Companies whose loyalty at times was suspect were disbanded.

The Disarming Act of 1725, devised to curb Jacobite activity, forbade the carrying of arms by private individuals, with severe penalties on those who did not comply. Bereft of their weapons the Highlanders were downcast and dispirited. But not for long.

The Independent Companies were reformed in 1725 by General George Wade, of bridge-building and road making fame throughout Scotland. The six units were designated Independ-end Highland Companies.

They immediately attracted young non-Jacobite Highlanders of good family. They were allowed to bear arms and wear High-land dress and many of the volunteers had gillies, or personal servants, who attended them in quarters and carried their bag-gage on the march. And a number of the *saighdearan* (Highland soldiers) rode ponies to and from parades.

Men from clans reckoned to be loyal – Campbell, Grant, Fraser and Munro – were prominently identified in the ranks. The spirit, discipline and bearing of the recruits was in sharp contrast to that in most regiments of Infantry of the Line which at this period had more than a leaven of ne'er-do-wells, outcasts, misfits and off-scourings of prisons.

The three principal units, with a strength of about 100 men each, were commanded by Lord Lovat, Sir Duncan Campbell of Lochnell and Colonel Grant of Ballindalloch. The three other companies, mustering around 75 men each, were led by Colonel Alexander Campbell of Finab, John Campbell of Carrick and George Munro of Culcairn.

In the ranks of the Independent Highland Companies the millennium was reached. For the Glencoe Massacre was forgotten and Campbells and MacDonalds soldiered side by side and were staunch comrades-in-arms.

At one period General Wade, under orders to enforce the hated Disarming Act, had four companies of this territorial militia under his command when Royalist forces were engaged in the construction of roads, bridges and forts. Object was the quick movement of troops and supplies to any threatened point and this was one of the factors which contributed to the Jacobite debacle of 1745-6.

In September 1739, King George II issued a Royal Warrant, or Letter of Service, forming the companies into the 43rd, or Highland Regiment of Foot and four more units were added. About 1,000 men assembled at the first muster, which took place on the banks of the River Tay near Aberfeldy, Perthshire, in May 1740. A cairn still marks the spot, and in 1885 a monument was erected portraying a soldier of 'The Watch' in the uniform of 1740.

A decade later, in 1749, the corps was re-numbered the 42nd, 'ancestor' of The Black Watch – *Am Freiceadan Dubh* in the Gaelic – Scotland's senior Highland regiment.

So that no ill feeling would be aroused by choosing a commanding officer from a particular clan, the command of the new regiment was given to a Lowlander – John, 20th Earl of Crawford. For three years it continued to perform the duties previously carried out by the Independent Companies.

The original uniform was similar to that worn by the Independent Companies – short red jacket faced with buff and white lace, red waistcoat, 12-yards long plaid – which also served as greatcoat, blanket and groundsheet – black leather belt with metal buckle, red and white hose, buckled shoes and blue bonnet. Sporrans were of badger skin and a cartridge-belt and sword-belt were worn.

The tartan was the 'Government Tartan', or 'Military Tartan', also known as the 'Universal Tartan'. In a slightly modified form – with coloured overstripes – this became the basis of several regimental and clan tartans. That worn by 'The Watch', however, has no clan significance and when it was adopted by the regiment it became known as the '42nd Tartan'.

The dark tartan is thought to have given the regiment its name – The Black Watch. But there is another opinion which associates it with the 'black Hanoverians', so long hated in many parts of the Highlands.

The Government provided each man with a musket, bayonet and broadsword but many of the Highlanders supplemented this issue with a brace of pistols, dirk and targe, or shield. Sergeants carried the Lochaber axe. The regiment at the outset was employed in detachments throughout the Highlands and in 1741 Hugh, 12th Lord Sempill, became its colonel.

Two stalwart gentlemen of 'The Watch', Privates Gregor MacGregor and John Campbell, were summoned to St. James's Palace, London, where they performed drill and weapon exercises before King George II, the Duke of Cumberland and General Wade. The 'musketeers' were much admired and as they took their leave each was 'tipped' with a golden guinea. This the proud Highlanders regarded as an insult, but concealing their indignation, they tossed the coins to a servant at the palace gates.

In March 1743, the 43rd was ordered to London and after concentrating at Perth the regiment commenced the long march south. Then there began an unfortunate train of events which culminated in The Black Watch Mutiny.

Though the corps was raised on a territorial basis the War Office had secretly decided to send it to Flanders. An inkling of this intention leaked out and there was bitter resentment among the Highlanders.

6

The authorities informed them that the move to London was for a Royal Review, and when the Highlanders expressed surprise that they had to march all the way to the capital to participate in this it was explained that the King, who had never before seen a Highland regiment, wished to honour the 43rd.

But the seeds of discontent had been sown. On the march they encountered recruiting cadres from regiments that had been practically wiped out on service in the disease-ridden West Indies and the Highlanders began to suspect a similar fate was in store for themselves.

When the 43rd paraded on Finchley Common transports were waiting at Gravesend to take the regiment to Flanders. Neither the King nor the Prince of Wales attended the review and this was taken as an insult. The veteran General Wade who had frequently commanded Independent Companies – took the parade and afterwards the Highlanders learned they were bound for service overseas.

Highland tempers flared. A secret plan was formulated and over 100 of them, bearing arms, assembled on Finchley Common at midnight on May 17. News of this gathering became known and two officers of the regiment tried to reason with the men before the affair went any further. They were driven off at bayonet point and a sergeant who accompanied the officers was struck by Private Farquhar Shaw.

The disaffected Highlanders marched for Scotland. Brigadier-General Blakeney was charged with their interception and arrest and Lord Sempill was ordered by General Wade to keep the remainder of his regiment under arms to prevent fresh incidents.

The companies adopted a threatening attitude and there was another march out in this case by about forty disillusioned Highlanders Again Finchley Common was the rendezvous. They were overtaken near Barnet by three of their officers and all but seven returned to duty. The recalcitrant seven later rejoined their fellows but four of them were court-martialled.

General Blakeney with a force of dragoons caught up with the main body at Lady Wood, near Oundle, Northamptonshire. He dispatched an officer with instructions to demand the immediate surrender of the mutineers.

The officer approached the Highlanders and delivered this ultimatum. They refused to lay down their arms and sought a free pardon from the General. Four, including Corporal Samuel Macpherson, trained their muskets on the officer and threatened to shoot him if he continued the parley.

The officer, Captain Ball of Wade's Regiment, gave the mutineers an hour to reconsider and asked for two of their number to accompany him through the wood. When he and his escort moved off he prevailed on one of them to come with him and persuaded the other to go back and advise his comrades to give up their weapons and surrender.

The latter soldier soon returned with 13 men and half an hour later 17 others followed. The officer blew the priming charges from each of their muskets and the 30 mutineers were marched before the General.

Captain Ball went back to Lady Wood and the remainder capitulated and were rounded up. Under heavy guard they were taken back to London and imprisoned in the Tower.

Before the Highlanders surrendered – or the court-martial warrant was signed – the Lords Justice, with the concurrence of King George II, had already decided that 'some of the most guilty' should be shot. The court-martial was, therefore, a gross travesty of justice.

It assembled in the Tower on June 8 with Major-General John Folliott, Colonel of the 1st Foot Guards presiding, and lasted a week. The proceedings were complicated by the fact that few of the 107 accused understood English and a Gaelic interpreter had to be summoned.

First to be tried was Private William Gordon, who presented a petition on behalf of all the mutineers. It complained that no allowance had been given them for the Highland weapons most of them carried; that they were not paid sufficient for the upkeep of their brogues and that they ought to have been issued with two shirts per year instead of one.

They pled guilty to the charge of mutiny. But the plea was made *'We were levied only to guard the Highlands and not to be employed elsewhere'*.

The officers gave the soldiers excellent character references but in spite of this, and the fact that several of them had not been properly enlisted, all except one man were pronounced guilty and sentenced to death.

The exception had deserted three days before the review and

was deemed not guilty of mutiny. He was sentenced to receive 1,000 strokes of the lash.

But pardons were forthcoming for most of the Highlanders on condition they joined regiments in the West Indies – the death sentence in another form!

But authority was adamant that an example must be made and three men were not reprieved – Corporal Samuel Macpherson, his brother Malcolm and Private Farquhar Shaw. Samuel Macpherson was a linguist and had studied law, Malcolm had assisted on his father's estate in Laggan and Shaw joined the regiment when his droving business failed.

Though Corporal Macpherson was suspected as the ringleader it was never proved. At the court martial the Highlanders denied under duress that they had a leader. The soldiers of 'The Watch' were loyal to each other in the face of death.

The three died bravely in front of a firing squad on Tower Parade at 6 o'clock on the morning of July 18, 1743, in the presence of their comrades and the garrison. And so a shadow was cast over British justice. . . .

The historian of The Black Watch Mutiny, H. D. MacWilliam, in 1910 wrote: 'On George II and his government must rest the responsibility for the mutiny, and the stigma for all time of the treacherous and tyrannical treatment accorded to the brave and loyal men of The Black Watch – men of whom it may be truly said, without any disparagement of the men of the Highland regiments to-day, "We ne'er shall see their like again".'

The remainder of the 43rd, totalling over 900, embarked for Flanders and fought with outstanding gallantry at Fontenoy in May 1745, during the War of the Austrian Succession. Dutch and Austrian resistance was half-hearted and the French were the victors. During this battle the war-pipes of the Scots and the Irish sounded on opposing sides as the Irish were in the service of France.

The Highlanders, after taking part in an unsuccessful attack, hurled themselves at the enemy to cover the withdrawal of their Allies and prevented retreat from developing into rout. 'The Highland furies rushed in upon us with more violence than ever did a sea driven by a tempest' was how a French officer described their onslaught.

After the doom of the Stewart cause at Culloden came the

Abolition and Proscription of the Highland Dress – an attempt by George II to smash the clan system and all it stood for. An excerpt read:

That from and after the first day of August, one thousand seven hundred and forty-seven, no man or boy within that part of Great Britain called Scotland, other than shall be employed as officers and soldiers of His Majesty's Forces, shall, on any pretext whatever, wear or put on the clothes commonly called Highland clothes – that is to say, the plaid, philabeg or little kilt, trouse, shoulder belts, or any part whatever of what peculiarly belongs to the Highland garb, and that no tartan or party coloured plaid or stuff shall be used for greatcoats or upper coats, and if any such person shall presume after the first day of August to wear or put on the aforesaid garments or any part of them, every such person so offending shall be liable to be transported to any of His Majesty's plantations beyond the seas, there to remain for the space of seven years.

And so the Sassenach scourge descended and lay heavily upon the Highlands. The repeal came in 1782, but by then many of the clan tartans had been lost, never to re-appear. Under the appropriate clause in the Abolition Act, however, the tartan of The Black Watch continued to be worn as the loyalty of the 43rd was never in doubt.

In June 1746, the regiment sailed for America, but the ships were driven back three times by contrary winds and the 43rd arrived in Ireland to be stationed in Limerick for several months. Later that year the regiment landed at Quiberon, capturing a fort and a number of guns from the French. The Highlanders proceeded to Flanders in 1747, and after an uneventful spell of duty returned to Britain towards the close of the following year.

While serving in Ireland from 1748 to 1756 The Highland Regiment of Foot was re-numbered, becoming the 42nd in 1751. In the spring of 1756 they sailed for America to operate against the French and their Indian allies.

From New York the 42nd went on to Albany where the Highlanders were trained in Indian warfare. The regiment was included in the force which General Abercromby led in June 1758, against Ticonderoga, a strongly fortified position between Lake George and Lake Champlain.

In July, without artillery support, an assault was launched

which was hurled back with heavy loss. The 42nd, in reserve, witnessed the frightful execution wrought by the enemy, and without waiting for the order, charged to avenge their comrades.

A few succeeded in reaching and mounting the fortifications and hacked their way inside only to fall under the murderous fusilades. Three times the Highlanders were ordered to retire from the shambles before they obeyed. In over four hours of ghastly fighting the regiment lost 647 men out of a total of 1,100.

A Royal Warrant in the same month conferred on the regiment the title 'Royal' and the uniform facings were changed to blue. About this time authority was given for the raising of a second battalion. This was completed at Perth by October, 840 Highlanders responding.

The 2nd was dispatched to the West Indies, and in 1759 formed part of the force which made a determined but unsuccessful attack on Martinique, after which it participated in the expedition against Guadaloupe. The new battalion later arrived in North America.

The 1st and 2nd were in the second assault on Ticonderoga, which fell after a brief action lasting only half an hour. The two battalions were present at the capture of Montreal in August 1760, as a result of which all Canada came under British control on the surrender of the French.

They were also in the force which in 1761 shared in the capture of the Windward Islands and, early in the following year, Martinique and Havannah. In 1763, on the disbandment of the 2nd Battalion a contingent from the 2nd joined the 1st.

For four years the 1st operated against the Indians, and the Highlanders distinguished themselves at Bushy Run in July 1763, during the relief of Fort Pitt. Here their stealth and craft outwitted the Indians who were ambushed in a deadly gauntlet of fire. Service followed in Ireland and early in May 1776, The Royal Highland Regiment embarked at Greenock to take the field against the American colonists.

A gale separated the transports and one was captured by an American fighting ship. A prize crew was put on board, but a few days afterwards the 42nd overpowered their captors. They brought the vessel safely into port only to find it was in American hands. The enemy vainly tried to enlist the

Highlanders to fight for their cause and two years later exchanged them for American prisoners, the Scots rejoining their corps.

The other transports made Staten Island. The 42nd fought well at Brooklyn – where George Washington narrowly escaped capture – and a few weeks later, at Bloomingdale, the Highlanders, though heavily outnumbered, repelled an attack.

In an assault at White Plains, north of New York, they cleared the Colonists from the heights after a long stiff climb. The Highlanders were heavily engaged at Brandywine, Germantown, Monmouth, Pisquatua, Charlestown and Yorktown. When peace came in October 1783, they moved to Nova Scotia.

In 1779 another second battalion was raised, on this occasion by Lieutenant-Colonel Norman MacLeod of MacLeod. With several of his officers from the 1st Battalion a nucleus was formed and the battalion was embodied at Perth in 1780. It was mainly a MacLeod formation.

The 2nd was ordered to India in 1782 for service against Hyder Ali and his French supporters. The battalion took part in the capture of Mangalore in 1783 and held it during a long siege. The small garrison of 400 British troops and 1,500 sepoys was attacked again and again by numerically superior forces of Indians and French but fought back for nine months.

Three relief attempts failed and, reduced by disease, famine and casualties to dire extremity, the defenders surrendered at the close of January 1784. The enemy commander, Tippoo, was so impressed by their resistance that he allowed them to march out with all the honours of war.

In 1786 the 2nd Battalion 'hived off' from the 42nd to become a separate corps – The 73rd Highland Regiment. In 1787 a teen-age officer was commissioned in the 73rd. He was Arthur Wellesley, later to become the Duke of Wellington – the man who out-generalled Napoleon Bonaparte.

Back in Flanders once more in 1794 the 42nd campaigned around Nijmegen, Arnhem and along the banks of the Rhine. They performed a *tour de force* at Geldermalsen in January, 1795. In the British retiral two companies, serving in the rear-guard, attacked the oncoming French cavalry and re-captured two abandoned guns. The Highlanders manhandled the pieces across rough ground to safety, fighting off the enemy and suffering considerable losses.

Geldermalsen was the one memorable engagement for the Highlanders in a disastrous campaign in which the British troops were very short of supplies and poorly supported by their allies. The ground lay deep in snow, the cold was intense, and they were without greatcoats. In spite of the appalling conditions, however, the losses of the 42nd were comparatively light due to the natural hardiness of the Highlanders.

At King George III's birthday parade on June 4, 1795, every soldier was presented with red vulture feathers. With the Highlanders of the 42nd this gift became a 'keepsake' and the distinctive Red Hackle in the bonnets of The Black Watch still identifies this grand old regiment.

In August 1822, an Army Order authorised its exclusive use by the 42nd. Many hold the belief, however, that the Red Hackle is a permanent reminder of the regiment's service in North America.

The badge of The Black Watch consists of The Royal Cypher within the Garter; the badge and motto of the Order of the Thistle; in each of the four corners The Royal Cypher is ensigned with the Crown; the Sphinx is superscribed 'Egypt'.

In October 1822, the regiment embarked for the West Indies but the ships were dispersed by severe gales. Five companies reached Barbados but Headquarters and other five companies were driven back to Portsmouth where orders were then received to proceed to Gibraltar.

The companies in the West Indies were at the capture of St. Lucia and St. Vincent after hard fighting in 1797. Re-united at 'Gib.', the regiment sailed for Minorca, which was seized in 1798. The 42nd was also included in the expeditions launched against Genoa and Cadiz.

The Highlanders led Sir Ralph Abercrombie's landing in Aboukir Bay early in March 1801, and with bayonets fixed fought their way up the steep sandhills. Taking up a defensive position they hurled back the French and captured the Colour of the 'Invincibles'.

Cavalry charged in great strength and burst in among them, but the Highlanders rallied in little groups and battled on. Casualties were severe, but reinforcements came up and the enemy retired with depleted numbers, the British in close pursuit. A Highlander saved General Abercrombie from being sabred by a French Dragoon officer, whom he tackled and bayoneted.

The Battle of Alexandria was one of The Royal Highland Regiment's finest actions and its sacrifice and gallantry earned it the right to bear the Sphinx superscribed 'Egypt' on the Colours. With the enemy surrendering the town this brief campaign in the Land of the Pharaohs came to an end.

In 1802 a second battalion was once more raised and in 1805 it was dispatched to Ireland. The 1st Battalion in July 1808, joined British forces at Lisbon to participate in the Peninsular War raging across Spain and Portugal.

General Sir John Moore advanced to link up with the Spaniards and join battle with the French. Near Salamanca he learned that the Spanish armies had been decisively beaten and that several strong French columns, totalling over 100,000 men, were converging on him. On Christmas Eve, 1808, he ordered a withdrawal to the coast for evacuation.

And so began the epic fighting Retreat to Corunna – a march of over 200 miles involving the crossing of the Cantabrian Mountains in the dead of winter. And Corunna was reached in 19 days. Chilled to the bone the British marched through howling blizzards and fought a series of desperate delaying actions in deep snow, freezing rain, mist, icy sleet and drizzle with the enemy always close behind.

Transport and commissariat broke down and often there was no food. The men were soon tattered, famished, footsore and there was no shelter. Sick and wounded succumbed by the score. It was march or die.

Again and again the 42nd was ordered to hold up the French advance and fought a number of violent rearguard actions in which they beat back the numerically superior enemy with rifle, bullet and bayonet. But for many of the Highlanders their last great fight was on the road to Corunna, their shroud a blanket of snow and the howling of the wind their requiem.

Thousands of gaunt, hollow-eyed limping scarecrows reached Corunna early in January only to find that the evacuation ships had not arrived. The French came up in considerable strength intent on administering the *coup de grace*. General Sir John

Moore rallied his pitiful remnant of an army and achieved the impossible.

They held the hills above the harbour and in a fierce four-hour battle sent the enemy reeling back in disorder. At Elvina on January 16, 1809, the 42nd poured a withering volley into the French and at once closed with the bayonet. Corunna is a proud battle honour of 'The Auld Forty-Twa'.

The ships were now waiting and the British troops went on board at night. Throughout the evacuation the French remained at a safe distance and made no attempt to interfere. But many of the ragged, barefoot verminous survivors were destined to wreak a terrible vengeance on Napoleon's colourful regiments at a later date.

Another ordeal of horror was the lot of the 1st Battalion several months later. It formed part of the ill-fated Walcheren expedition in July 1809, intended for an attack on Antwerp. Walcheren lay well below sea-level and the force of 40,000 men was soon ravaged by fever. Several thousand died, and there was an evacuation from the Dutch coast within a few weeks with 11,000 sick.

The 2nd Battalion was sent to Portugal early in 1809. Principal actions were Busaco, the assault on Ciudad Rodrigo, 'bloody Badajos' and Fuentes d'Onor. In the spring of 1812 the 1st Battalion arrived and absorbed what was left of the 2nd.

The Royal Highland Regiment joined battle at Salamanca and was active at the siege of Burgos. The regiment was well to the fore in the numerous engagements in the Pyrenees, at Nivelle and Pampeluna, made an assault-crossing of the Nive, and took part in the bitter fighting at Orthes.

At Toulouse the retreating French made a determined last stand. The Highlanders led the British onslaught on their re-doubts which they cleared at bayonet point in concentrated fire. The few survivors formed a battle-trained nucleus when the regiment was brought up to strength.

After Toulouse the Duke of Wellington led his army into France and Napoleon abdicated. In June 1814, the 1st arrived in Ireland, and in October the 2nd Battalion was disbanded at Aberdeen.

On the escape of Napoleon from Elba war again broke out, and in May 1815, the 42nd sailed for Belgium. At Quatre

Bras – prelude to Waterloo – The Royal Highland Regiment was drawn up in a cornfield. In a charge by French Lancers their squares suffered severely but the Highlanders closed their ranks and fought back to empty numerous saddles among the enemy cavalry.

The magnificent bearing of the 42nd at Quatre Bras and Waterloo under the concentrated fire of the French artillery, their calm and courage when facing the massed cavalry charges and their desperate unyielding defence during attack by close-packed lines of infantry won the regiment a special mention in the Duke of Wellington's dispatches.

At Waterloo an ensign of the 92nd (Gordon Highlanders) was killed and the French would have captured the Colour had not a Grenadier of the 42nd rushed forward. On finding he could not disengage it from the dead officer's grasp he lifted ensign and Colour and bore them to safety. The gallant Colonel of the French Imperial Guards ordered his men not to fire on the Highlander.

The Royal Highland Regiment spent several months with the occupation forces in Paris. The 2nd Battalion was 'resurrected' in 1842, but while both battalions were stationed in Bermuda the 1st absorbed the 2nd in 1850.

The 42nd landed at Scutari in June 1854, and formed part of the Highland Brigade, which distinguished itself in the grim fighting by the Alma during September. The brigade put to flight eight Russian battalions and forced the retiral of another four. A month later The Highland Brigade again drove back the Czar's hordes, on this occasion at Balaclava.

In May 1855, the 42nd was included in the two expeditions sent against Kertch, and on returning from the second took up position before Sevastopol. After the failure of the British assault on the Redan Redoubt in September, The Highland Brigade moved into the trenches.

The Highlanders were to attack on the following day, but a patrol got into the enemy position and found the Redan abandoned. Mines were sprung, and with a shattering roar this key bastion in the Russian defence system went up in smoke. The enemy evacuated Sevastopol and the Crimean War ended with the rumble and flash of explosions.

This campaign was a masterpiece of muddle and incompetence. Almost criminal negligence was responsible for shortages of equipment, food, clothing, shelter and medical supplies, particularly during the severe winter. Casualties were heavy, and cholera and dysentery rife. The hero was the common soldier. And there was a heroine – Florence Nightingale, the Lady of the Lamp.

In December 1857, the regiment marched from Allahabad to the relief of Cawnpore with General Sir Henry Havelock's column, covering about 80 miles in 56 hours during the rainy season and fighting several sharp engagements en route with sepoy mutineers. Without waiting for the artillery to come up, the Highlanders rushed the enemy guns outside Cawnpore with the bayonet and silenced them, then hurled back a cavalry charge.

On entering the town the relief force found that all British residents and troops had been overwhelmed and massacred. The Highlanders went berserk when they caught up with the retreating mutineers at Seria Ghat. The sepoys and sowars made a run for it, abandoning seventeen guns and a large amount of equipment and baggage.

During 1858 the 42nd experienced further severe fighting, principally at the siege and capture of Lucknow, where Captain F. E. H. Farquharson won the Victoria Cross, and in the attack on Fort Rooyah. In this assault Quartermaster-Sergeant John Simpson, Lance-Corporal Alexander Thomson and Privates James Davis and Edward Spence also won this coveted award. Another Victoria Cross was earned by Colour-Sergeant William Gardiner at Bareilly, where he saved the life of his commanding officer.

The severity of the fighting and heroism of the 42nd was reflected in further awards of the Victoria Cross – to Privates Walter Cook and Duncan Miller at Sissaya Ghat. With all the officers and N.C.O.s down, they organised the defence of 37 men from sunrise till sundown and kept at bay over 2,000 mutineers. On the collapse of the Indian Mutiny detachments scoured the country in general mopping-up operations.

On September 12, 1861, Queen Victoria authorised The Royal Highland Regiment to be distinguished, in addition to that title, by its earliest name – The Black Watch. The full designation then became the 42nd, or The Royal Highland Regiment (The Black Watch.

In early December 1873, the regiment sailed for the Gold Coast and about a month later marched on Kumasi, 150 miles inland, capital of the murderous King Coffee Calcalli, scourge of West Africa. The brief hard Ashantee campaign was fought over difficult terrain in intense heat, the Highlanders hacking their way through dense jungle and battling out of frequent ambushes.

Often the first sign of impending action was the jettisoning of their loads and sudden headlong flight by the native porters. Disregarding flank attacks and ambuscades to delay their rapid advance, the Highlanders shot and bayoneted their way through the enemy, who broke and fled before their onslaughts.

The pipes skirled amid the crack of rifles, the clash of steel, the roar of King Coffee's warriors and Highland cheers. Kumasi was entered and burned with all its array of skulls and shrines of torture and human sacrifice.

Principal engagements were at Amoaful and Ordashu. In the wild melee at Amoaful Lance-Sergeant Samuel McGaw won the Victoria Cross. The Ashantee Campaign was marred by the unfortunate death of so many soldiers not from the bullet but as a result of eating salt beef which had been packed by the authorities for the Crimean War, some nineteen years previously.

Under the Army reforms of 1881 the regiment was styled The Black Watch (Royal Highlanders), and in the same year the 73rd Regiment – which had been the 2nd Battalion since it was raised in 1779 until it became a separate corps in 1786 – returned to the 'fold', resuming as the 2nd Battalion.

The 73rd Highland Regiment was in the force which in 1791 toiled across the Ghats. Guns and heavy equipment were manhandled among the rocks and paths had to be cut through the jungle. In spite of strenuous efforts the expedition failed and the troops had to backtrack through torrential rain and were frequently harried by Tippoo's cavalry.

The regiment was in the attack on his stronghold, Seringapatam, and, in 1793, at the taking of Pondicherry. It campaigned against the Dutch in Ceylon in 1795. The power of Tippoo was finally broken in 1799 with the assault and capture of Seringapatam after bitter fighting. Tippoo was killed, 1,000 guns taken and over £1,000,000 in cash. With the fall of his capital, Mysore, the war ended.

The 73rd returned to Scotland in 1806 and raised a second battalion. In 1809 the regiment was ordered to discontinue wearing Highland dress and adopt the uniform of Infantry of the Line. Thus, until 1881 the 73rd lost its Highland identity. In 1809 the 1st Battalion sailed for Australia and on arrival was employed in suppressing disorders among the colonists and hunting down bushrangers in the outback.

The 2/73rd was sent to Stralesund to aid the Swedish Army in 1813. In mid-September the battalion entered the fray at Ghorde just in time to turn the tide of battle, the Scots attacking the French centre which was rolled back by their impetuous charge. The battalion next served in Holland and was in action at the capture of Antwerp in 1814.

The 2nd acquitted itself valiantly at Quatre Bras, again arriving at the crisis of the engagement. At Waterloo it was exposed to the full shock and impact of eleven cavalry charges and also withstood the terrific artillery bombardment unleashed by the French. The battalion re-crossed the Channel and was disbanded in May 1816, 300 of its officers and other ranks joining the 1st Battalion in Ceylon.

The 1st Battalion had arrived in Ceylon in August 1814, and was engaged in operations against the King of Kandy, whose capital was entered in February 1815. Split up into detachments, the 1st maintained order, continuing in this role until 1816. One detachment was trapped at Badulla, but help arrived in time to save it from annihilation.

While in Canada in 1838 the regiment was on duty during political unrest. In 1846 the 73rd sailed from Cork, and, arriving at Rio de Janeiro, moved to Montevideo, which it defended for seven months against the attacking Argentinian forces. In the same year the regiment sailed for South Africa, the transport coming near to disaster in a gale which swept the mouth of the Great Fish River.

Arriving at Port Elizabeth, the 73rd marched off to deal with the marauding Kaffir tribesmen – operations which dragged on intermittently until 1856. It was during this protracted campaign that the troopship Birkenhead was wrecked near Simonstown in the early hours of February 26, 1852.

Reinforcements for several regiments, including the 73rd, were on board, and their splendid discipline when the ship struck a rock and began to sink ensured the survival of all the women and children – the families of soldiers.

There being insufficient lifeboats, the troops – after assisting the women and children into the boats – silently lined up on deck and did not break ranks until the vessel began to settle. And when they struck out for the shore they avoided the crowded lifeboats though in shark-infested waters. Fifty-six men of the 73rd drowned – the largest number of deaths suffered by any of the regiments represented on the Birkenhead.

The 73rd sailed for India in 1858 and arrived in time to take part in the final round-up of the mutineers. From Calcutta it marched for Benares and detachments were employed on a series of punitive expeditions and general pacification duties. In 1861 it was back in England, and in August 1862, was styled the 73rd (Perthshire) Regiment.

The remainder of its existence as a separate regiment was uneventful. The 73rd returned to the U.K. from India in 1881 to rejoin its 'parent' formation – the 'Auld Forty-Twa' – as its 2nd Battalion.

On the outbreak of Colonel Arabi Pasha's rebellion against the Khedive of Egypt and the wanton slaughter of Europeans in Alexandria, the 1st Battalion The Black Watch joined The Highland Brigade at Ramleh in August 1882. The transports steamed up the Suez Canal and landed the troops at Ishmailia. Action followed at El Magfar, Tel-el-Mahuta and Kassassin.

The Black Watch marched across the desert and surprised the enemy at first light on September 13 at Tel-el-Kebir. The order 'Fix Bayonets!' rang out and the buglers sounded the 'Charge'.

Pipes skirling, the Highlanders rushed forward and cleared the Egyptians and Soudanese from their strong entrenchments. Soon they were marching into Cairo, Arabi Pasha and 10,000 of his men surrendering without firing a shot. The battalion then spent a long term on detachment duty in Lower Egypt.

The 1st Black Watch went to Suakin in February 1884, as part of the force assembled to deal with the hostile tribes of the Eastern Soudan led by the Mahdi, who was preaching a *jehad*, or holy war. Principal actions were at El Teb and Tamai. In the fierce encounter with the Dervishes at Tamai Private Thomas Edwards – attached to The Naval Brigade as a mule driver –

though wounded by a spear thrust displayed conspicuous bravery in defending his gun when all the crew had been killed.

The Black Watch – forming the front of a square – were ordered to charge a mass of tribesmen. They obeyed with alacrity, but into the gap created poured the 'Fuzzy Wuzzies', and it became a general *sauve qui peut* ere the howling slashing warriors were downed or ejected. This was one of the very rare occasions when a British square was breached.

In the forced march to the relief of General Gordon, trapped at Khartoum, the battalion shattered the onrush of fanatical tribesmen at Kirbekan in 1885. The *pibroch* sounded as the Highland charge drove them from the ridge at bayonet point.

The fighting resolved into a series of clashes for the possession of water-holes and there were fierce engagements at Abu Klea and Abu Kru wells. At Abu Klea the British square was again penetrated but as at Tamai few of the tribesmen who broke in lived to tell the tale.

The relief column pushed on, but news came in that Khartoum had fallen and General Gordon was dead. It had arrived in sight of Khartoum 48 hours too late. The expedition retired through hostile territory to Wadi Halfa, some 800 miles down the Nile. The Black Watch was on duty in Cairo until May 1886. In 1893 a detachment effectively dealt with the marauding natives of Matabeleland who were attacking the settlers.

There is a pipe march which is eerie, mournful and strident. It is 'The Highland Brigade at Magersfontein', played by Highland regiments in 'Retreat' ceremonies. The wailing piercing notes make 'Magersfontein' a lament as well as a march, for it recalls a day of dool and grief in the Highlands and islands, North and North-East of Scotland.

On Sunday, December 10, 1899, the smartest, finest and toughest infantry brigade in the British Army advanced under popular hard-soldiering General 'Andy' Wauchope, of The Black Watch, to dislodge the Boers from Magersfontein Hill and so open the road to besieged Kimberley for the relief column. No pipes, no drums. A night march and a wild Highland charge in the dawn light was decided upon – a stratagem that had vanquished many a foe.

General Wauchope led his men across five miles of flat open ground. The 2nd Battalion of 'The Auld Forty-Twa' was leading, followed by the 2nd Seaforths, 1st Highland Light Infantry and 1st Argyll and Sutherland Highlanders. For three hours The Highland Brigade plodded silently steadily on shoulder-to-shoulder through the rain and murk. The Highlanders formed a solid compact rectangle of brawn and muscle tipped with steel.

The dim misty outline of the hill became visible as the horizon began to brighten, and it looked as though another of Scotland's glory days had come. But it was not to be. General Wauchope ordered the brigade to deploy. While this movement was being carried out the silence was shattered by the snarling crackle of musketry.

Within a few minutes the ground was strewn with bodies as the Highlanders went down in swathes before the murderous close-range fire. The Highland Brigade was doomed in this death-trap, with thousands of Boer marksmen pouring a hail of lead into its confused swaying ranks. The hill had been pounded by the artillery for several hours on the previous day but the Boers had descended and taken up positions on the level, thus escaping the full effect of the bombardment.

The Highlanders lay down among their dead, wounded and dying and returned the enemy fire, fighting back gamely until 2.30 p.m. Officers and N.C.Os. rallied them and there were several local successes but the dwindling bands of Highlanders could not exploit their gains.

In a gallant attempt to extricate the sadly depleted brigade pinned down by the continuous well-directed fire under a blazing sun, the 1st Gordons rushed through the storm of bullets, but they too were levelled by the score. The Scots Guards fared no better, and in the withdrawal there were further heavy losses. Wounded were borne back by their comrades, but when they were set down many were found to be dead – hit again during the retiral.

General Wauchope died at the head of The Highland Brigade on that stricken field, and 46 officers and over 700 other ranks were killed or wounded – excluding the severe casualties of The Scots Guards and Gordons. Commandant Cronje, the noted Boer leader, later referred to the 'sublime courage' of the Highlanders at Magersfontein. It is believed that the vivid flashes of lightning during a sharp thunderstorm revealed the brigade in its approach march.

General Gatacre had been repulsed at Stormberg, General Buller had suffered a reverse at Colenso – then Magersfontein. This came to be known as 'Black Week' – but it was the turning point of the war.

One of Scotland's finest soldiers, General Hector MacDonald – Ross-shire's 'Fighting Mac' – took over the shattered Highland Brigade. Reorganised and reinforced its elan and dash was born anew under the able leadership of this renowned ranker-officer of the 92nd Highlanders (Gordons).

Revenge came for The Highland Brigade at Koodoosberg Drift, and at Paardeberg Commandant Cronje surrendered with 4,000 of his fighting men. The 2nd Black Watch took part in the actions at Poplar Grove and Driefontein then marched into Bloemfontein, capital of the Orange Free State, in mid-March 1900. The battalion was also prominent at Baviaans Berg and at Retiefs Nek another 4,000 Boers led by Prinzloo put up their hands.

The 2nd was later employed on detachment duties and operated with mobile columns in Natal. In May 1902, the battalion was sent to Harrisburg, in the Orange Free State, where the 1st Battalion – which had arrived in South Africa in late December 1901 – was already located. The 1st and 2nd served together for about six months.

Battle honours of The Black Watch at the turn of the century were: Guadaloupe 1759, Martinique 1762, Havannah, North America 1763-4, Mangalore, Mysore, Seringapatam, Corunna, Busaco, Fuentes d'Onor, Salamanca, Pyrenees, Nivelle, Nive, Orthes, Toulouse, Peninsula, Waterloo, South Africa 1846-7, 1851-2-3. Alma, Sevastopol, Lucknow, Ashantee 1873-4, Tel-el-Kebir, Egypt 1882, 1884, Kirbekan, Nile 1884-5, Paardeberg, South Africa 1899-1902. These battle honours are emblazoned on the Regimental Colour.

On the outbreak of war in August 1914, the 1st Black Watch, forming part of the 1st Guards Brigade of the 1st Division, arrived in Belgium in time to take part in a series of desperate encounters with the onrushing German Army during the Retreat from Mons. This epic fighting withdrawal ended within fifty miles of Paris.

But an unbroken line was maintained and all enemy attempts to break through and outflank the Allies were frustrated. And so time was won with the blood of the British Expeditionary

Force and the French for new armies to be equipped, trained and sent into battle.

The 1st Black Watch was heavily engaged in the stand on the Marne, which checked the Germans, and in the consequent advance to the Aisne during the autumn. The 1st entered the grim fighting at the First Battle of Ypres in November and put an entire battalion of Prussian Guards *hors de combat.*

The 2nd Black Watch, with the 21st Brigade of the Meerut Division, arrived in France from India early in October and entered the firing line near Givenchy. The two battalions fought practically alongside each other for close on a year. They were heavily committed at Givenchy. The 2nd distinguished itself at Neuve Chapelle the following March, and both battalions acquitted themselves valiantly at Festubert in May.

In this sector, at Rue du Bois, Corporal John Ripley of the 1st and Corporal David Findlay of the 2nd each won the Victoria Cross. At Festubert the 1st Black Watch was the only battalion in its division to reach the enemy trenches.

The two battalions were in the Loos bloodbath in September, locked in a desperate battle with the Germans in their intricate network of strongly defended trenches. They carried their objectives with heavy casualties, but had to retire as their flanks were exposed, the attack as a whole having failed. After Loos the 2nd Battalion was sent to Mesopotamia with the Meerut Division.

The 1st Battalion fought splendidly on the Somme in July 1916, and names like Contalmaison, High Wood, Delville Wood and Longueval revive Black Watch memories. The 1st were again conspicuous in the bitter fighting at the Third Battle of Ypres.

When the Germans launched their last mighty offensive in March 1918, the 1st Black Watch met the shock of its impact on the Lys. It looked like a wipe-out of the battalion. The long field-grey waves of German infantry came on in close-packed lines, and when they were mown down still more loomed up over the trenches.

For five days the dwindling companies held on to Givenchy Ridge. Several times they were surrounded. And after counter-attacks they were still surrounded – but by German dead. The few score survivors of the 1st Black Watch were subjected to gas, artillery concentrations and assailed with flame-throwers, but fought off the enemy from positions littered with a ghastly shambles of dead, wounded and dying – German and their own.

In the massive British counter-offensive unleashed in the autumn the 1st Black Watch was prominent in the highly successful assault on the strategic Drocourt-Queant switch-line early in September, and battled on to and over the St. Quentin Canal in pursuit of the shattered retreating German Army.

The 'cease-fire' found the battalion on the banks of the Oise-Sambre Canal near the point where it had concentrated with the 1st Division of the British Expeditionary Force in August 1914. And so 'Highland Laddie', the Regimental March of 'The Auld Forty-Twa', sounded loud and clear as the 1st Battalion marched into Cologne to serve six months with the Army of Occupation.

The 2nd Black Watch was in the force rushed to the relief of General Townsend surrounded at Kut-el-Amara, on the banks of the Tigris. After a twenty-mile march, with no opportunity to reconnoitre, the battalion went into action early in January 1916, at Sheikh Saad. The order was 'attack where the fire is thickest'.

The Black Watch charged the strong Turkish entrenchments but several hundred men were cut down by the hail of rifle and machine-gun fire. The remainder had to take whatever cover they could find and, raked by the enemy guns, they lay until nightfall before retiring. Memories of Magersfontein. . . .

The relief attempt failed and the garrison at Kut-el-Amara surrendered. The survivors of the 2nd Black Watch were amalgamated with the remnant of the 1st Seaforths, this battalion having also been decimated. The composite formation was styled 'The Highland Battalion', but a few months later, on the arrival of reinforcements, the two battalions resumed their separate identities.

In March 1917, the 2nd Black Watch marched on Baghdad with General Maude and were the first troops to enter the town. Later that month the battalion was engaged in operations to the north, and on April 21 there was a spirited action at Istabulat, where Private Charles Melvin gained his Victoria Cross. A few days afterwards the 2nd was in Samarra and the battalion was represented in the force sent to capture Tekrit in November.

Dispatched to Palestine, the 2nd Battalion entered the firing line a few miles north of Jaffa in April 1918. It was given an important role in General Allenby's attack which broke Turkish resistance at the Battle of Sharon in September. The Black Watch onslaught bit deep into the enemy defences and numerous prisoners were taken. The breakthrough was followed by a pursuit of the rapidly retreating enemy to Tripoli, where news was received of the Armistice with the Turks. In 1920 the title was changed to The Black Watch (Royal Highland Regiment).

Sixty-eight battle honours were awarded to the 'Auld Forty-Twa' for valour in World War I: Retreat from Mons, MARNE 1914, '18, Aisne 1914, La Bassée 1914, YPRES 1914, '17, '18, Langemarck 1914, Gheluvelt, Nonne Bosschen, Givenchy 1914, Neuve Chapelle, Aubers, Festubert 1915, LOOS, SOMME 1916, '18, Albert 1916, Bazentin, Delville Wood, Pozières, Flers-Courcelette, Morval, Thiepval, Le Transloy, Ancre Heights, Ancre 1916, ARRAS 1917, '18, Vimy 1917, Scarpe 1917, '18, Arleux, Pilckem, Menin Road, Polygon Wood, Poelcappelle, Passchendaele, Cambrai 1917, '18, St. Quentin, Bapaume 1918, Rosières, LYS, Estaires, Messines 1918, Hazebrouck, Kemmel, Béthune, Scherpenberg, Soissonnais-Ourcq, Tardenois, Drocourt-Quéant, HINDENBURG LINE, Epéhy, St. Quentin Canal, Beaurevoir, Courtrai, Selle, Sambre, France and Flanders 1914-18, DOIRAN 1917, Macedonia 1915-18, Egypt 1916, Gaza, Jerusalem, Tell 'Asur, MEGIDDO, Sharon, Damascus, Palestine 1917-18, Tigris 1916, KUT-EL-AMARA 1917, Baghdad, Mesopotamia 1915-17. (The ten battle honours printed in capitals are borne on the Sovereign's Colour.)

The 1st Black Watch arrived in France with the 4th Division in October 1939, and after uneventful service in the north and in front of the Maginot Line, the battalion joined 154 Brigade of the 51st (Highland) Division in early March 1940. The 51st held a section of the 'Maginot' near Metz. In these days of desultory rifle and machine-gun fire, occasional raids and patrol actions our American cousins called it the 'phoney war'.

May 10 dawned – and *blitzkreig* became an English word. German tanks and infantry flowed across Holland, Belgium and France like the deluge released by the collapsing wall of a dam.

Three days later a heavy bombardment was sprung on the divisional area and furious fighting developed, with the Highland Division giving as good as it got. On May 15, however, it was ordered to withdraw in conformity with the French defence plan.

And so began the epic 60 miles fighting retreat which was to end in the German tank-trap at St. Valery-en-Caux. March, dig in and fight. . . . March, dig in and fight. And this went on amid air raids, chaos, killing and havoc. Rumours of disaster and surrender came in daily. But for the Highland Division it was still march, dig in and fight.

Brigades changed position; battalions moved forward; companies deployed, attacked, defended, retired; other units moved up, lost contact and were never heard of again; orders, countermanded orders, fresh orders followed in quick succession . . . the crash of shells, the drone of aircraft, the whistle of bombs, the chatter of machine-guns, the crack of rifles . . . smoke, flames, confusion, torn, maimed broken bodies, rubble, debris, shattered villages, bomb and shell-pocked roads, fleeing refugees. March! Dig In! Fight!

On reaching Etain and Varennes it was learned that the Germans had broken through on a wide front, the French armies were disintegrating and that a deep wedge of fast-moving enemy armour and infantry was between the Highland Division and the British Expeditionary Force. The 51st retired to defend Paris, then news came in that King Leopold of the Belgians had surrendered.

March, dig in, fight – no 'phoney war' now! The exhausted battle-weary men of the Highland Division toiled, they sweated, they swore – but they marched, dug in and fought. The division changed direction and retired on a new defence line stretching from the north of Abbeville to the sea. By this time the B.E.F. was being evacuated at Dunkirk.

Attacking an enemy bridgehead on the Somme, south of Abbeville, 'A' Company of the 1st Black Watch carried its objective but as positions on the flank were overrun in a German counter-attack a retiral was ordered. The brigade took up a defensive line near the sea but more ground had to be given up at the junction of the Bethune and Varenne under powerful enemy pressure.

The 1st Black Watch blocked the German advance on the Varenne until pulled back through Ouville to St. Pierre-le-Viger, within a few miles of St. Valery. The enemy tank ring drew closer.

They were bombed, they were battered, they were shelled, they were shattered, the artillery thundered, the rifles cracked, the machine-guns rattled and the enemy armour came rumbling on. The tattered, famished and footsore Highlanders retired still fighting a desperate, hopeless, rearguard action against overwhelming odds. So it went on, day after day, night after night.

The divisional guns fell silent – no shells; the rifle and machine-gun fire slackened then died fitfully away – no ammunition; men staggered with exhaustion – no rest, no food, no reinforcements. But The Black Watch closed their ranks as they did in days of yore.

Was that the *pibroch*'s eerie notes shrilling through the din of battle? Maybe the 'wee folk' of the mountains, glens, woods and lochs played a dirge for them as they went down before the rain of shot and shell in that ever-narrowing circle of fire and steel. As consciousness lapsed and life ebbed away the valiant soldiers of *Am Freiceadan Dubh* heard elfin pipes lament the passing of The Highland Division. . . .

The French capitulated at 8 o'clock on the morning of June 12. And at St. Valery by the misty sea, surrounded by the enemy, the port ablaze, under heavy air attack and bombarded by artillery, with no hope of evacuation, came the last fateful order from the divisional commander, Major-General Victor M. Fortune, two and a half hours later – SURRENDER!

General Fortune's cup of bitterness was full. He was a man of The Black Watch, commissioned into the regiment at the beginning of the century. Surrender was foreign to his nature.

Highlanders angrily flung down their useless weapons, many with tears in their eyes and curses – Gaelic curses – on their lips. And there were those who mumbled a few words of prayer. *Saoraidh e mi bho mo Namhaid is treasa, agus uathasan tha toirt fuath dhomh.* (He shall deliver me from my strongest enemy and from them which hate me.) But the 1st Black Watch, unaware of the surrender order, fought on for another three hours.

The skirl of the pipes ushered in a new 51st (Highland) Division. At 21.40 hours (9.40 p.m.) on October 23, 1942, one gun banged. It was the signal. Then the roaring reverberating boom of the British batteries thundered, echoed and re-echoed far out across the desert to open the Battle of El Alamein.

The artillery – including the 51st Divisional gunners – had the first crack with 800 guns, spaced at intervals, and stretching for over six miles across the sands. The vivid gun-flashes illuminated the desert and blazed, flickered and rippled to and fro along the horizon like summer lightning. No man who heard the mighty cacophony of the Eighth Army's guns at El Alamein is ever likely to forget it.

Then the infantry went in. Each battalion of the Highland Division was led by its pipers, and the long steel-tipped lines pushed through to the throat of the enemy. And red were the bayonets of the Highlanders under the desert moon.

Advancing with them were the Australians, New Zealanders and South Africans, and *am piob mhor* – the great war-pipe – never sounded more defiant and triumphant than across the sand-dunes at Alamein. So the tide of war turned in North Africa after many months of ebb and flow fighting, disappointments, reverses and stalemate.

In this, their 'baptism of fire', the new Highland Division avenged St. Valery and hurled Rommel's Afrika Korps back into the open desert. The armour rumbled, clanged and clanked through the gap torn by the infantry and soon the prison cages filled with gesticulating nerve-shattered Italians glad to be out of it and sullen dejected Germans.

The '*mir-cath*' – battle frenzy – came upon the men of the 1st Black Watch and they went berserk with their bayonets among the German and Italian infantry. Both waves took their objectives and on several occasions had to wait until the artillery raised the barrage before they could resume their onslaught and *mac siccar*. After eleven days of ghastly close fighting the battalion was moved back for a well-earned respite.

In pursuit of the retreating enemy the 1st Black Watch worked round Mersa Brega in a dust storm followed by torrential rain and succeeded in cutting the road, but not without some casualties in rough going across mine-sewn ground. In January 154 Brigade was poised for the assault on the strong defensive position at Buerat, launched about the middle of the month. The attack bit deep into the enemy lines, and the 1st Black Watch by-passed Misurata and pushed hard for Homs at the heels of the German rearguard.

Four miles to the west was a fort – dubbed 'Edinburgh Castle' – which was the hinge of the enemy line. The battalion moved forward only to be pinned down by well-directed artillery and small arms fire. On resuming the advance it was found that the Germans, on discovering they were outflanked, had evacuated 'Edinburgh Castle'. The Eighth Army entered Tripoli on January 23 and the Red Hackle of The Black Watch was prominent in the Victory Parade.

From March 21-28 the battle raged to crack the Mareth Line, where the Germans and Italians rallied and launched a determined attack. This was repulsed but they came on again and made several slight penetrations. These were sealed off in the counterblow.

There were further desperate engagements at Wadi Akarit and for the possession of Roumana Ridge. After bitter fighting and severe losses the Eighth Army broke through the Gabes Gap early in April, opening the vital road to Sfax, Sousse, Enfidaville and Tunis.

With the enemy once more in full retreat the British advance was rapid and Tunis was entered in May. The massed Pipes and Drums of The Highland Division stole the show at the Victory Parade. The 51st moved to Djidjelli and Bougie, on the Algerian coast, where a series of landing operations was carried out – a portent of things to come.

After concentrating around Sfax and Sousse the Highlanders sailed for Malta on July 5, arriving next day. The battle for Sicily began on the 10th, the Highland Division landing on the Pachino Peninsula, on the south-easterly 'jut' of the island.

As the weather was stormy the element of surprise was in their favour and the Italian gunners manning the coastal defences discreetly retired inland or surrendered. Encountering only light opposition the infantry brigades advanced into the interior.

The 154 Brigade crossed the River Monaci and entered Ramacca with enemy resistance showing signs of stiffening. The Dittaino bridgeheads secured, the brigade approached the village of Gerbini, the 1st Black Watch leading. The battalion captured the road junction then headed for the barracks and railway station. But here the advance 'over-reached' itself.

The barracks and aerodrome were held in considerable strength and the going was rough – tanks, machine-guns and concentrated fire. With casualties mounting the brigade was pulled back behind the Dittaino line. The enemy had also suffered severely and was later observed withdrawing from Gerbini.

Fighting over farmlands, open country, olive groves and orchards the Highland infantrymen pursued the Germans and Italians into the Sferro Hills to the east of Adrano early in August. The 1st Black Watch was heavily committed on Pietraperciata Ridge and battled on to Cocola, and, the Simeto River crossings secured, the battalion skirmished up to Biancavilla where its last shots were fired amongst the bullet-swept hills.

In mid-August 154 Brigade arrived at Messina, the enemy having crossed the straits to Italy. The battalion was set to guard bridges and other strategic points against sabotage and took the surrender of groups of Italians abandoned by the Germans during the evacuation. They also kept the straits under constant observation to cover the landing of the 13th Corps on the mainland.

The corps went over the narrows without difficulty, and on September 5 the brigade followed to hold the important bridgehead around Reggio and the aerodrome. This mission successfully accomplished, 154 Brigade was ferried back to Messina three days later and enjoyed a brief respite from the alarms of war.

The Highland Division embarked at Catania towards the close of November, and on a cold, bleak wintry morning sailed up the Clyde. There was only a fleeting glimpse of the Old Country, however, as the division immediately entrained for the Home Counties to prepare for the great battles of destiny across the Channel.

At the end of March the 51st (Highland) Division was dispatched to East Anglia, and in April left the 30th Corps of North Africa renown to join the 1st Corps. Leave spent in Scotland was only a pleasant memory as troops of the division boarded invasion craft in the Thames a few weeks later. The curtain was already rising on the stark drama of the Normandy beachheads.

Landing in the early hours of D Day plus 4 the 1st Black Watch, with 154 Brigade, moved east across the Orne in mid-June and was temporarily placed under orders of the 6th Airborne Division. The brigade took up positions in defence of the Orne bridgeheads in the 'Triangle' containment area. It came under intense mortaring and shelling in the Bois de Bevant, where enemy infiltration attempts were successfully countered.

The Highland Division, under orders of the 2nd Canadian Corps, took – and gave – heavy punishment in holding and later breaking out from the 'Triangle'. In early August the brigade moved against St. Aignan with armoured and air support.

The 1st Black Watch skirmished among uncut crops interspersed with strips of woodland, along sunken roads, up steep embankments, through orchards and thick high hedges in the crucial stage of the battle to end the Caen stalemate and close the Falaise 'gap'. The battalion carried its objectives and dug in.

The inevitable German counter-attack soon followed with accurate artillery fire and mortaring. American planes joined in this concentrated 'stonk', but unfortunately dropped some bombs in the battalion area and there were several casualties. Enemy Tiger tanks and infantry entered the melee but the Germans were held after a hard fight.

The first phase of the breakout completed, the Highland Division was set to clearing the road to Lisieux. The brigade assailed the woods around St. Sylvain and suffered severely from machine-gunning. The brigade headed for St. Pierre-sur-Dives, crossed the river and fought on to the high ground at Le Godet with tank support, encountering stubborn opposition.

The 1st Black Watch pushed on and entered St. Julien in the face of light resistance. In clearing the Germans from Tilly to Lisieux the Highland Division had a 'star' role in the battle for Normandy, and the speed of its subsequent advance probably accounted for the occasional unfortunate bombing of its lines by the R.A.F. and U.S. Air Force.

The 51st battled eastwards through the *bocage* of Normandy and advanced on the Seine with the Germans in full pelt retreat. The artillery and machine-gunners opened up on the barges ferrying the rearguards across the river, then the infantry brigades went over in their wake. From Elboeuf and Rouen the Highland fighting men surged forward to liberate St. Valery of unhappy memories.

Garlanded, kissed, cheered, dined and wined they were welcomed back to St. Valery-en-Caux via the battlefields of North Africa and Sicily, and the pipes skirled in the square. Divisional H.Q. was established in the chateau at nearby Cailleville, and on September 3 – fifth anniversary of the outbreak of war – the Massed Pipes and Drums of the 51st (Highland) Division played 'Retreat'. It was a proud day for Scotland's senior Highland regiment – *Am Freiceadan Dubh*.

Mais, c'est la guerre! – the Highlanders' stay was short. The German garrison at Le Havre was holding out though the peninsula had been cut off by the sweeping advance of the Scots and Canadians. It was anticipated that this would prove a tough nut to crack, so the Highlanders were ordered to deal with the situation.

The German infantry were in poor shape, and after a brief token resistance – principally by the artillery – Le Havre surrendered. This was one of the very few occasions when the 1st Black Watch was not committed. The 154 Brigade moved against the troublesome German garrison at Dunkirk, but after some brisk skirmishing the brigade was relieved early in October and sent off to rejoin the 51st in the Eindhoven-Nijmegen area.

En route, however, the brigade received an order over the radio to concentrate at Zeelst airfield, near Eindhoven. A German raiding party had made a night crossing of the Wilhelmina Canal and penetrated to the edge of the airfield before withdrawing on being detected.

The defending units of the R.A.F. Regiment had several casualties and there was a 'flap' as His Majesty the King was expected at Zeelst within a few days on a visit to troops in the Eindhoven-Nijmegen 'corridor'. It was decided to bring in the battle-trained 154 Brigade as a precautionary measure.

The 1st and 7th Battalions of The Black Watch and the 7th Battalion The Argyll and Sutherland Highlanders of 154 stood to but the Germans lay low and the Royal visit passed off without incident. The brigade then re-joined its division in the 'corridor'.

In this area a platoon of 'C' Company and several H.Q. personnel of the 1st Black Watch had a 'passage d'armes' with a German fighting patrol. The enemy at first had the initiative and advantage but after taking three prisoners decided to call it a day and made off.

The Black Watch men followed up, hurled 'crackers' and opened rapid fire on the withdrawing Germans. Out of the 20-strong patrol only five escaped minus their officer. The three prisoners accounted for 'Herr Leutenant' in a breakaway from their captors!

In the Battle of the Maas the Highland Division took part in a number of operations to clear the Germans from the south bank of the river and free the port of Antwerp to supply the Allied armies. Its thrust from Schijndel to Geertruidenberg and the series of actions fought east and north of s'Hertogenbosch liberated about 300 square miles of Holland and denied the enemy their intended bridge escape route at Geertruidenberg.

They captured or wiped out enemy 'pockets' of resistance and rearguard formations, made assault-crossings of two rivers, forced the narrow causeway from Waspik to Geertruidenberg and fought across the Afwaterings Canal. The 154 Brigade was conspicuous in these operations, which began in late October and drew to a successful conclusion in mid-November.

The Dommel and Halsche were crossed by 154 Brigade on 'kangaroos' and strong bridgeheads were quickly established. The 1st Black Watch went over the Halsche at Helder under a smoke screen, one company picking its way carefully across the wreckage of a bridge blown by the enemy.

The battalion led the brigade advance to the west with the object of preventing the enemy crossing to the north of the Maas. The 1st moved on the bridge at Hooge which was strongly defended and violent action flared up at the village of Waspik.

The brigade was then sent to s'Hertogenbosch where it launched diversionary attacks while the other two brigades – 152 and 153 – cleared up the partially flooded 'Island' area. Light opposition was met and numerous prisoners taken.

The Germans had launched a powerful assault on the Americans holding a section of the line along the banks of the Meuse, on the Dutch-Belgian frontier. They penetrated twelve miles west of Roermond, established themselves about

20 miles from Eindhoven – which was now threatened – and extended their bridgehead across the Maas.

This area was the locale of the Highland Division's next battle. The role of the 51st was to clear the Germans out to the south of the Weert-Roermond road a few miles north of the Belgian border and then push them across the Maas to Venlo.

The assignment of 154 Brigade was the capture of the lock-gates at Nederweert, at the junction of the Norder and Wessem canals, as the Germans holding these gates could empty or flood the waterways as strategy demanded. This objective was carried in mid-November in the face of light resistance.

But before the crossing an enemy patrol infiltrated and took several prisoners among The Black Watch and Seaforths. They were not captives for long, however, as the Germans ran into a standing patrol of the 42nd which scattered them and the prisoners escaped.

The Black Watch advanced to Leveroi on 'kangaroos' and fought through Bong and Baarlo. There the operation across the water barriers of the Lowlands of Holland ended. The Highland Division was given the task of holding the 'Island' bridgehead in the Nijmegen sector towards the end of the month.

In this area troops had striven hard but in vain to link up with the airborne forces dropped around Arnhem. Early in December the Germans blew the Lek dyke and with the water level rising steadily only the 1st and 7th Black Watch remained north of the Maas. Civilians were evacuated from their derelict homes and farmhouses in a bleak, miserable flooded wilderness.

In the push for Kessel and Goch the 1st Black Watch made a night crossing of the Niers in 'buffaloes'. The battalion came in for heavy shelling, ran into stiff opposition from defended houses and the enemy began to infiltrate. Aircraft plastered the German positions and the bridgehead was secured, Kessel falling soon afterwards.

Crocodile tanks equipped with flame-throwers came up and The Black Watch advanced with them to capture Hassum. The enemy put down a concentrated bombardment which caused a deal of casualties.

The battalion moved to the outskirts of Goch and crossed Kendel to take Winkel then entered Robbenhof. About the close of the month 154 Brigade was relieved and returned to Goch. The battle for the Reichswald was over and won.

When Hitler made his final desperate offensive in the Ardennes in mid-December the 51st was rushed south from Nijmegen to plug the deep gap torn between the U.S. and British armies. Held in reserve for the counter-offensive, the division guarded several of the Maas crossings between Namur and Liege towards the close of the year.

When the Allied attack was sprung the infantry brigades of the Highland Division moved into action down the snow and ice-bound Ourthe Valley. Preceded by armoured bulldozers which cleared away the drifts and enemy obstructions, trees and fallen masonry, 154 Brigade headed for Laroche, which the 1st Black Watch entered and then fought the enemy off a ridge on the other side of the town.

They drove on into Erneuville and the following day established contact with the Americans coming up from the south. The breach closed and the position now restored, with the Germans once more in retreat, the 51st left the deep snow of the Ardennes and headed north to clear the enemy from the Maas to the Rhine alongside their old comrades of the 30th Corps.

Early in February the divisional assault swept towards the Reichswald – an extensive forest on the Dutch-German frontier – spearheaded by 154 Brigade. The 1st Black Watch broke in and were the first troops to carry the war on to German soil. The brigade fought into Hekkens, a strongpoint of the Siegfried Line, with the Black Watch battalion well to the fore.

Came 'Monty's' clarion call 'Over the Rhine then let us go' – and first to go were the 15th (Scottish) Division and the 51st (Highland) Division at 9 p.m. on March 23. The 52nd (Lowland) Division was also heavily committed in the battle for the Rhine. The infantry crossed on 'buffaloes' under a smoke-screen which cloaked their movements from the enemy gunners.

Supported by a tremendous barrage reminiscent of El Alamein, the Highland Division attacked on a two-brigade front, and throughout the entire operation there was direct communication between the brigades and fighter-bomber aircraft. On the extreme left of the assault-crossing was 154 Brigade, which went over from the Honnepel area. Their 'buffaloes' grounded in less than three minutes.

Enemy artillery fire during the crossing was less heavy than anticipated, but when 154 Brigade reached the German-held bank infantry reaction was violent. The 1st Black Watch attacked Klein Esserden and came under intense mortaring.

Klein Esserden and Speldrop were both entered, but a powerful counterblow hit 'C' Company hard at the latter and 'B' and 'C' Companies were pulled back to a creamery at the approaches to Klein Esserden. Reinforced by some tanks, anti-tank guns and a machine-gun platoon the 1st Black Watch re-captured Klein Esserden next morning. An advance by a Canadian Highland regiment made contact with isolated parties which had fought on at Speldrop.

After two days of furious fighting there was a new Watch on the Rhine – The Black Watch! But victory was tempered with sorrow. Among the fallen was Major-General Thomas G. Rennie, C.B., D.S.O., M.C., commander of the 51st (Highland) Division.

On a visit to 154 Brigade Tactical H.Q. on March 24 a pattern of mortar bombs exploded, the General's jeep receiving a direct hit. The Highland Division took its last farewell of this outstanding soldier of *Am Freiceadan Dubh* at Appledorn where the pipes and drums joined in lament.

As Major Rennie of the 51st Divisional Staff he was taken prisoner at St. Valery-en-Caux, but made a dramatic escape and commanded the 5th Black Watch in 153 Brigade of the reconstituted Highland Division in North Africa. He took over command of 154 Brigade in Sicily and was later given command of the 3rd Division – first to land on the Normandy beaches.

General Rennie was wounded several times, and when he returned to the 51st as its commander at the end of July 1944, his arm was in a sling. Thomas Rennie was a man with a mission – to lead the Highland Division back to St. Valery. History records how well he accomplished it.

He was succeeded by Major-General Gordon H. A. MacMillan, C.B., C.B.E., D.S.O., M.C., a distinguished officer of The Argyll and Sutherland Highlanders – who had taken the 15th (Scottish) Division to France in June 1944. General MacMillan was a 'weel kent' face in the Highland Division, having commanded 152 Brigade in Sicily. He came back to the 51st from the 49th Division.

Exploiting the success on the Rhine, 154 Brigade made for the bridge at Empel on the road to Isselburg. The 1st Black Watch ran into some trouble with enemy self-propelled guns, but took Empel village. The build-up was on for the assault on Dinxperlo, and 154 Brigade resuming their advance entered the town early in April.

The Highland Division was sent some 40 miles north to concentrate near the Dutch town of Enschede. Here preparations were made for the advance through Arnhem to clear the Germans from the North-east of Holland and the coastal strip along the mouth of the Elbe.

The 154 Brigade thrust south of the Lingen-Furstenau area and captured several villages, the 1st Black Watch on 'kangaroos' accounting for Badbergen and Dinklage. There were frequent surrenders by the Germans and hospitals were taken over crowded with their wounded.

The brigade led the division's advance on Delmenhorst, entering Ippener and Annen. Now the 51st made its push for Bremen, with 154 Brigade clearing the Germans from the banks of the Wumme and moving quickly through Robertburg. The 1st Black Watch captured Ottersberg, Otterstedt and Vorwerk.

It was obvious that the German military Collossus was tottering and about to fall. Enemy resistance was sporadic, ineffective and half-hearted. Only the fanatics made a stand – and they too were fewer after the crossing of the Rhine.

The Germans were beaten – and they knew it. Surrenders of entire formations became more numerous and there were many occasions when units were found lined up, waiting and ready to be marched off as prisoners. The will to resist had gone. The days of the Third Reich were numbered.

On May 3, 154 Brigade skirmished forward with Lintig as the objective. The 1st Black Watch pushed through Grossenham at the ready. It was their last advance. Overtures for peace were being made to Brigadier J. A. Oliver (The Black Watch), C.B.E., D.S.O., T.D., at 154 Brigade H.Q.

The surrender soon followed of the 15th Panzer Grenadier Division, a reconstituted Afrika Korps formation. The 'original' had been the 51st's old and honourable adversaries in the Western Desert until capitulating in Tunisia in May 1943.

Peace came with the glorious bloom of spring flowers and the fluting notes of the song-birds. And so dawned VE Day, May 8, 1945. The roar of the guns and the metallic clanking rumble of the tanks was stilled. Stilled too was the deadly chatter of machine-guns, the sharp crack of rifles, the crump of mortars and the whistle and crash of bombs. The curse of Hitler had been lifted from the brows of men.

Four days later the Massed Pipes and Drums of the Highland Division took part in the memorable Victory Parade through Bremerhaven. The Highlanders made a brave show. The kilts, sporrans and bare knees swung in rhythm, the bayonets gleamed and glinted – and the Red Hackle of The Black Watch 'brightly beamed abune them a!'

The 2nd Black Watch arrived in Palestine in the autumn of 1937 and began operating against elusive bands of Arab raiders who supported the Mufti of Jerusalem. The battalion provided escorts for convoys, took part in patrols and 'sweeps' over the rugged, stony hills of Judea and Samaria and carried out snap checks and searches of villages for wanted men and hidden arms.

They had a full round of guard and communication duties in the sweltering heat and experienced several exchanges of fire with marauding Arabs. They were engaged in this role when war broke out in early September 1939.

At the beginning of May 1940, the 2nd Black Watch arrived in Egypt's Canal Zone and towards the end of August the battalion left Aden for Berbera to defend British and French Somaliland against the expected Italian invasion.

The defection of the French, however, allowed the Italians to cross the frontier near Jibouti and The Black Watch moved to block the enemy in a defile at Tug Argan, about 60 miles from Berbera. The battalion was bombed at Laferug, several miles north of Tug Argan, on August 11 but came through the attack unscathed. Their small arms fire downed one plane. First blood to the 'Auld Forty-Twa!'

The Italians were observed in great strength and the defenders – Indians, East Africans, North Rhodesians and Somalis – had to give way. The Black Watch took up a position on a long low range of hills called Barkasan and dug in.

First clash with the enemy occurred on the 13th at Tug Argan. 'A' Company ran into an ambush while taking 'ammo', rations and water into this area. A brisk fire – anti-tank, mortar and small arms – was opened but the company successfully extricated itself with a few casualties.

When the decision was taken to evacuate the Protectorate the 2nd Black Watch was given the task of holding Barkasan to cover the withdrawal from Tug Argan and the embarkation at Berbera. There was no armoured support or air cover, artillery was weak, and the Italians had complete freedom in the skies. The prospect was grim and smacked of disaster.

But the retiral and embarkation operations proceeded according to plan. Italian reaction was limited to an air raid on Berbera. The enemy, though possessing heavy numerical superiority, did not force the issue. As later events proved, the Italian Army was much more skilled at avoiding action than seeking it.

On August 17, after being cut off, two platoons of Punjabis came back with the enemy close behind. The Black Watch opened fire. The enemy trucks reversed into one another, milled around in confusion and then made off leaving about 100 Italians and native troops high and dry. 'D' Company engaged and quickly sent them scampering for cover.

The enemy began crawling along wadis in an attempt to infiltrate. A larger force, comprising a battalion of native 'askaris', came up and launched an attack which was easily beaten back. The enemy again went to earth to escape the lashing fire of The Black Watch.

Another battalion advanced with artillery support and succeeded in penetrating the position. All mortar 'ammo' expended and communications cut by shelling, the 42nd went at the enemy with the bayonet and Bren and the Italians and their native levies were chased back beyond their start-line.

But the enemy build-up continued. The bayonets flashed out again, and 50 men of The Black Watch made a daring exposed downhill charge while the right flank poured in supporting fire. The Italians rose from cover in their hundreds and ran like March hares, discarding rifles and equipment as they fled before the yelling Highlanders.

This headlong charge earned several valuable hours respite but it was observed that the enemy was still gathering strength and that tanks were now arriving on the scene. A few probing attacks were made on the flanks but the spirited reaction encountered was too much for the enemy who again sought cover with alacrity.

To escape mortaring and sniping, when the Italians got on to higher ground, outlying platoons were pulled back. Then tanks opened fire and another assault was launched. 'C' and 'D' Companies being heavily engaged.

A dangerous situation was developing. Small arms and machine-gun ammunition was running low and the mortars were all silent now. Communications were still cut and the Italians were seen working round the flanks in an enveloping move. They were observed urging on their native troops while they themselves brought up the rear. More tanks rumbled up, but several were destroyed by fire from a Bofors.

The 2nd Black Watch was ordered back behind Laferug. The Italians followed but showed no inclination to renew combat. The evacuation having been successfully completed and the advancing enemy held in check by The Black Watch rearguard, the Highland battalion entered Berbera and within a few hours was under way for Aden, arriving on August 19. From there it moved to Suez, disembarking a week later.

Black Watch casualties had been very light in the fighting against tanks, artillery, aircraft and infantry – seven killed, sixteen wounded. Enemy losses at the hands of the Indians, East Africans, Somalis, North Rhodesians and Highlanders were estimated at close on 2,000.

Five Italian brigades had been held up for several days and at times fought to a standstill by five battalions with weak artillery support, no armour and without air cover. And sporting fans in the 2nd Black Watch expressed the opinion that the Italian challenge in running events at the post-war Olympic Games would be serious!

There followed a spell of duty at the Citadel, Cairo, and in October the battalion embarked at Port Said. Destination – Suda Bay, Crete. After preparations to defend the island the 2nd Black Watch battled desperately with invading paratroops flown in from German-occupied Greece in May 1941.

After concentrated bombing and machine-gunning of the British positions scores of large Junkers troop-carrying aircraft came over. Every available gun was brought to bear and a heavy accurate fire was opened.

Aircraft hit plunged down in smoke and flames and parachutists hurtled earthwards in blazing harness. Planes were seen turning away from the fire and making off with paratroops draped over their wings. Other aircraft, driven out of formation, flew in among the descending parachutists. Germans were obligingly slaughtering Germans.

Paratroopers tangled in telegraph wires and in trees and were speedily dealt with, but the enemy rained down reinforcements and the position gradually began to deteriorate. There were heavy supporting air raids and at Heraklion The Black Watch defenders were bombed and machine-gunned from high and low level.

From their slit trenches they replied with rifle and automatic fire and many of the parachutists were riddled ere they grounded. The carnage went on for three weeks, The Black Watch denying the enemy the use of the airfield, and there was bitter disappointment when the evacuation order was received.

In June the Royal Navy brought off the defenders under great difficulty owing to the numerous concentrated air attacks, and off Crete and in running the bomber gauntlet across the Mediterranean to Egypt, a number of ships were lost. The resulting casualties among the troops were much heavier than those incurred during the fighting on the island.

Early in July the 2nd Battalion left Cairo for the Plains of Sharon, and for a time it was stationed near Damascus. Arriving at Zahle, in the eastern foothills of Mount Lebanon, a series of hard training exercises was carried out.

The scene changes to Tobruk – shelled, bombed, attacked, isolated – but still defiant. The 2nd Black Watch disembarked from destroyers late in October and joined the beleagured garrison. General Sir Archibald Wavell's army, after routing the Italians, had to retire to the Egyptian frontier before the powerful armoured formations Hitler dispatched to North Africa to bolster up the feeble morale of his allies.

But at Tobruk General Wavell – a Black Watch officer (Colonel of the Regiment from 1946-50) – left behind an Australian Brigade which the 2nd Black Watch reinforced. The 'Diggers' and 'Jocks' teamed up well together and held their positions on the perimeter against all comers, proving an exceedingly sharp and troublesome thorn in the side of the enemy.

The counter-offensive – Operation Crusader – intended to drive Rommel out of Cyrenaica and raise the long siege – was launched at first light on November 18. Tactical surprise was achieved and by the following evening the British were in control of the all-important Sidi Rezegh area.

Sidi Rezegh was the key to Tobruk, some 20 miles away, but the defenders were not content to sit and wait. In any case it was part of the pre-arranged plan that they should co-operate by breaking out in strength, seize El Duda, and link up with the relief force.

The troops for this sortie assembled on the night of November 20. First objective was the capture of 'Jill', a German strong-point, and then they were to take 'Tiger', a formidable defence system 3 miles south-east of the perimeter. The twin spearheads were the Tank Brigade and the 2nd Black Watch.

But they did not know that Rommel had been massing his guns and troops at these points in preparation for an all-out assault on Tobruk on the 23rd. Had the enemy's concentration of fire-power been known it is extremely unlikely that the ill-fated sortie would have been embarked upon.

The tanks were to drive straight for 'Jill' with 'B' Company close behind, but in the murk they went off course and the infantry advanced unsupported across the open desert. The distance narrowed. The Germans were holding their fire. Again the range lessened as the lines of infantry came on. Then the enemy opened up a murderous hail of flying lead.

The men of 'B' Company were mown down in swathes. There was no cover, and if they had flung themselves into the sand, or retired, they would still have remained in the German gun-sights. This was a 'no surrender' battalion. They fixed bayonets and charged.

The deadly chatter of automatic weapons was punctuated by a series of sharp explosions. The tanks – now on course – had run into an extensive minefield. In a few minutes the Black Watch company shed its life-blood and ceased to exist.

Men stumbled, staggered, swayed and fell in long lines as the enemy machine-guns wove their pattern. But a little group of Highlanders raced through the maelstrom of shot and shell to capture 'Jill' at bayonet point – and the eleven survivors immediately pushed towards 'Tiger' with the other companies.

43

The battalion withered away under the accurate concentrated fire from hundreds of machine-guns, mortars and rifles. For a moment the attack faltered, then, rising and falling over the desert air and penetrating the cacophony of battle, came the rousing strains of 'The Black Bear', played by Pipe-Major Roy – shot three times – and Pipe-Sergeant McNicol.

The effect was electrifying! The tanks lumbered up, several heading straight for 'Tiger', others making a wide sweep to outflank the position. With the pipes skirling the survivors of the 2nd Black Watch hurled themselves at 'Tiger' and took it with bloody bayonets. And they consolidated under a deluge of fire.

That sacrificial charge was probably the finest hour in the long eventful history of the 'Auld Forty-Twa'. But glory's price was dearly paid. When it was all over 25 officers and about 400 other ranks lay dead, wounded or dying on the body-strewn Plain of Tobruk.

The Tank Brigade also suffered appalling losses. A total of 169 armoured fighting vehicles had joined in the sortie. Now 120 blazing, glowing, smoke-belching tangled wrecks littered the desert – a funeral pyre for their crews and the fallen of The Black Watch.

A cairn of rough hewn stone on the Bardia road marks the spot. The inscription reads:

IN MEMORY
of those gallant officers and men of
the
2nd Bn. The Black Watch
who fell in this area on
21st Nov. 1941
in the attack from the Tobruk Defences

Early in 1942 the remnant of this elite battalion left Tobruk for the Delta. Reorganised and brought up to strength it was dispatched to Syria to counter the expected Axis thrust through Anatolia. Victory in the Western Desert, however, ended this threat. The 2nd Black Watch formed part of reinforcements bound for Burma but, with the fall of Rangoon and the rapid advance of the Japanese, the convoy was diverted to Bombay.

The battalion trained for several months in jungle warfare

and in August maintained order in West Bengal during civil unrest. In a brief spell in the Arakan in May 1943, the 2nd Black Watch took part in a successful patrol action against the Japs. Then it was selected for a Chindit role – long-range penetration of enemy-held territory with air-dropped supplies.

On joining General Orde Wingate's Special Force in March 1944, the battalion was re-organised in two formations – 42 and 73 – taking the old numbers of the regiment. Each had a strength of about 400. Fully trained and re-equipped The Black Watch Chindits moved to Assam about the middle of the month and arrived at Lalaghat on the 21st.

Next day 73 flew into 'Aberdeen', a Dakota airstrip in the Meza Valley, near Manhton, 42 following on the 25th. Seventy-three moved out and while assembling 42 was bombed and had several casualties.

Moving south on its way to the Banmauk-Indaw Road, 73 had its first brush with the enemy near Sittaw towards the close of the month. Both columns ambushed a Jap force at night on this road on April 5. The leading truck was attacked and most of the occupants killed. Those in the second jumped down and suffered heavy casualties. The third vehicle made off.

Following a reconnaissance a few days later 42, with three platoons of 73, carried out a sharp attack with direct air support. Bombers and fighters were homed on to their target by radio and as a result a Jap dump at Singgan was set ablaze and destroyed. The defenders were badly shot up as they ran through the exploding bombs and ammunition into the jungle.

Early in May the Chindits of 73 and 42 advanced along the broad shallow waters of the Naumi Chaung, and on the 3rd were within sight of White City – several hills on the edge of the Indaw-Myitkyina railway. White City had been held by Brigadier Calvert's force since the middle of March in the face of several determined Japanese attacks.

A patrol from White City contacted the two Black Watch formations on the 4th and led them across the open valley without incident. Soon they were ascending the Kachin Hills and heard the din of battle at White City.

An ambush was laid on to the north of Nathkokyin on the 5th. Three platoons of 73 took up position in the gathering darkness. A few hours later a long line of Japanese troops appeared, led by a mounted officer. When the Chindits had them in their sights they let them have it. Scores of the enemy went down in their tracks and the remainder ran into the jungle.

On the night of the 7th a much more ambitious trap was sprung south of Nathkokyin. Six platoons totalling about 200 men engaged over 1,000 Japs and fierce fighting ensued. Recovering from their surprise the enemy counter-attacked strongly. The Chindits succeeded in inflicting heavy losses before retiring. While this sharp action was in progress the diversion allowed Brigadier Calvert's troops to evacuate White City without interference.

Following operations in the Kachin Hills towards the close of May, the columns met 111 Brigade retiring from 'Blackpool' – a position straddling the railway about eight miles south-east of the top of Kyusunlai Pass. There were several bitterly fought engagements here and a determined Jap attempt to drive the Chindits from the crest was repulsed early in June. Further enemy attempts to break out were also frustrated and there was a particularly fierce patrol clash at Kontha.

The two Chindit columns headed north and toiled up the Nawku Pass early in July in torrential rain. Several swollen fast-flowing rivers had to be crossed and there was a spirited patrol action at Latang.

Three platoons of 73 surprised the enemy at Loikum Bum and the Japanese again had the worst of the encounter. The other column also had a hectic collision with the enemy, in this case at Pungan, and after indecisive fighting the Japs withdrew leaving the Black Watch masters of the area.

Exhausted, sodden, foot-sore, ravaged by typhus, their clothes and equipment rotting on their bodies, they fought their last engagement in this theatre of operations on August 4 – the attack on Labu. The Chindits mortared the enemy out of a strong position in front of the village. The Japs rose and ran for it pursued by the Black Watch, tommy-guns spitting and bayonets gleaming. And that charge was made to the skirl of the pipes – played by a Sassenach 'Jock' named Lark!

For the Chindits of 'The Auld Forty-Twa' the campaign was over. There was a rendezvous on the 9th with forward elements of the British 36th Division, and on the 17th Piper Lark played his Scottish comrades down the main road on the first lap of the long journey by rail, air and 'shank's mare' back to Assam.

During the Burma Campaign The Black Watch Chindits moved swiftly, unseen and unheard in front of, among and behind the Japanese. They lived almost like animals, creeping stealthily silently through the jungle in exhausting heat or monsoon downpour, worming over scrub-covered hills, snaking across arid rocks and wading through evil-smelling swamps, rivers and rushing torrents.

Frequently they 'ghosted' through the blackness of jungle night to surprise and rout the enemy at first light. They caused confusion, havoc and heavy losses among the Japanese who prided themselves on their 'creepcraft' and infiltration tactics which earlier won them an easy conquest.

Thus the Black Watch Chindits did much to explode the unfortunate myth of Jap invincibility. Nursed back to health in India after their five months of hard campaigning the 'bonnie fechters' of the 2nd Black Watch were training as airborne troops for the invasion of Malaya when hostilities ended.

Sixty-two battle honours were granted to the Regiment for dedicated service and achievement in the campaigns of World War II: Defence of Arras, Ypres-Comines Canal, Dunkirk 1940, Somme 1940, St. Valery-en-Caux, Saar, Breville, Odon, Fontenary le Pesnil, Defence of Rauray, Caen, Falaise, FALAISE ROAD, La Vie Crossing, Le Havre, Lower Maas, Venlo Pocket, Ourthe, Rhineland, Reichswald, Goch, RHINE, North-West Europe 1940, '44-45, Barkasan, British Somaliland 1940, TOBRUK 1941, Tobruk Sortie, EL ALAMEIN, Advance on Tripoli, Medenine, Zemlet el Lebene, Mareth, AKARIT, Wadi Akarit East, Djebel Roumana, Medjez Plain, Si Mediene, TUNIS, North Africa 1941-43, Landing in Sicily, Vizzini, Sferro, Gerbini, Adrano, Sferro Hills, SICILY 1943, CASINO II, Liri Valley, Advance to Florence, Monte Scarlari, Casa Fortis, Rimini Line, Casa Fabbri Ridge, Savio Bridgehead, Italy 1944-45, Athens, Greece 1944-45, CRETE, Heraklion, Middle East 1941, Chindits 1944, BURMA 1944. (The ten battle honours printed in capitals were selected to appear on the Sovereign's Colour.)

After the war the 1st Battalion served in Germany with the occupation forces. The 2nd Battalion was the last British unit to leave Pakistan at the end of February 1948, and when infantry regiments were reduced to one-battalion strength, the 2nd joined the surviving 1st in July that year at a parade in Duisberg, Germany.

In 1952 it was announced that The Black Watch was one of the seven infantry regiments authorised to raise a second battalion, and the 2nd was duly re-formed in the spring. In February 1952, its stint in Germany over, the 1st Black Watch arrived in Crail, Fife, its place in Germany being taken by the 2nd.

The 1st Black Watch moved from Pusan to enter the fray in Korea with the Commonwealth Division in June 1952. In flooded dug-outs and trenches in the hills the battalion operated in torrential rain, which turned the red clay into thick, clinging slippery mud. But this did not bog down the aggressive patrolling of the Black Watch, and there were several successful clashes with enemy prowlers and raiding parties.

Their principal action was the defence of The Hook, an important salient jutting into enemy territory. In November the North Koreans and their Chinese allies were on three sides of the crest of the ridge. The Hook was the key to the strategic Samichon Valley, on the road to Seoul, the South Korean capital.

The enemy heavily shelled the area and attacked in great strength. Bitter fighting followed in 18 degrees of frost, and when ammunition ran out The Black Watch companies charged with bayonets and spades. On several occasions they called the supporting artillery to barrage their positions to clear them of the enemy.

With their horns and trumpets sounding the North Koreans and Chinese swarmed across the hills and poured into the assault, coming on through their own artillery fire and the United Nations counter-bombardment. Long irregular gaps were torn in their lines, but more attacking waves were thrown in, and the enemy came on, howling in frenzy – until they met the bayonets of the Black Watch.

The gleaming barrier of cold glinting steel stopped them and when the crisis of the battle was over there was a crazy pattern of bodies lying in no man's land in front of the United Nations positions. The costly fighting for The Hook continued into 1953.

In one of the furious Imjin River engagements, on November 4, 1951, Private (later Sergeant) William Speakman, a 6 ft.

7½ in. Black Watch stalwart attached to the 1st Battalion The King's Own Scottish Borderers, won his Victoria Cross.

Wave after wave of 'Gooks' came at the Borderers. 'Big Bill', of B Company H.Q., on hearing that the section holding the left of the company's position had suffered severe casualties and was in danger of being overrun, quickly collected a party of six men with an abundant supply of 'crackers'.

He led them in a series of grenade throwing charges which broke up several attacks. Despite wounds in a leg Private Speakman continued to lead his little band, showering the oncoming enemy with grenades and keeping them at bay long enough for his company to withdraw and regroup.

The cease-fire was on July 27, 1953, and in the same month the 1st Black Watch left Pusan for Kenya to curb the activities of Mau Mau. Black Watch Hill is a permanent memorial to the valour of the 'Auld Forty-Twa' during thirteen months in Korea. Battle honours awarded were The Hook 1952 and Korea 1952-53. They are emblazoned on the Queen's Colour.

Arriving at Nairobi in August the battalion was at once employed in pursuing and tracking down murdering marauding bands of Kikuyu tribesmen. The Black Watch scoured the Aberdaré Mountains and had a number of clashes with Mau Mau. After 'Operation Anvil' the members of this cult of barbarism were considerably less.

In September 1954, the 2nd Black Watch was dispatched to British Guiana to relieve The Argyll and Sutherland Highlanders and continued the pacification duties initiated by the Argylls during a period of political tension and unrest. In 1955 the 2nd returned to Scotland and was disbanded, a contingent joining the 1st.

Towards the end of 1958 the Soldiers of the Red Hackle arrived in Cyprus – 'Trouble Island' – where they operated against the EOKA terrorists in the closing months of the state of emergency. In an internal security role they guarded Government buildings, police posts and strategic points, provided escorts in danger zones, set up road blocks and check points and took part in searches for suspects, arms and ammunition. The battalion came home in late 1961.

Early in 1962 it became the Demonstration Battalion at the School of Infantry, Warminster, Wilts – a unique distinction.

And no regiment in the British Army was better qualified than the 'Auld Forty-Twa' – Chan 'eil na's fhearr (Second to None). After two years on 'demos' the 1st Black Watch received an overseas posting and arrived in Germany. The battalion had resumed its odyssey.

During November 1966, they moved from Minden to Cyprus, and on arrival joined the United Nations peace-keeping force. While in Cyprus the Highlanders reluctantly discarded their distinctive headgear and adopted – temporarily – the blue beret of the international force. The battalion returned to Minden in May 1967.

Thirty soldiers were selected from a large number of volunteers for nine months service with The Argyll and Sutherland Highlanders in Aden. After a home leave they left the Highland Brigade Depot, Aberdeen, in mid-June 1967, and made their rendezvous with the Argylls at Plymouth. They were air-lifted with them from Gatwick at the end of the month and arrived at Aden then in a turmoil with terrorists 'spite' outrages following the Arab debacle in the brief war with Israel.

The Black Watch and The Argyll and Sutherland Highlanders were in the dramatic re-capture of the Crater district – a nationalist stronghold and hide-out – early on July 4. The pipes and drums sounding loud and clear was the first indication the inhabitants had that the British had moved in, raising the 13-day siege of this maze of narrow alleys and rabbit-warrens.

The Highlanders quickly consolidated, dug-in, established road-blocks and check points and set up a number of sandbagged gun positions and posts at vantage points. It was a textbook operation carried out with great dash, split second timing and precision – in spite of the doubts of the civil authorities. There were no British casualties in the fitful resistance but several Arabs were downed.

A few days later the fire of a patrol toppled an enemy marksman from his perch on the heights of a mosque. This internal security role to assist the South Arabian Federation to maintain law and order was danger-fraught and thankless and the timely arrival of the Argylls and Black Watch volunteers was a welcome reinforcement.

And thousands of miles away, in Germany, the soldiers of the 1st Black Watch were giving the thumbs-up sign. Their thirty volunteers were worthily upholding the traditions of 'Am Freiceadan Dubh'. Their four years 'stint' over the battalion sailed from Bremerhaven to disembark at Leith in mid-March 1968, and took up their abode at Kirknewton, a few miles from the Capital.

In mid-August 1969, they were off again. The first parties of the battalion were airlifted from Turnhouse Airport, Edinburgh, to Gibraltar. And so 'The Watch' were on the alert when General Franco again cast envious eyes on the 'Rock', but no doubt his informers told him that 'The Black Watch of the Battles' was ready.

After nine months on this island in the sun the 'Auld Forty-Twa' was flown back to Edinburgh in mid-May 1970. Within a few weeks, however, the battalion was hurriedly dispatched to Ulster and on arrival immediately joined the Peacekeeping Force. History repeats. . . . The Black Watch once more reverted to its original role as armed police.

In 1970-71 they experienced three spells of duty, serving in Belfast, Londonderry, Enniskillen and Armagh.

In Belfast and elsewhere the soldiers of the Red Hackle countered the violence of political, religious and other rabble-rousers, a dangerous and thankless task which they discharged with commendable firmness and tact in the best traditions of Scotland's senior Highland regiment.

The British troops frequently became targets for the warring factions and I.R.A. extremists while endeavouring to keep them apart. They were stoned, grenaded, nail-bombed, petrol-bombed and sniped and on several occasions had to open fire in self defence. Snatch parties sallied forth to arrest obvious ringleaders and other known trouble-makers.

Though scores of soldiers were injured in incidents and in dismantling street barricades and other obstructions erected by rioters the troops showed wonderful restraint under intense provocation. But they harboured no grudges or malice and when Irish tempers cooled they went to the aid of the injured, distressed and homeless.

In addition to anti-riot duties they guarded communications centres, public service installations and police establishments against sabotage attempts, provided street and vehicle patrols, set up road blocks and made spot searches of cars and took part in searches of houses and buildings for arms, ammunition and explosives. These activities extended over a wide area of Belfast and the surrounding hills, including the Blue Mountain.

There were occasions when units of the Peacekeeping Force slept with clothes on during five or ten minute standbys, ready for instant action. Due to local conditions they lived hard and ate and slept when they could.

Night patrols were liable to ambush and their vehicles being mined and the danger of booby-traps was ever present. When off-duty soldiers went into town they did so in groups. With the approach of the Irish 'parade season' and the Battle of the Boyne anniversary the entire province was a flashpoint, but the vigilance of the police and military kept the number of incidents to the minimum.

The Timmies and Jocks will long remember the Belfast 'battles' in Falls Road, Crumlin Road, Coates Street, Shankill Road, Unity Flats and Artillery Flats . . . And during the troubles there was another 'bombardment' – of Cupid's darts. Many soldiers of the Peacekeeping Force wed *colleens*.

CHAPTER II

The Queen's Own Highlanders— Regiment of the Clans

From misty islands beloved of artist and poet, from shieling, clachan, thatched croft and windswept moorland, from mountains, glens and rugged sea coves, from lochs and purple heather hills, from the great silences where golden eagles soar and are heard strange bird calls, came the men who marched behind the pipes and drums of the Seaforths and the Cameron Highlanders.

Hardy sons of the sea and the soil these, whose forebears had followed the standards of the Old Pretender or Bonnie Prince Charlie. But, their loyalty won for the new Royal House, they fought gallantly and gloriously on many a foreign field and around the outposts of the Empire.

The separate lives of The Seaforth Highlanders and The Queen's Own Cameron Highlanders came to an end on February 7, 1961, when the two Regular Army battalions amalgamated at a ceremony in Redford Barracks, Edinburgh, to become The Queen's Own Highlanders with H.R.H. the Duke of Edinburgh as Colonel-in-Chief.

At 9 a.m. four subalterns, wearing the Mackenzie tartan kilts of the new regiment and the cap badge of The Highland Brigade, paraded in the officers' mess with the Queen's Colours and Regimental Colours of the two battalions and placed them in one group, giving effect to the amalgamation order.

First public duty, at 10 a.m., was the taking over of the guard at Edinburgh Castle from The Queen's Own Cameron Highlanders. The changing completed the old guard of the Camerons who, led by a piper, marched off with a soldier of The Queen's Own Highlanders on duty at the castle entrance.

The two regiments had been 'next door neighbours' for several generations – the Seaforths at Fort George and the Camerons at Inverness – and there was a close affinity between them, also a stimulating healthy rivalry. They had similar ancestry born in the clan tradition.

In many a battle Seaforth and Cameron had charged together with the same war cries, their pipes sounding in unison – and their blood had mingled. Thus the amalgamation was a union

55

of strength between kinsmen and an alliance of clans. Old Comrades of the two regiments – and others – hailed the fusion as 'the finest Highland blend unbottled!'

All ranks in The Queen's Own Highlanders, except pipers and drummers and military bandsmen, wear the Seaforth kilt – the Seaforth sett of the Mackenzie tartan – and Cameron trews. The musicians wear the Cameron kilt and Seaforth trews. The facing colours are buff and blue. Buff was the facing colour of the Seaforths and blue that of the Camerons.

The badge of The Highland Brigade incorporates the Seaforth motto 'Cuidich 'n Righ' (Help the King), the Stag's Head and the Cross of St. Andrew. The collar badge of The Queen's Own Highlanders portrays the elephant of the Seaforths super-scribed with the battle honour 'Assaye' and the sporran crest is the Camerons' crowned thistle.

Until the amalgamation early in 1961 the sagas of the two regiments are best chronicled separately.

The Seaforth Highlanders
(Ross-shire Buffs, The Duke of Albany's)

The 1st Battalion The Seaforth Highlanders – the old 78th and later the 72nd Highlanders – was raised in 1778 by Kenneth, Earl of Seaforth, Chief of Clan Mackenzie. On May 15, 1778, at Elgin, Major-General Robert Skene subjected the muster of over 1,000 Highlanders to a thorough inspection. He then described them as 'stoute men, hardy and active, and in a short time will make a remarkably fine regiment'. Prophetic words!

The Mackenzies of Seaforth supported the Jacobite cause in the 1715 Rising and William, the fifth Earl, was deprived of his title and estates. His eldest son, however, upheld the Government during the 1745 Rebellion. Kenneth, William's grandson, was allowed to purchase the estate from the Crown and he was created Earl of Seaforth in 1771.

To show his gratitude Kenneth Mackenzie offered to raise a Highland Regiment of Foot on his estate for service against the American Colonists. King George III readily accepted in December 1777, and the Earl received authorisation to proceed and was appointed Lieutenant-Colonel Commandant.

Kenneth Mackenzie rallied round him many clansmen from his Ross-shire lands and from the estates of the Mackenzies of Scatwell, Kilcoy, Applecross and Redcastle. The Macraes of Kintail were so well represented that for some time the new formation was known as the 'Regiment of the Macraes'. Several hundred men came from the Lowlands, England and Ireland.

Numbered and designated the 78th Regiment, Seaforth's Highlanders, the Mackenzie tartan was adopted. The stag's head badge with the motto *Cuidich 'n Righ* is the crest of the Mackenzies of Seaforth.

The crest and motto were granted to Colin Fitzgerald, founder of the family, in 1255, by King Alexander III, whose life he saved from a stag. *Tulloch Ard* on officers' sword-belts is a war-cry of the clan. It means high hill, the allusion being to the meeting or council place of the Mackenzies. And Highland mothers put the *sian* – the luck sign – on sons leaving to join the regiment.

Three months after embodiment the 78th arrived in Leith. The regiment was under orders for the East Indies. As it was raised for service in North America this news caused immediate resentment. The angry Macraes formed up with two plaids on poles as their 'colours' and led by pipers they marched defiantly out of barracks and entrenched themselves on Arthur's Seat.

The Macraes had numerous kinsmen and many other sympathisers in the area and they climbed the hill to provide the Highlanders with food. Through the efforts of Lord Dunmore and General Skene a settlement was soon reached and the soldier clansmen trooped back to barracks. The order dispatching the regiment to the East Indies was countermanded and the 78th was sent to the Channel Islands.

In May 1779, the French made a surprise landing on Jersey but the Seaforths and local militia drove them back to their ships in disorder. Early in January 1781, the French returned, seized St. Helier, took the Governor prisoner and demanded the surrender of the islands. The Seaforths and other units surrounded the enemy after street fighting and forced them to capitulate.

At the beginning of June the 78th embarked at Portsmouth for India without incident. The voyage was disastrous. It lasted

E

about ten months, the Colonel, Lord Seaforth, died off St. Helena and one of the ships was so badly damaged in a gale that she had to shape a course back to Portsmouth for repairs. When the regiment disembarked at Madras at the end of March 1782, about 250 men had succumbed to scurvy and other diseases.

The French and Dutch encouraged the Indian princes to rise against the British and Hyder Ali, Sultan of Mysore, took the field with a large well-equipped army. Less than 400 soldiers of the 78th were fit for duty but early in June the depleted regiment took part in the Battle of Arnee.

In early September detachments from the 78th served on the fighting ships of Admiral Sir Edward Hughes which engaged the French in Indian waters. The Highlanders, in the role of sailors and marines, were encouraged by their pipers who played during the action. The battle raged all day before the enemy was finally defeated.

A welcome reinforcement in October was the arrival of the company which had been on the disabled ship forced to leave the convoy. With the company was a draft of over 100 men. In January 1783, operations were resumed against Tippoo, who had succeeded as Sultan of Mysore. The French and their native allies were engaged at Cuddalore fort which was entered when peace was negotiated.

The truce was soon broken and a contingent from the 78th in a surprise attack during a severe storm overpowered the defenders of Palgautcherry fort. Coimbatore surrendered and when the enemy capital, Seringapatam, was threatened peace was made in March 1784. Owing to a reduction in Army Establishment the regiment was re-numbered the 72nd in September 1786.

Britain went to the aid of the State of Travancore in 1789 when Tippoo again became bellicose. The 72nd was engaged in long marches and a series of assaults on hill forts and were in the forefront at the capture of Coimbatore, Morglee, Savendroog, Outradroog, Outra Durgam, Dindegul, Palgautcherry and Seringapatam. The storming of the fortress of Bangalore – considered impregnable by the enemy – was another 'tour de force' of the 72nd.

This hard-fought campaign successfully concluded, the Seaforths were dispatched with the expedition sent in 1793 against the French settlement at Pondicherry, which the enemy surrendered in August. In July 1795, the regiment landed in Ceylon to operate against the Dutch, allies of France.

Trincomalee fort was captured, then Batticola and Manaar. The fortress of Colombo surrendered in February 1796, and Ceylon was ceded to the Empire. The 72nd returned to Scotland in 1798 and served in Ireland. A second battalion of the regiment was raised in 1804 when Napoleon threatened invasion. It was formed in Aberdeenshire and functioned as a 'feeder' for the 1st Battalion. The 2nd was disbanded in 1816 while serving in Ireland.

The 72nd was included in the British force which captured the Cape of Good Hope from the Dutch. Early in January 1806, the Seaforths, forming part of the Highland Brigade, overcame stubborn resistance on the Blaauberg, or Blue Mountains, and a few days afterwards the Dutch capitulated. Cape Colony then became a British possession.

It was decreed in 1809 that five regiments should be taken off the Highland Establishment and assume the uniform of infantry. The 72nd ceased to wear the Mackenzie tartan kilts and yellow facings on their doublets and reluctantly donned the white facings and pantaloons of the Infantry of the Line.

The 72nd departed from the Cape in 1810 to participate in seizing Mauritius from the French. Three years later the regiment was back in Cape Town. In 1815 it was ordered to India but the Nepal War was over ere the Seaforths landed. The 72nd returned to the Cape and from 1817-21 half of the battalion was on frontier duty along the Great Fish River protecting the settlers from Kaffir raids.

The Seaforths came home in 1822 and received the welcome news that King George IV had approved of the regiment again becoming a Highland corps but wearing tartan trews instead of kilts. As a further token of Royal esteem the Commander-in-Chief, H.R.H. the Duke of York and Albany, granted the Seaforths the use of his Scottish title, cypher and coronet and permitted the regiment to assume the Prince Charles Edward Stuart tartan.

Thus the 72nd took the title 72nd, or The Duke of Albany's Own Highlanders. It was the only Highland regiment to wear the feathered bonnet with trews.

Following a six year round of duty in the U.K. the Seaforths sailed for the Cape in 1828. From 1832-35 they operated against the marauding Kaffir tribesmen. The next homecoming was in 1840. The 72nd went overseas in 1844 and was stationed at Gibraltar, Barbadoes, Trinidad, Nova Scotia and New Brunswick, returning to Britain in 1854.

In June 1855, the Seaforths landed in the bleak disease-ridden Crimea. The regiment was represented in the force sent to Kertch but the troops did not land and a number of soldiers and sailors succumbed to an outbreak of cholera on board the ships.

On its return the 72nd joined General Sir Colin Campbell's Highland Brigade. The Seaforths entered the trenches in front of Sevastopol and were poised for an assault when the Russians evacuated the fortress blowing up magazines and defences as they retired. The ghastly Crimean War over, the 72nd sailed home in 1856.

Landing at Bombay during the Bengal Army Mutiny The Duke of Albany's Own Highlanders joined a field force advancing on the walled fortified town of Kotah in Central India. Towards the close of March 1858, Kotah was carried by assault with the Seaforths forming the bayonet-tipped spearhead.

On March 30, in forcing the entrance of a house commanding a gateway Lieutenant Aylmer Spicer Cameron won the regiment's first Victoria Cross. Under a withering fire he led a small party of Seaforth's up the narrow staircase to close with a band of rebels. In a desperate encounter he accounted for three of his assailants before going down wounded. The enemy was later blasted out with gunpowder.

The regiment was deployed in detachments to take up the pursuit of bands of mutineers and their adherents. In October 1858, the timely arrival of the 72nd with brigade saved the State of Bhopal from the enemy. For several months detachments were engaged in rounding up rebel groups and in general pacification duties over a wide area.

Early in 1866 the regiment was back in the homeland remaining until the spring of 1871 when it returned to India. In October 1878, the 72nd Highlanders were in the force sent against the Amir of Afghanistan. The right wing of the regiment distinguished itself in the grim battle for Peiwar Kotal. The enemy were strongly entrenched in a pass near Kohat but the

Highlanders and Gurkhas in a flank attack dislodged the tribes-men who abandoned the heights.

Peace was made in May 1879, but after the murder of the British Embassy staff at Kabul operations were resumed in September. In the march on the enemy capital the 72nd and Gurkhas were heavily engaged in assaults on the heights at Charasiah. The Afghans were driven back and Kabul was entered a few days later.

A *jehad*, or holy war, roused the tribesmen and there was further bitter fighting for the possession of the Deh-ma-Zung gorge and on Bala Hissar hill and Takht-i-Shah. The Seaforths fought off thousands of Moslem religious fanatics – known as Ghazis – and on December 14, Lance-Corporal George Sellar won the Victoria Cross for his courage and leadership in clear-ing an enemy *sangar*, or strongpoint, on the Asmai Heights.

The hill tribes rallied and on being reinforced the Afghans came on in dense masses and a retiral was ordered into Sherpur. After a ten day siege the enemy attacked but their numbers were thinned by the concentrated artillery and rifle fire of the defenders and they retreated into the hills pursued by cavalry.

In August 1880, after a British column had been overwhelmed at Maiwand, the regiment formed part of the force which marched with General Roberts to the relief of Kandahar. It covered 320 miles in 22 days and engaged and routed the enemy to the north of the town on September 1. The 72nd operated on the flank. Thus ended the Afghan War fought in the arid passes and eternal snows of the mountains.

Under the Army reforms of the 80's the 72nd, The Duke of Albany's Own Highlanders, became the 1st Battalion, The Sea-forth Highlanders on July 1, 1881, and the 78th Highland Regi-ment (Ross-shire Buffs) entered the corps as the 2nd Battalion, The Seaforth Highlanders. This was a singularly appropriate union as the 72nd and 78th had similar origin.

On its return from foreign service in 1882 the 1st Battalion – formerly the 72nd – resumed wearing the Mackenzie tartan kilts, the dress it had to discard under the unpopular order of 1809. This garb was also reverted to by the 2nd Battalion – formerly the 78th – after an interval of over 70 years.

The 78th was raised in the spring of 1793. France and Britain were then at war and on February 2 Francis Humberston

Mackenzie of Seaforth offered to recruit a Highland regiment on his estates in Ross-shire and Lewis. Authorisation followed from the King in a Letter of Service dated March 7, and he was appointed Lieutenant-Colonel Commandant.

Numbered the 78th, the formation paraded at Fort George on July 10 and was inspected by Lieutenant-General Sir Hector Munro. The establishment was soon raised to 1,110 and the regiment arrived in Guernsey in the autumn. In 1794 it was dispatched to the Netherlands where it participated in an unsuccessful campaign against the French.

The new Highland regiment, however, had three successes. Early in November it headed a sortie at Nijmegen and routed an enemy battalion in the trenches. At the close of December the 78th was in the counter-attack at Tuyl which drove back the French, and at the beginning of January 1795, the Highlanders, in defending Guildermalsen, repulsed a cavalry charge followed by an infantry attack.

The campaign was fought against numerical odds and in atrocious weather conditions. There was a retiral into Germany and troops were evacuated from Bremerhaven in the spring of 1795.

In 1794 a second battalion of the 78th was raised and granted the title of The Ross-shire Buffs. The commanding officer was Lieutenant-Colonel Alexander Mackenzie of Fairburn. The 2/78 sailed for the Cape of Good Hope in early March 1795, and took part in wresting Cape Colony from the Dutch after a two months' campaign.

The 2nd Battalion was absorbed by the 1st at Cape Town in June 1796, and the 78th sailed for India in mid-November. In the campaign against the Mahrattas, who were aided by the French, the 78th formed part of the forces commanded by Major-General Sir Arthur Wellesley (later the Duke of Wellington). The regiment was engaged at the capture of Ahmednagger in mid-August 1803.

The advance south continued and on September 23 battle was joined at Assaye. Here British and Indian troops defeated a Mahratta army estimated at six times their own strength after ghastly close fighting. The Highlanders braved the concentrated enemy bombardment, captured the guns and then stood firm against the swords and lances of the cavalry.

The King honoured the British regiments which broke the power of the Mahrattas by decreeing that an elephant super-scribed *Assaye* should be borne on their Colours. In addition, the East India Company presented each of the regiments with an *Assaye* Colour. Thus the Battle of Assaye was a glory day for the 78th Highlanders.

The Mahrattas rallied at Arguam but were again vanquished and, with the destruction of their fort at Gawalghur the war ended in December 1804. In 1811 the 78th was sent with an expedition to clear the French from the Dutch island of Java.

Batavia, the capital, was entered and the enemy retired on Weltevreeden. On being ejected the French retreated to the fortified line at Cornelis, which fell in August. After another stand at Samarang in mid-September the French surrendered and evacuated the island.

Clashing with the forces of the rebellious Sultan of Djocjocarta, the Highlanders participated in the capture of his stronghold in late June 1812. Returning to India in November 1816, the transports conveying the 78th were wrecked in the Bay of Bengal and the baggage, records and funds were lost.

The Highlanders were marooned on the island of Preparis for about a month and suffered considerable hardship through lack of provisions. After their rescue the 78th sailed for the home country at the beginning of March 1817.

In 1804 another second battalion of the 78th was raised, on this occasion by Major-General Alexander Mackenzie Fraser. Most of the recruits came from the Western Isles. The 2nd Battalion, 850 strong, was inspected the following year by the Marquis of Huntly at Fort George.

After duty at Gibraltar and in Sicily the 2/78 landed in Italy towards the end of June 1806, to take the field against the French. During the advance inland there was skirmishing and on July 4 the main enemy force confronted the British at Maida, in Calabria. Though heavily outnumbered the new battalion went at the French with the bayonet and drove them back in disorder.

In 1807 the 2nd Battalion formed part of a British expedition sent to Egypt to engage the Turks -- allies of France. Alexandria was occupied in mid-March and at the close of the month an attack was delivered on the Turks in their strong position at

Rosetta. The Highlanders sustained severe casualties and the survivors of units cut off at El Hamet were forced to surrender. Egypt was evacuated in September and the 2/78 returned to the homeland in January 1808.

The battalion was represented in the disastrous Walcheren expedition dispatched in July 1809, with the object of attacking Antwerp. Over 40,000 troops were involved but fortunately encounters with the enemy were few as disease was rife. The British force was withdrawn in December with over 11,000 men suffering from 'Walcheren fever'. The 2nd Battalion was still further depleted by the furnishing of drafts to the 1st Battalion serving against the French in Java.

The 2/78 was again sent to Holland early in January 1814, but on this occasion the Highlanders operated with outstanding success. In the advance on Antwerp they drove four French battalions from Merxem and later joined the Allied Army of Occupation. In 1816 the 2/78 returned to the U.K. to be amalgamated with the 1st Battalion.

The 78th experienced tours of duty in Ceylon, India and Aden and in early January 1857, the regiment proceeded with a division commanded by Brigadier-General Havelock to join the Persian Expeditionary Force led by Lieutenant-General Sir James Outram. The 78th disembarked at Bushire, on the Persian Gulf, at the beginning of February and after a series of long marches over difficult country in torrential rain the Shah's army was brought to battle at Koosh-ab.

The Persians were soon in flight and there was a further engagement at Mahommerah before the end of March. Light vessels of the Royal Navy engaged the enemy batteries and the Highlanders, disembarking from a fighting ship, were preparing to attack the entrenchments when the Persians were observed withdrawing with all speed. The campaign over, the British expedition returned to India.

Meanwhile the Bengal Army had mutinied and reports of uprisings and massacres were coming in as the troops disembarked at Bombay about the middle of May. The 78th was at once ordered to Calcutta by sea and on arrival the Highlanders disarmed several battalions of disaffected troops. The regiment was rushed to Allahabad where it joined General Havelock's small column which marched to the relief of Cawnpore.

The mutineers were routed at Futtehpore, Aong and Pandu Nuddi. The column pressed on to Cawnpore where a group of Europeans were putting up a stout resistance in the defence of some 200 women and children against several thousand rebels.

The 78th moved well ahead of the main body and had no artillery support when it rushed and silenced the enemy guns at Cawnpore and then repulsed a cavalry charge. Their pipes skirling the Highlanders burst into the town in mid-July only to find the little garrison had been massacred along with the women and children. Two days earlier they had been tricked into surrendering on the promise of safety.

Two attempts were initiated to relieve Lucknow where the garrison, comprising about 1,600 British troops, loyal sepoys and armed civilians were facing a similar fate. And in their charge were numerous women and children. There was bloody close fighting at Bithur, Mangalwar and Bashiratganj. In the initial bid to break through Lieutenant Andrew C. Bogle won the 78th's first Victoria Cross.

On July 29, at Onao, Lieutenant Bogle headed an assault party in entering the narrow doorway of a loopholed house from which the enemy was pouring a concentrated fire. Lieutenant Bogle and his Highlanders fought their way into the courtyard which was crowded with mutineers and in the ensuing melee he and many of his men were wounded.

On August 12, during the second attempt Lieutenant Joseph P. H. Crowe led a frontal attack on the batteries at Boorbia-ki-Chauki. Lieutenant Crowe was also awarded the Victoria Cross for his inspired leadership and conspicuous gallantry.

On September 23, after receiving reinforcements, General Havelock's column again battled forward. The mutineers and their adherents were driven from the Alambagh, a walled fortified enclosure about two miles from Lucknow, and the advance continued against mounting opposition.

The canal at Charbagh was crossed and the enemy batteries silenced in wild bayonet charges. The relief force, though suffering severe casualties, fought through the maze of narrow winding streets under a hail of fire from houses, walls and rooftops and the Residency was entered on the 26th.

A further six Victoria Crosses were won by soldiers of the

78th during the relief operations: Lieutenant Herbert T. Macpherson; Surgeon Joseph Jee; Assistant-Surgeon Valentine T. MacMaster; Private Henry Ward; Private James Hollowell; and Colour-Sergeant Stewart Macpherson.

Lieutenant Macpherson led a bayonet charge which captured two field guns. The bearing and spirit of Private Hollowell so heartened nine of his comrades that they defended a house against several hundred rebels and saved several wounded men. Under fire Colour-Sergeant Macpherson rescued a wounded private from an exposed position in the Residency. Surgeon Jee, Assistant-Surgeon MacMaster and Private Ward performed many acts of valour in evacuating and attending to the numerous casualties.

The depleted column joined the defenders of the Residency and together they kept the rebel hordes at bay for six weeks until General Sir Colin Campbell's force arrived from Cawnpore in mid-November. The 78th was represented in the relief force and in the garrison there was a reunion.

General Sir Colin Campbell left a division at Lucknow as a reinforcement and marched against the rebels who were now threatening his communications and base at Cawnpore. He returned to Lucknow with sufficient troops in March 1858, and the mutineers were finally cleared from the city.

The 78th joined the Rohilkund Field Force and was engaged at the capture of Bareilly. General pacification duties followed and The Ross-shire Buffs sailed for home in May 1859. After tours of duty at Gibraltar and in Canada the regiment returned to India early in 1879 and though it operated in the Afghan War of 1879 the 78th was not committed to battle. The Highlanders garrisoned Kandahar from 1880-81.

In the spring of 1882 the 1st Battalion The Seaforth Highlanders – the former 72nd – left India for Aden. In August the battalion arrived in Egypt to suppress the Egyptian Army mutiny organised by Colonel Arabi Pasha and engaged the rebels at Shaluf.

In mid-September the 1st Seaforths were prominent in the dawn bayonet charge which surprised the enemy at Tel-el-Kebir. Their rush overran the guns and the infantry after a feeble resistance fled across the desert. Cairo was entered, the mutiny collapsed and the battalion was homeward bound in October.

At the close of 1897 the 1st Seaforths were in the International Occupation Force which was dispatched to Crete. In March 1898, the battalion landed in Egypt and joined General Sir Herbert Kitchener's Anglo-Egyptian Army for the recovery of the Sudan.

The Khalifa's dervish army had advanced to a position on the bank of the Atbara River and the Anglo-Egyptian force approached by means of the Nile and marches across the sands. Early in April, after a lashing bombardment, the assault went in, the Seaforths 'leapfrogging' the Camerons. The enemy commander, Emir Muhmoud, was captured and after half an hour's hard fighting the dervishes broke and scattered into the jungle.

Four months later the Anglo-Egyptian expedition marched on Omdurman. On September 2, about ten miles from his capital, the Khalifa barred the way with over 60,000 of his desert warriors. The screaming war-cry of their faith was drowned in the thunder of artillery and the rattle of musketry. It was more of an execution than a battle and the charging masses of dervishes went down in thousands before the concentrated well-directed fire of the 20,000 Britons, Egyptians and Sudanese.

The Khalifa fled from the shambles, Omdurman was entered and then Khartoum. The campaign was over – and the murder of General Gordon avenged. Throughout the South African War the 1st Battalion was stationed in Egypt but sent drafts to the 2nd Battalion in the field. The 1st also dispatched two mounted infantry companies.

In 1903 the 1st Seaforths were serving in India. The battalion joined a punitive column in February 1908, and operated against the Zakka Khel Afridis. The 1st Seaforths were again in action some three months later, their adversaries being Mohmand tribesmen – a 'sept' of the Pathans. These frontier 'wars' were successfully concluded within a few weeks.

After the 78th became the 2nd Battalion The Seaforth Highlanders in 1881 it again experienced active service in India. The battalion was with the punitive force which in the autumn of 1888 skirmished with the Asakis and Hassanzais in the rugged Hazara or Black Mountain region beyond the North-West Frontier. There were sharp engagements, particularly at Kotkai, but early in November peace returned to the high passes – but not for long.

In 1891 there was further trouble in the Hazara necessitating the dispatch of another expedition in March. The Seaforths sniped and were sniped at among the boulders, crags and defiles during sixteen months of hide-and-seek guerilla warfare until the tribesmen surrendered in mid-May.

When the garrison at Chitral was attacked by the hill tribes in 1895 the 2nd Battalion was with the relief column which set out at the end of March. This force fought through the Malakand Pass into the Jandol Valley and was on the final lap of the operation when news came in that Chitral had been relieved by another column advancing from Gilgit.

The 2nd Seaforths voyaged home in 1897 and in mid-October 1899, the battalion left Fort George for Cape Town. It joined the Highland Brigade on the Modder River early in December with Britain at war with the Boers of the Transvaal and Orange Free State.

In a determined bid to relieve Kimberley the Highland Brigade made an approach march to Magersfontein Hill on the night of December 10/11. It was intended to take the Boers by surprise at first light but the advance bore too far to the left and during a thunderstorm the flashes of lightning are believed to have revealed to the enemy the nearness of the brigade.

As the Highlanders rectified their course in the lifting darkness and deployed to launch the assault a sudden blast of fire levelled them in scores. With men falling on every side the survivors rallied and charged. There were several local successes but lack of numbers ruled out further progress.

The 2nd Seaforths got into the trenches of the Scandinavian Commando and destroyed this formation with bullet and bayonet. Hopelessly intermingled the companies attacked the key position on the hill only to be enfiladed by their own batteries. For several hours they lay out in the blazing sun exchanging fire and rushing the entrenchments.

The Boers began an outflanking movement and the shattered brigade was ordered to retire. The Highlanders again came under the deadly fire of the enemy marksmen and though covered by the artillery the Gunners could accomplish little against the narrow deep Boer trenches.

At the beginning of February 1900, the Highland Brigade seized Koodoosberg and repelled an attack. There was hard fighting at Paardeberg resulting in a Boer surrender at the end of the month. The enemy was driven from Poplar Grove and Driefontein and Bloemfontein, capital of the Orange Free State, was entered in mid-March.

The Highland Brigade held Roodeport in the face of a powerful attack, Heilbron was taken and after the capture of Retiefsnek about the close of the month there was another Boer surrender. The advance on Pretoria, capital city of the Transvaal, gathered impetus.

The 2nd Seaforths were engaged in several actions notably at Jagersfontein, Fauresmith and Philloppolis and until the end of the war – in May 1902 – the companies manned a number of blockhouses from which they cleared the enemy from the surrounding territory, area by area. The battalion came home early in 1903 and proceeded to Ireland.

Early in the twentieth century the following battle honours appeared on the Regimental Colour of The Seaforth Highlanders: Carnatic, Hindoostan, Mysore, Cape of Good Hope 1806, Maida, Java, South Africa 1835, Sevastopol, Koosh-Ab, Persia, Lucknow, Central India, Peiwar Kotal, Charaslah, Kabul 1879, Kandahar 1880, Afghanistan 1878-80, Tel-el-Kebir, Egypt 1882, Chitral, Atbara, Khartoum, Paardeberg, South Africa 1899-1902.

At the outbreak of World War I the 1st Seaforths were stationed at Agra, India. With the 7th (Meerut) Division of the Indian Expeditionary Force the Highlanders arrived in France in October 1914. The battalion was the only British formation in the 19th Indian (Dehra Dun) Brigade.

During the winter of 1914-15 the Seaforths manned the trenches in the Richebourg-St. Vaast-Neuve Chapelle area and several German attacks were driven back, particularly at Givenchy in mid-December. The battalion was heavily engaged at Neuve Chapelle in early March 1915, and in taking a front-line trench and repelling a counter-attack the Seaforths had heavy losses.

A month later the battalion took part in an attempt to drive the enemy from Aubers Ridge but again it was stalemate. During the onslaught at Loos the Indian Corps created a diversion on the flank. In November the 1st Seaforths were withdrawn with their Indian comrades to serve in another theatre of war – Mesopotamia.

Arriving at Basra the battalion was transported along the Tigris and after a week's voyage disembarked at El Gharbi. Early in 1916 the Seaforths attacked over flat coverless ground in an effort to break through the Turkish entrenchments and relieve the garrison trapped at Kut-el-Amara. Casualties at Sheikh Saad, Wadi and El Hannah were such that the 2nd Black Watch and 1st Seaforths were amalgamated to form 'The Highland Battalion'.

At the beginning of April another attempt pierced the defences at El Hannah but an assault on the key position at Sannaiyat failed. On April 6, at Sannaiyat, Corporal Sydney W. Ware won the Victoria Cross. The order was given to retire to the cover of a communication trench and Corporal Ware, who had distinguished himself earlier, brought back several wounded in various acts of gallantry during two hours under heavy fire.

Despite the sacrifice of the relieving force the dwindling, disease-ridden famished garrison at Kut-el-Amara was forced to surrender at the end of the month. A lull in the fighting ensued and in the autumn, with the arrival of reinforcements, the 2nd Black Watch and 1st Seaforths resumed their separate identities.

Towards the close of February 1917, the Dehra Dun Brigade re-entered the fray and three lines of trenches were wrested from the Turks at Sannaiyat. And another Victoria Cross was won by Lance-Sergeant Thomas Steele.

On February 22 an enemy counter-attack temporarily regained several trenches. Lance-Sergeant Steele ran across open ground under artillery and small arms fire and helped to get a machine-gun into position. He kept it in action and was instrumental in holding the remainder of the line.

Some hours afterwards in another onslaught the Turks succeeded in re-occupying parts of trenches they had lost. Lance-Sergeant Steele rallied the defenders and they fought on and assisted in re-establishing the line. In this second act of gallantry he was badly wounded.

Enemy resistance was weakening and within a few days the 7th (Indian) Division left the flies, sand, torrential rain and mud to advance, via Kut and Ctesiphon, cross the Tigris and converge on Baghdad, which fell in mid-March. Beyond Baghdad there

were sharp engagements with the retreating Turks at Mousha-
dieh, Beled, Istabulat and Tekrit.

The 'Mespot' campaign successfully concluded, the Seaforths
moved south to Basra and arrived in Egypt early in January
1918. The division then joined the 21st Corps in Palestine for
General Allenby's final victorious advance. In late September
the 1st Seaforths were in the hard fighting which presaged the
capture of Beit Lidd.

The battalion trekked north to enter Beirout and was later
stationed at Tripoli. It was back in Beirout when hostilities
ceased early in November. In March 1919, the 1st Seaforths
proceeded to Egypt and left the Land of the Pharaohs bound for
Fort George in June.

The 2nd Battalion crossed the Channel to arrive in France on
August 23, 1914, as part of the 10th Brigade of the 4th Division.
It joined the British Expeditionary Force battling on the left of
the French against the German invaders. In the unforgettable
Retreat from Mons companies operated in spirited rearguard
actions as the battalion retired fighting from Hurlevant to
Chevry, covering 130 miles in little over a week.

When the enemy was checked on the Marne the Seaforths
were prominent at the capture of Meteren and were engaged
round Frelinghien during October. As the war of movement had
ended the B.E.F. manned the hastily constructed lines of
trenches.

The 2nd Seaforths distinguished themselves at St. Julien in
the Second Battle of Ypres towards the close of April 1915.
Early in May the Germans sent over gas. With handkerchiefs
bound over their mouths and noses the Highlanders kept their
trenches intact.

Later in the month, while in reserve, the battalion was rushed
forward to recapture several trenches and the mission was
accomplished despite severe losses. In July the Seaforths were
switched to the Albert-Arras area, a comparatively quiet stretch
on the Third Army's 'front'. Nevertheless the battalion featured
in several minor operations.

In the Somme offensive the 2nd Battalion went into the
assault near Beaumont Hamel and took several trenches. Here,
on July 1, 1916, Drummer Walter Ritchie won the Victoria
Cross. He stood up on the parapet of an empty trench and though

under machine-gun and bomb attack he repeatedly sounded the 'Charge'. Leaderless soldiers of various units, who were showing signs of wavering, immediately rallied and throughout the fighting Drummer Ritchie carried messages over fire-swept ground.

The Seaforths fought in this onslaught during the summer and autumn and after another grim winter in the trenches they entered the Battle of Arras early in April 1917. The battalion attacked near Roeux and in this sector, at Fampoux, another Victoria Cross was earned.

On April 11 Lieutenant Donald Mackintosh, though wounded in a leg, continued to lead his Highlanders and captured a trench. He gathered men of another company and drove back a counter-attack but was again hit. Unable to stand, Lieutenant Mackintosh kept control of the situation and ordered the fifteen survivors to advance on the final objective. With great difficulty he got out of the trench and received a third wound. The award of the Victoria Cross was posthumous.

Though reduced by appalling casualties to two companies the Seaforths were well to the fore in further attacks early in May. In October, they entered the Third Battle of Ypres and were prominent in the assaults on Passchendaele Ridge.

The winter of 1917-18 was spent in a merciless war of attrition in frozen or waterlogged exposed trench lines -- raids, counter-raids, bombing forays, sniping and thundering artillery concentrations. On March 21, 1918, the 2nd Seaforths faced the mighty German spring offensive at Arras.

With the 4th Division they fought like men possessed in stemming the seemingly endless lines of field grey as the Germans came on shoulder-to-shoulder till swept away by artillery, rifle and machine-gun fire. The battalion was later rushed to La Bassée where the enemy had broken through the positions of Portuguese troops and after desperate fighting the line was stabilised.

In this massive offensive, delivered on a wide front, the German Army spent itself. Following initial gains the enemy wavered and then reeled before the combined counter-offensive of the Allies. The Germans streamed back in disorder towards the Meuse and thousands of prisoners were taken daily.

Rearguards at first fought stubbornly and skilfully but their resistance broke though in a number of instances there was frenzied close fighting ere they were overwhelmed. There were rumours of unrest in the Fatherland and early in November Germany sued for peace.

The following battle honours were later awarded to the Regiment: Le Cateau, Retreat from Mons, MARNE 1914, '18, Aisne 1914, La Bassée 1914, Armentieres 1914, Festubert 1914. '15, Givenchy 1914, Neuve Chapelle, YPRES 1915, '17, '18, St. Julien, Frezenberg, Bellewaarde, Aubers, LOOS, SOMME 1916, '18, Albert 1916, Bazentin, Delville Wood, Pozieres, Flers-Courcelette, Le Transloy, Ancre Heights, Ancre 1916, ARRAS 1917, '18, VIMY 1917, Scarpe 1917, '18, Arleux, Pilckem, Menin Road, Polygon Wood, Broodseinde, Poelcappelle, Passchendaele, CAMBRAI 1917, '18, St. Quentin, Bapaume 1918, Lys, Estaires, Messines 1918, Hazebrouck, Bailleul, Kemmel, Bethune, Soissonais-Ourcq, Tardenois, Drocourt-Queant, Hindenburg Line, Courtrai, Selle, VALENCIENNES, France and Flanders 1914-18, Macedonia 1917 18, Megiddo, Sharon, PALESTINE 1918, Tigris 1916, Kut-el-Amara 1917, BAGHDAD, Mesopotamia 1915-18. (The names printed in capitals appear on the Queen's Colour.)

Early in 1919 the 2nd Battalion reorganised at Fort George and in the autumn was ordered to India. In mid-August, 1930, the Seaforths were engaged against frontier tribes which were threatening Peshawar. The battalion, serving with the 9th Jhansi Brigade, operated from a fortified base camp set up at Miri Khel. The Afridis were brought to heel and in August, 1931, the brigade was withdrawn. The battalion was stationed in Palestine during 1932 and voyaged home in the following year.

The 1st Battalion was in Dublin in 1921 during the 'troubles' and at the close of 1933 left the south of England for Palestine and for several months the 1st and 2nd Battalions were on the same station. When the Italians invaded Abyssinia in 1935 the 1st Seaforths were rushed from Cairo to Mersa Matruh as a precautionary move but Mussolini's blackshirts showed no inclination to advance from Libya towards the Nile Delta.

The battalion was back in Palestine in 1936 and was employed on an internal security role in maintaining order during racial and anti-British strife. Later that year the Seaforths were again in Cairo. The battalion was dispatched to Hong Kong early in 1937 and in March 1938, moved to Shanghai.

F   73

While the Sino-Japanese War was raging the companies were on duty in the British sector of the International Settlement. In late September, following the Munich crisis, the battalion embarked 'on the double' and a cruiser rushed the Seaforths over to Hong Kong. Early in October, however, the battalion was again stationed in the International Settlement in Shanghai.

At the end of August 1940, the 1st Battalion arrived in Singapore and early in 1941 was dispatched to Agra. The Seaforths joined the 23rd (Indian) Division near Kohima in March 1942, and in May took up defensive positions which facilitated the withdrawal of the Burma Army across the Chindwin.

The British and Indian forces of South East Asia Command made a fighting comeback and in 1943 the 1st Seaforths were prominent in a series of actions along the Chindwin. These engagements aided Major-General Orde Wingate's Chindits in returning from their first successful mission deep in enemy-held territory.

In 1944 the battalion featured in operations intended to give the Japanese the impression that a crossing of the Chindwin was imminent. At the same time the Seaforths and other units diverted enemy attention from General Wingate's second long-range penetration when his destroy-disrupt-and-kill force was flown into Burma.

In the spring the Japanese launched an invasion on India. The 1st Seaforths moved from Wangang through hilly country and led the brigade group towards the west of Imphal to get behind the enemy surging down the Ukhrul road. In mid-April the battalion was in the attack on Kassom which followed the seizing of features known as North Pimple and South Pimple.

Light opposition was encountered as Kassom was entered. The Japanese struck but were repulsed and the companies moved north towards Sokpao and came under mortaring followed by grenade attacks. Infiltration attempts by enemy groups failed and a link-up was effected with a brigade approaching from Litan.

The Japanese retired into the hills lying south of Imphal and the Seaforths headed for Lammu. Automatic bursts and mortaring checked progress and artillery shelled the village. A limited withdrawal was made to allow an air strike and a further bombardment.

The assault went in and the enemy was cleared out of Lammu. These operations resulted in disrupting the Japanese drive along the Ukhrul road and they abandoned their thrust on Imphal from this direction. In mid-May the companies were engaged in patrolling difficult country in the Shenam area.

At the close of the month the battalion took over forward positions in the hills and in strengthening the defences there were appreciable casualties as a result of grenade-lobbing by the enemy. In mid-June the monsoon deluge inundated trenches, dug-outs and emplacements.

A fortnight later a sudden attack was delivered on the Japanese near Mitlong Khunou. They were taken by surprise but soon retaliated in strength and were finally pinned down by an artillery concentration. The battalion returned to Shenam and in mid-July took part in the general advance.

One company was involved in a violent action on Nippon Hill and wiped out the Japanese defenders in their maze of bunkers. The enemy was now in retreat but the 1st Seaforths were not in at the 'kill'. The battalion was withdrawn and on VE Day was training in India for the recovery of Malaya.

The 1st Seaforths later received honourable mention in the history of the 23rd (Indian) Division – which lived and fought for two years in the hills and valleys round Imphal. The Seaforths were the first troops of this division to arrive on the Chindwin 'front'. On three occasions the 23rd covered fighting withdrawals of British and Indian formations from Burma.

The chronicle of the division relates how the battalion patrolled the river and later maintained a vigil on the strategic Ukhrul road. It enthuses over the battalion's part in the operations which slowed down the Japanese crossing of the Chindwin. When the enemy succeeded in cutting the withdrawal route of the 17th (Indian) Division the Seaforths, with other units of the 23rd, battled off determined attempts to annihilate the 'tail' of the hard-pressed 17th.

The 23rd also fought hard in assisting the 17th back from Tiddim. The division's references to the Highlanders enthuses about their aid to the Chindits. The Seaforths were proud to be associated with this noted division and its achievements – and their feelings were heartily reciprocated by their Indian comrades.

Reconnaissance missions and patrols well behind the enemy lines were Seaforth specialities. They operated in the sweltering steamy heat of jungle and swamp, over arid hills and mountains and along dried-up watercourses – which became raging torrents during the monsoon. The torrential rain, sweat and humidity rotted clothes and 'harness' on their bodies.

Engagements with the Japanese were invariably violent bloody affairs and frequently the enemy had to be blasted out of their cunningly concealed camouflaged bunkers. Sickness and casualties reduced the strength of the companies and often they were on tight rations and short of supplies – and mail was usually several months late. But the Fourteenth Army – 'The Jungle Bashers' – battled through to final victory and exploded the myth of the Japanese super-man – even to the Japanese.

The 1st Seaforths landed at Port Dickson, in Negri Sembilan, Malaya, in mid-September 1945, and later they were dispatched to Java to disarm Japanese troops on the island and undertake general pacification duties. At one period unrest and looting resulted in Japanese soldiers and Seaforths standing guard together.

In March 1940, the 2nd Battalion The Seaforth Highlanders joined 152 Brigade of the 51st (Highland) Division. The 6th Seaforths (T.A.) left this brigade of the 51st to take the place vacated by the 2nd Battalion in 17 Brigade of the 5th Division. The 2nd Seaforths were brigaded in 152 with the 4th Seaforths (T.A.) and the 4th Queen's Own Cameron Highlanders (T.A.). The Highland Division and attached troops at this time was known as the Saar Force.

In the spring, in support of the French, the Highland Division was located in a sector of the Maginot Line defences and at the beginning of May took over forward trenches. In aggressive night patrolling by both sides the Highlanders had much the better of the exchanges.

On May 10 the Germans invaded the Low Countries – the 'phoney war' was over. Three days later – on the memorable 13th – a mighty bombardment fell on the divisional lines and the advancing enemy infantry was engaged in the Saar region in front of the Maginot Line.

Bitter confused fighting ensued as German pressure mounted and on the 15th the Highland Division, which was under French command, was ordered to retire to new positions to conform with the defence plan. Then the 51st entrained near Metz, the intention being to link up with the British Expeditionary Force at Rouen.

But by this time a wedge of German armour had been driven between the Highland Division and the B.E.F. and the Dunkirk evacuation had begun. The 51st joined the line of the 9th French Corps on the Somme. The position here too was precarious as the enemy had established two firm bridgeheads, one at St. Valery-sur Somme and the other to the south of Abbeville.

Two French assaults had failed to smash the Abbeville bridgehead and on the morning of June 4 the Highlanders and General de Gaulle's armoured division delivered another attack, the 2nd Seaforths going in on the left. A number of tanks was lost and though some initial progress was made, particularly by 152 Brigade, several units were isolated and, with no reserves available, the situation quickly deteriorated. A withdrawal was then made to the start-line.

The following day the enemy launched a counter-attack and forward positions were overrun, dive-bombers joined in and it became a fight for survival. A further retiral was decided upon, 152 Brigade withdrawing from the Blangy-Monchaux area to the Foret d'Eu to cover a similar move by the French on the right flank.

Fighting back to the line of the River Bethune with the division 152 Brigade manned positions from Dieppe to Arques. The Germans drove hard for the Channel ports and their offensive gathered impetus from St. Quentin to the sea, splitting the 10th French Corps. When the enemy established bridgeheads across the Seine the 51st was fighting its last battle in withdrawing to St. Valery-en-Caux.

Behind the Highlanders were the cliffs and the sea. In front and on each flank were Rommel's tanks and infantry. Even then there were hopes of an evacuation but the German artillery pounded St. Valery and forced the waiting ships out to sea. A rain mist cloaked the coast. The Highland Division was doomed.

The French capitulated at 8 o'clock on the morning of June 12. The Highlanders ignored a demand that they too should surrender and they fought on alone for over two hours. The divisional guns fell silent – they had fired all their ammunition. And around Le Tot and St. Sylvain, on the defence perimeter of St. Valery, the 2nd Seaforths made it a fight to the finish.

After a month of withdrawals, holding actions and costly attacks, the failure to join the British Expeditionary Force at Rouen as a result of French vacillation and, for the same reason, the loss of the opportunity to evacuate the division from Le Havre, Major-General Victor Fortune knew his men had done all that was expected of them – and much more. And he had obeyed his orders to cover the French flank.

With a heavy heart but with a clean conscience he gave his last order – to surrender. The silent, exhausted, tattered remnant of the Highland Division filed past him and began the long march into Nazi prison camps. Round One had gone in favour of the German Colossus.

Within a few months the Regular Army battalions of the lost division were re-raised – and the 'reincarnation' of the 2nd Seaforths took its rightful place in the new 152 Brigade. With the 2nd Battalion were the 5th Seaforths (T.A.) and the 5th Queen's Own Cameron Highlanders (T.A.). And the 'mor-chuis' (proud bearing) of the old 51st was at once evident in the reconstituted division.

The 'gong' which sounded for Round Two was the thunder of the massed artillery at the Battle of El Alamein on October 23, 1942. The Highland Division arose and surged across the desert sands to silence the chattering German and Italian machine-guns. And the *pibroch* skirled eerily amid the artillery's roar and the metallic rumble of the tanks.

The new 51st (Highland) Division punched a gap in the enemy line and the armour passed through to administer the knock-out. The 2nd Seaforths came out of reserve on the 24th to form a bridgehead over a minefield which had been holding up the armour.

Later the battalion was 'loaned' to the New Zealand Division for the final infantry onslaught in the north. And so in a fortnight of mortal combat the reconstituted 51st (Highland) Division avenged St. Valery.

Back streamed long straggling lines of prisoners – gesticulating Italians and sullen dejected Germans. The 2,000 miles pursuit began with the 51st on several occasions spearheading the Eighth Army's rapid advance. In mid-December the enemy vacated Mersa Brega as 152 Brigade approached and a company of the 2nd Seaforths entered Misurata in the wake of a German rearguard.

The bayonets of the battalion cleared the Corradini-El Nab area on January 20-21, 1943 – an action which was appropriately named the Battle of the Hills. Two days afterwards a company was in the force of tanks and infantry which entered Tripoli. And the pipes and drums of the Highland Division sounded loud and clear in the Victory Parade.

The enemy took up a strong position in the Mareth Line – originally a French defence system. Time was running out for Rommel and on March 3 he attacked with tanks and infantry on the divisional front. This was repulsed and on the 6th he tried again with dive-bombers co-operating. Some inroads were made but these were sealed off by counter-attacks. In the 'riposte' the Mareth defences were pierced by other formations at considerable cost.

In the assault on Wadi Akarit on April 6 the infantry brigades of the 51st took part in the hardest fighting since El Alamein. The Germans and Italians were positioned behind the wadi which was protected by a minefield and an anti-tank ditch. And they held the dominating Roumana Ridge.

Objective of 152 Brigade was the hill feature. At dawn the infantry battalions scrambled over the jumble of rocks to clear the heights and Djebel Roumana was almost theirs when the enemy launched a furious counter-attack. The fighting went on all day and the timely arrival of reinforcements again turned the tide. At first light it was found the Germans and Italians had withdrawn.

With their retiral from Wadi Akarit the bottleneck pass known as the Gabes Gap was opened to the Eighth Army for the final advance. The Highlanders were in positions in the Garci Hills, in the Enfidaville region, until early May. On the 12th the Axis Forces in North Africa surrendered. And the pipes and drums of the 51st had a field day in the Victory Parade through Tunis.

In the invasion of Sicily on July 10 the Seaforths landed on 'Amber' Beach and moved inland without meeting opposition.

But on the 14th, at Francofonte, a battalion of German para-chutists barred the way. The Gunners pounded the village, the Seaforths went in with their bayonets and the enemy withdrew considerably reduced in numbers.

On the other side of the Monaci and Gorna Lunga rivers the battalion was in operations round Gerbini. The River Dittaino crossed, 152 Brigade attacked into the Sferro Hills and, supported by a barrage, drove the Germans from the slopes and crest.

The enemy struck back with tanks and infantry but made no headway against the volume of defensive fire. Over the River Simeto, on the slopes of Mount Etna, 152 Brigade captured Biancavilla and the 2nd Seaforths entered Fleri. A few days later the Axis Powers conceded victory in Sicily.

The Highland Division was withdrawn from Sicily as the Allied Forces were preparing to invade the Italian mainland. In November the transports bearing the 51st sailed into the Clyde Estuary and on disembarking the brigades left for train-ing grounds in the South of England.

Early in April 1944, the 51st was transferred to the 1st Corps and left the 30th Corps with which it had served in the Desert War and in Sicily. The division moved to the embarkation zone on the Thames early in June.

'Fair stood the wind for France!' Disembarking from the 7th to 9th at Courseulles, Normandy, 152 Brigade crossed the River Orne on the 11th and moved into positions near Escoville, in the precariously-held 'Triangle'. The brigade's assignment was to maintain the vital Orne bridgehead.

The 'Triangle' was isosceles with a base of 300 yards, each side being 800 yards. It was enveloped by woods and pointed south. The Germans held two sides including the south and east apexes, which were formed by cross-roads. The 'Triangle' was a killing ground and its defence was costly. As the days passed in this area some pessimists styled it the 'Eternal Triangle' and prophesied a stay in it 'for the duration!'

Detachments of the 2nd Seaforths aided the 5th Camerons to capture the village of St. Honorine in mid-June. About a month later the battalion fought south past an apex of the 'Triangle' and down the fire-swept Troarn road.

On July 18, following artillery bombardment and attacks by Allied bombers, the Highland Division – now under command of the 1st Canadian Corps – broke out of the containment area at Caen to initiate a war of movement. The 2nd and 5th Seaforths were heavily engaged at Tilly-la-Campagne, which was not cleared of the enemy until early August. There was further hard fighting around Favieres.

In this phase of operations the 51st fought from Tilly to Lisieux – 17 days and nights of practically non-stop action. And the punishment inflicted on the enemy had much to do with the German High Command order that their forces begin a retiral from France and Belgium to defences in Holland and behind the Siegfried Line.

The infantry brigades of the 51st advanced to the Seine dealing with rearguard opposition en route. They crossed the river at Duclair and Mauny and liberated a string of picturesque villages. And on September 2, 1944, the Highland Division, via the battlefields of North Africa, Sicily and Normandy, returned to St. Valery by the misty sea.

Thus the Highlanders kept faith with the Auld Alliance between Scotland and France. And they kept faith too with the creed of the clans – *Na diobair caraid 's a charraid* – Forsake not a friend in the fray.

The *pibroch* sounded in the square, there were flowers, flags, wine, handshakes, kisses, singing and dancing for St. Valery was en fête to welcome the Highland Division. And there were happy reunions with families who had befriended and assisted the soldiers of the original 51st in June 1940.

The division was returned to 1st Corps for the attack on Le Havre. This fortress was bombarded from land, sea and air and 152 Brigade approached from the north-east. The 2nd Seaforths were held up by a minefield but nevertheless took all their objectives. Le Havre surrendered on September 12.

The Germans were retreating so quickly from France and Belgium into Holland that the 51st had no further contact until the beginning of October when the division moved into positions between Tilburg and St. Oedenrode. But three weeks later came the Battle of the Maas, which began on the 23rd – the anniversary of El Alamein.

The Seaforths and Camerons of 152 Brigade were assigned to clear the woods east of the Dommel. This accomplished the brigade headed for Vught and s'Hertogenbosch with the maximum of artillery support. Early in November 152 was switched to attack the 'Island', an area located at a loop in the Maas where an enemy 'pocket' was holding out.

The battalion established itself on the Drunen crossroads and there was a series of 'boating parties' on the Afwaterings Canal. And on the 5th the Gunners had a noisy Guy Fawkes night with an abundance of 'fireworks' and 'illuminations'.

The infantry brigades then left the bleak dismal 'Island' and were soon engaged in a succession of actions to capture the locks and sluice-gates which controlled the water level in the canal network. German patrols were active and mines were laid in the channels.

After arriving at Nederweert 152 made assault-crossings of the Norder and Uitwaterings canals. The 2nd Battalion reached its objective at Beringen and cleared up the surrounding country. The division, having ousted the enemy from Baarlo, Bong and Zoterbeke, was ordered to the Nijmegen bridgehead towards the close of the month.

Early in December the 51st made a hasty retreat – before rising floodwater. The Germans had blown the Lek dyke which necessitated evacuating the area. The civilian population was assisted in an exodus across the Nijmegen bridge and later waterborne patrols fought several 'naval engagements' in this flat desolate wilderness which oozed mud and water.

Hitler's last offensive, unleashed on the Americans in the Ardennes in mid-December, overran their forward areas. The Highland Division was rushed south to the Liege-Namur region to guard the Maas crossings. A week later it made an advance to contact along the Ourthe Valley.

The Ardennes was in the grip of snow and ice which restricted the use of tanks and artillery. It was a job of work for the infantry. The Seaforths and Camerons of 152 Brigade advanced from Hotton and took part in the capture of Mierchamps, Ronchamps and Halleux and were engaged around Laroche.

On January 12, 1945, there was a link-up with the Americans coming up from the south and, its mission successfully completed, the 51st was withdrawn from the Ardennes. The stag's horns of the Seaforths gave the enemy another prod in mid-February when the Highland Division, backed by a barrage reminiscent of El Alamein, crossed the German frontier and thrust into the Reichswald.

The 2nd Battalion, with 'Crocodile' tanks co-operating, took its objective in the forest. The 'Crocodiles' literally 'chewed up' the enemy. Overcoming stubborn resistance the Highlanders got on to the Kranenburg-Hekkens road and, resuming the attack, the Seaforths entered Grafenthal and Asperden and breached the anti-tank 'moat' at Goch – a bastion of the Siegfried Line.

Asperheide captured, the brigade went on to take Boeckelt in its stride and the 2nd Seaforths fought some sharp actions around fortified farmhouses. By early March the entire west bank of the Rhine had been cleared of the enemy and the 21st Army Group was poised for the crossing.

The Allied Air Force and the massed artillery pounded the opposite bank and just before midnight on the 23rd the 2nd and 5th Seaforths – under command of 153 Brigade for this operation – went over in assault craft, the crossing being effected in less than five minutes. Assembling under sporadic shelling the 2nd Battalion attacked the north of the ruin that was Rees and later skirmished along the road to Isselburg, entering its outskirts by a bridge the Germans had only partially destroyed.

The companies raced for Dinxperlo, the 5th Seaforths securing an undamaged bridge. The 'head' was threatened by fire from a nearby wood and aircraft made a delivery run – with rockets. There was no more trouble from this quarter and Hohenhorst was entered. With the guns now across the Rhine, the artillery ranged on Hagesfeld and Fredricks and the 2nd Battalion skirmished through and mopped up the surrounding area.

The enemy had withdrawn from Isselburg and was in disorderly retreat. The Germans showed more inclination to surrender than to fight. Prisoners were coming in at the rate of 10,000 a day – including entire formations. The Germans had no reserves available and they appeared to have more soldiers in the Allied prisoner-of-war 'cages' than effectives in the field. The Luftwaffe was in moult – and the Russians were converging on Berlin.

Early in April the Highland Division moved about 40 miles from around Isselburg to Enschede and embarked on operations to drive the Germans from the north-east of Holland, and also the coastal belt up to the mouth of the Elbe. From Lingen the infantry battalions of 153 Brigade led the divisional advance to Ippener and Annen.

While moving towards Delmenhorst the 5th Camerons, with artillery and armour co-operating, ejected the enemy from Adelheide. The 2nd Seaforths did likewise with a force of paratroops at Ganderkese – the last fanatical resistance to be encountered by units of the 51st. It was found that the Germans had vacated Delmenhorst and at the close of the month 152 Brigade was established at Selsingen.

From the east bank of the River Oste 152 Brigade spearheaded the 51st in its night approach to Bremervörde at the beginning of May and the 2nd Seaforths crossed a bridge spanning the eastern channel. The German artillery was troublesome but as the fighting progressed their infantry showed a willingness to put their hands up.

Overtures for peace were made and negotiations began. In the closing hours of the war the Highland Division took the surrender of the 15th Panzer Grenadiers, a resuscitated Afrika Korps formation – and the 51st's old and respected adversaries in the Western Desert.

A captured German document paid a high tribute to the Highland Division in World War I. The Highlanders, it stated, 'were the most to be feared division in the whole of the British Army'. In World War II the 51st was the only division to go from El Alamein to Berlin, via the battlefields of North Africa, Sicily, France, Holland, Belguim and Germany.

The ten World War II battle honours which appear on the Queen's Colour are: St. Valery-en-Caux, Caen, Rhineland, El Alamein, Akarit, Sicily 1943, Anzio, Madagascar, Imphal, Burma 1942-44.

The other battle honours awarded to the Regiment for the campaigns of 1939-45 are: Ypres-Comines Canal, Somme 1940, Wihdrawal to Seine, Odon, Cheux, Troarn, Mount Pincon, Quarry Hill, Falaise, Falaise Road, Dives Crossing, La Vie Crossing, Lisieux, Nederrijn, Best, Le Havre, Lower Maas, Meijel, Venlo Pocket, Ourthe, Reichswald, Goch, Moyland, Rhine, Uelzen, Artlenberg, North-West Europe 1940, 1944-45, Advance on Tripoli, Mareth, Wadi Zigzaou, Djebel, Roumana,

North Africa 1942-43, Landing in Sicily, Augusta, Francofonte, Adrano, Sferro Hills, Garigliano Crossing, Italy 1943-44, Middle East 1942, Shenam Pass, Litan, Tengnoupal.

At the beginning of October 1946, the 1st Battalion left Java for the Ipoh area of Malaya. In 1947, when Regular Army infantry regiments – except the Guards – were reduced to one battalion establishment, the 2nd Battalion amalgamated with the 1st the following year. In mid-June 1948, the 1st Seaforths moved from Singapore to counter Communist terrorist activity and for three years the companies were engaged in Johore, East and Central Pahang and Perak.

Far from their base camps patrols penetrated deep into the jungles, hills and swamplands to ambush or track down murder gangs. Frequently these missions developed into hide-and-seek operations and there was a number of running engagements with terrorist bands.

The patrols brought back information which proved invaluable to the security forces in future operations. Close on 100 'jungle cats' were accounted for and there was over a score of 'probables'. The battalion lost fourteen in these actions. The 1st Seaforths returned home in mid-June 1951, and within a few weeks departed for Germany.

Coming back in May 1954, the battalion trooped for the Middle East in June and served in Egypt's Canal Zone. In July 1955, it was flown to Aden and took part in punitive expeditions directed principally against the warriors of the Shamsi section of the Rabizi tribe.

The Seaforths were engaged in desert and hill country protecting convoys from raids and in co-operating with Protectorate troops and levies in beleagured forts and outposts. Later the battalion was employed in general pacification duties.

The battalion left the Protectorate in the spring of 1956 for Gibraltar and it was ordered to Germany in the spring of 1957. The 1st Seaforths were back in Scotland early in 1961 to be fused with the 1st Queen's Own Cameron Highlanders.

The Queen's Own Cameron Highlanders

It's a far cry to April 16, 1746, when the bloodied remnants of Lochiel's Camerons, shattered by the Hanoverian cannon at Culloden, trudged wearily homeward and the cry *A bhean, a bhean, thoir dhuinn deoch* ('Woman, woman, give us water") was heard at farm and croft as they went by. That was in the year of *Am Prionnsa* – the Prince . . . But their descendants were to add lustre and glory to the saga of a regiment which perpetuated the proud name of their clan and its septs – The Cameron Highlanders.

The regiment was raised at Fort William on August 17, 1793, by Major Alan Cameron of Erracht, son of Ewen Cameron, who was second-in-command of Clan Cameron during the '45. Unfortunately young Cameron killed a clansman – Cameron of Morsheirlich – in a duel and fled to Canada.

Alan Cameron joined the Royal Highland Emigrant Corps and served against the American Colonist forces in the War of Independence. He was captured in the winter of 1775 while bound for Norfolk and was imprisoned in Philadelphia. With the aid of an American loyalist he escaped though badly injured in the process.

He reached the New Jersey coast but again fell into the hands of the enemy. He made another attempt to regain his freedom and was finally liberated under a prisoner exchange scheme and returned to Scotland in 1778.

Britain was then at war with Republican France and regiments were being formed in many parts of the country. Alan Cameron, anxious to prove that the old sores of the Jacobite risings were now healed and that there were no more loyal subjects in the realm than the clansmen of Lochaber, Appin, Morven and Mull, made several applications to the War Office for permission to raise a regiment.

Eventually he received a Letter of Service authorising him to proceed and stating that the soldiers recruited would not be drafted into other corps. But the Government was still suspicious of the Camerons and no bounty was offered to those who enlisted, and when the corps was formed it was styled the 79th or Cameronian Volunteers. Thus the authorities played down the clan association.

Nevertheless the following year – 1794 – the title was changed to the 79th Regiment, or Cameron Highlanders. For once Clan Cameron had won a bloodless victory! And the clan rallied as though the fiery cross had been carried through its lands.

In recruiting Alan Cameron received considerable assistance from his brother, Captain Ewen Cameron – *Eoghainn Mor* (Big Ewen) as he was locally known – and from Macdonell of Keppoch, whose father had featured in a gallant last stand against the 'Sassenach' at Culloden.

Financial support was forthcoming from Alan Cameron's father-in-law, Nathaniel Phillips, a Pembrokeshire landowner. Alan married his daughter, Anne, at Gretna Green in 1779 after a romantic runaway escapade. His heiress wife also helped to defray the cost of raising the new Highland regiment.

In his native Lochaber – a traditional Cameron stronghold – Alan Cameron received numerous pledges of support. He made his peace with the family of the man he had killed by promising commissions to several of his near relatives.

It was considered that red, the prevailing colour of the Cameron tartan, would not harmonise well with the scarlet military coatee. On the suggestion of Alan Cameron's mother the Macdonald sett was selected with the addition of the yellow stripe of the Cameron and the omission of three of the thin red lines of the Macdonald. The design became known as the Cameron of Erracht tartan.

The Letter of Service authorised the raising of the corps within three months and decreed that it should consist of a company of grenadiers, one light infantry company and eight battalion companies. The regiment was recruited to a strength of 750 in less than two months.

The first muster of the 79th was at Fort William in December 1793. The regiment then set out for Stirling where it was inspected, pronounced efficient and presented with a stand of Colours. When the Camerons marched away from rugged Lochaber the pipes were playing *Gabhaid sinn an rathad m'or* (We'll take the high road) and the clansmen were accompanied for several miles by a large number of their kinsmen and womenfolk.

While stationed in Belfast in June 1794, the kilts of Cameron of Erracht tartan attracted much attention and admiring comment. The uniform was similar to that worn by other Highland regiments, but the facings on the red coatees of the 79th were green.

The Cameron Highlanders first experienced active service during 1794-95 in the Duke of York's ill-conducted campaign in the Netherlands against Republican France. As the regiment was not committed to battle it had no opportunity to distinguish itself. The 79th lost about 200 men – most of them frozen to death. Half-starved, poorly-clad and inadequately equipped the British force took part in the ghastly winter retreat across Hanover and Westphalia to Bremen and the mouth of the Elbe.

When the 79th returned from Germany it was proposed to disband it and draft the Highlanders into other corps. This was in violation of the terms of the Letter of Service granting permission to raise the regiment.

Colonel Alan Cameron sought an interview with the Duke of York, the Commander-in-Chief, and legend has it he angrily informed him that 'to draft the 79th is more than you or your Royal father dare do'. The Duke just as heatedly replied, 'The King, my father, will certainly send the regiment to the West Indies.' Colonel Cameron stormed back, 'You may tell the King, your father, that he may send us to Hell if he likes and I'll go at the head of them – but he daurna draft us.'

The Duke was impressed by the vehemence of the fiery Cameron, the drafting order was rescinded, but the threat to dispatch the 79th to the West Indies was unfortunately implemented. The regiment was sent to Martinique and within two years it lost close on 300 men from fever and other tropical diseases.

While the Camerons were in the West Indies the 'no drafting' promise was broken. Soldiers of the depleted regiment were made 'volunteer' to serve in The Black Watch and other corps. The officers, senior N.C.O.s and the band, however, returned to Inverness in 1798 and the regiment was saved from extinction by recruiting up to strength.

The Camerons again took the field against the French in Holland in 1799 and in the grim fighting at Egmont-op-Zee on October 2 the regiment gained its first battle honour. Colonel

Cameron was wounded and the day after the battle the Duke of York rode up to the 79th and, doffing his hat, said to the acting commanding officer, 'Major MacLean, nothing could do the Regiment more credit than its conduct yesterday.' And so the Commander-in-Chief made piece with the clansmen.

Eighteen months later, after participating with a naval squadron in an unsuccessful attempt to destroy Spanish shipping and the arsenal at Ferrol, the 79th joined Lieutenant-General Sir Ralph Abercromby's force. Early in March 1801, this expedition effected a landing in Aboukir Bay and defeated the French at Mandora and Alexandria.

The Camerons were in the march on Cairo where the enemy surrendered and then evacuated Egypt. For its outstanding part in these operations the 79th was granted Royal authority to bear upon its Colours and appointments the Sphinx superscribed 'Egypt'.

A rifle Corps was formed in 1800 which became the 95th and later The Rifle Brigade. Originally raised on an experimental basis, it comprised detachments of picked men from fourteen regiments. The 79th contributed a kilted company.

A second battalion was added to the 79th in 1804. It was commanded by Alan Cameron's second son, Lieutenant-Colonel Nathaniel Cameron, and functioned as a 'feeder' for the 1st during the Peninsular campaigns. On the conclusion of peace with France the 2nd Battalion was disbanded at Dundee towards the end of 1815.

The 79th was engaged with the force sent against Denmark in 1807. It was feared that if the Danish fleet fell into Napoleon's hands this would change the balance of sea power. The Danish Government was asked to surrender the fleet and its return after the war was guaranteed. The Danes refused but after a bombardment of Copenhagen they complied with the British terms.

At the close of 1808 the Camerons were with Lieutenant-General Sir John Moore in his advance from Lisbon to join up with the Spanish Army and engage the French. On nearing Salamanca it was learned the Spaniards had been defeated, Madrid had fallen and that several large enemy columns – one led by Napoleon – were marching hard to trap the comparatively small British force.

G

On Christmas eve Sir John Moore's four divisions embarked on the hazardous 200 miles retreat to Corunna, which entailed crossing the snow and ice-bound Cantabrian Mountains. Food supplies gave out, transport was inadequte and desperate rearguard actions were fought en route. The walking wounded trudged or limped on using their rifles as crutches and others were cut down by the French cavalry operating on the flanks and rear.

Arriving at Corunna the ragged, famished and exhausted troops turned and hurled back their pursuers after four hours of violent close fighting in which Sir John Moore was killed. The battle ensured a successful evacuation on January 11, 1809, without interference from the enemy. During the ghastly winter retreat the 79th marched with the reserve.

In July of the same year the 79th took part in the expedition to Walcheren in an attempt to capture Antwerp and destroy French shipping on the Scheldt. After the seizure of Flushing no further progress was made as the force was ravaged by fever and had to be withdrawn in the autumn with several thousand sick, wounded and dying.

In the protracted Peninsular campaign the Camerons defended Cadiz and fought in the battles of Busaco, Fuentes d'Onor and Salamanca. The regiment took part in the occupation of Madrid, the siege of Burgos and the battles of the Pyrenees – Nivelle and Nive – and in the assault on Toulouse, which ended the war.

A detachment of 49 soldiers from the 79th entered the fray at Talavera. Only 12 came out. At Busaco Captain Alexander Cameron with an outlying picquet held on although surrounded and went down fighting against overwhelming odds.

At Fuentes d'Onor Lieutenant-Colonel Philips Cameron, a son of Alan Cameron, was mortally wounded. The shout *Thuit an Camshronach!* (Cameron is dead) went up. The Highlanders retaliated with a furious charge which drove the French Imperial Guard and Grenadiers out of the disputed village and turned looming defeat into victory.

The sole success at Burgos was achieved by the 79th who broke into the outlying Hornwork. At the Battle of Toulouse they stormed and carried the Colombette Redoubt and Tour des Augustins, the strongest features in the defenceworks.

During some of the long exhausting marches, when the

services of a piper were not available, the Camerons resorted to *puirt a' beul*, mouth-music, and their flagging feet invariably responded to the lilting airs of the islands.

Their onslaughts struck terror into the hearts of the French. The pipers commenced the *siubhal*, or going forward movement of the *pibroch*, then they broke into the blood-tingling 'charge' which sent the Camerons racing with levelled bayonets at the enemy. Portrayals of these wild charges never fail to draw applause at a military tattoo.

Before the 1850's the pipes and drums never played together. The Corps of Drums, under the drum-major, beat the cadence of the march and relayed commands represented in the 'pattern' of the beats. At a time when soldiers fought standing in lines, in columns or in squares the massed drums would penetrate the din of battle, direct and control the pace and movement and inspire the fighting men.

Just as the Colours were the rallying point of the regiment, the drums were its heart-beat. Later, when tactics changed, commands were passed by bugle-calls. These were sounded by the drummers, who still carry a slung bugle.

The Camerons arrived in Cork in December 1814 and on the escape of Napoleon from Elba they left for Ostend early in May 1815. The 79th proceeded to Brussels and the officers were attending the historic eve of Waterloo ball given by the Duchess of Richmond on the night of June 15 when news was received that Napoleon had crossed the River Sambre and battle was imminent.

The pipes and bugles sounded the alarm, the officers quietly left the bright lights and gay music and rejoined their units. The Camerons formed up on the Place Royale and, headed by the pipers, marched to engage the French at Quatre Bras. Soon they heard the distant boom of cannon.

Stationed on the left of the British line the 79th suffered severe losses. The Camerons were detached to cover some guns threatened by the French and on scattering them they entered on a vigorous pursuit. On reforming the regiment formed square and again stood firm under several charges by the Cuirassiers.

The Duke of Wellington retired his forces to a position he had selected at Waterloo. In the decisive battle here on June 18, 1815, the Camerons with the 1st Brigade, 5th Division helped to hurl back attack after attack by columns of infantry. For several hours they braved the terrific cannonade and faced the surging charges of the massed cavalry attempting to hack their way through to Brussels.

Piper Kenneth Mackay, a native of Tongue, Sutherland, stepped outside the compact square to *brosnachadh* (cheer) his comrades. He played the stirring air *Cogadh na Sith* (War or Peace) during the onrush of Napoleon's élite 'Old Guard'.

Then came the Highland charge which routed the Emperor's shattered formations. Close on 500 Camerons were killed or wounded and the remnant ended the battle commanded by a sub-altern, Lieutenant Alexander Cameron, a nephew of the founder – now Major-General Sir Alan Cameron. The 79th was one of only four regiments, three of them Highland, which were mentioned by name in the Duke's famous Waterloo dispatches.

The Cameron Highlanders entered Paris and served with the Army of Occupation for three years. The regiment experienced tours of duty in the U.K. and at Gibraltar and was twice stationed in Canada. On the outbreak of the Crimean War in 1854 the 79th left Portsmouth to join the Highland Brigade.

The Camerons were engaged in the Battle of the Alma and at Balaclava. They were also in the expedition to the Sea of Azov and at the siege of Sevastopol. There was stubborn fighting on the slopes by the banks of the River Alma. The 79th crested a hill in battle array, Colours flaunting in the breeze and pipes skirling, and soon The Highland Brigade had a panoramic view of the Russians retreating on Sevastopol.

Early in September 1855, the 79th was preparing for a dawn attack on Sevastopol. During the night, however, the enemy retired blowing up the defenceworks and the Highlanders quickly moved into the silent deserted Redan Redoubt which had defied several determined assaults.

The privations of the Crimean War over, the Camerons had a welcome spell of home service before being ordered to India. The regiment arrived in Calcutta towards the end of 1857 – the 'Mutiny' year – and participated in the relief of Lucknow. The Highlanders fought through the narrow winding streets and when the rebels made a run for it they at once took up the pursuit, capturing the Colours of the 7th Oude Irregular Infantry and four guns.

There was further hard fighting at the Battle of Bareilly, at the storming of Rampore Kussia and in operations in Oude and Rohilkand. A wing of the 79th was represented in a force sent against the troublesome Mohmand tribesmen on the North-West Frontier during 1863 and there were several sharp skirmishes in the Shubkudder Pass. The regiment returned to Britain in 1871.

In April 1873, Queen Victoria decreed that the 79th should in future be styled 'The Queen's Own Cameron Highlanders, and that the facings on the uniform be changed from green to blue, as befitted a Royal regiment. Throughout her long eventful reign the Queen showed a marked interest in the 79th and frequently referred to the regiment as 'My Own Cameron Highlanders'.

The Queen's Own Cameron Highlanders contributed a detachment of two officers and 135 other ranks to accompany The Black Watch to the Gold Coast for the Ashanti Campaign. These Cameron volunteers were engaged in the fighting at Amoaful and at the capture of the notorious King Coffee's capital, Kumasi.

Under the Army reforms of 1881 two-battalion infantry regiments were formed by linking two regiments as first and second battalions and it was proposed that the 79th should become the second battalion of the 42nd (The Black Watch). On being asked if this would be acceptable the Commanding Officer of the 79th sent firm refusals by wire and by letter.

In April of that year, the Secretary of State for War announced in Parliament that the Camerons would continue as the only single-battalion regiment in the Army. And so it remained until a second battalion was raised in 1897 with a nucleus provided by the 1st Battalion. In 1881, however, the numeral '79' had to be dropped.

The Queen's Own Cameron Highlanders sailed from Gibraltar in August 1882, and joined The Highland Brigade at Alexandria. In mid-September, after a night march across the desert, the brigade attacked Colonel Arabi Pasha's Egyptian Army mutineers at Tel-el-Kebir.

The Highland charge at first light broke through the enemy entrenchments and after a feeble resistance the insurgents fled with 'The March of the Cameron Men' ringing in their ears.

The insurrection collapsed but the Camerons remained in Egypt and in 1884-45 they served with the expedition which ascended the Nile in an attempt to rescue General Gordon trapped by the Mahdi's dervishes at Khartoum.

When news came in that Khartoum had fallen and General Gordon had been murdered, the operation was abandoned and the regiment withdrew to Wadi Halfa, about 800 miles down-river. Throughout December 1895, at Fort Koseh, with the 9th Sudanese Battalion, a detachment of Egyptian troops and an armed steamer, the Highlanders fought off over 7,000 desert fanatics who had followed up the retiring Nile Expedition.

On the arrival of reinforcements the 'fuzzy-wuzzies' took severe punishment near Ginnis, losing all their guns and river craft. The Camerons came home in 1887 and entered another troubled period in their existence. That year, and in 1893, it became known that the authorities were contemplating the conversion of the regiment into a third battalion of The Scots Guards.

Consternation and dismay gave way to a storm of protest and resentment and Queen Victoria once more championed the cause of her Cameron Highlanders and saved the regiment from virtual extinction. Service followed at Malta and Gibraltar and in 1897 the 2nd Battalion of The Queen's Own Cameron Highlanders was formed at Fort George by Colonel J. M. Hunt.

At the beginning of 1898 the 1st Camerons joined the expeditionary force assembling at Berber for the re-conquest of the Sudan. At the Battle of Atbara on April 8 the Camerons tore gaps in the enemy *zareba*, or defences, for the advancing brigade. In the frenzied fighting Piper Stewart played until he fell riddled with bullets and Private Cross dispatched with his bayonet a tribesman who attempted to spear Brigadier-General Gatacre.

Led by their holy men and standard-bearers about 60,000 of the Khalifa's desert warriors advanced across open ground at Omdurman on September 2 and hurled themselves on the waiting British line. Their massed rushes met with such an intensity of artillery and rifle fire that they went down in thousands.

There was a last stand around the great flaunting black flag of the Khalifa, but their leader fled leaving his fanatical retinue to meet their death shrieking and transfixed by the bayonets of the Highlanders or the lances of the cavalry. The Khalifa was killed later.

Khartoum – the enemy capital – was entered and the pipers of the Seaforths and Camerons played a lament in front of General Gordon's residence. And so the surgery of rifle and bayonet ended the reign of terror in Egypt and the Sudan.

A company of Cameron Highlanders along with a battalion of Sudanese troops accompanied General Sir Herbert Kitchener on his mission in mid-September to Fashoda, on the White Nile, about 450 miles south of Khartoum. This brought Britain and France to the brink of war. Major Marchand at the head of a French force had arrived in the area, but the British and Egyptian flags were hoisted as a sign of possession and only after high-level political activity the tension eased and the French withdrew from the disputed zone.

Towards the close of the century the battle honours of The Queen's Own Cameron Highlanders were: Egmont-op-Zee, Corunna, Busaco, Fuentes d'Onor, Salamanca, Pyrenees, Nivelle, Nive, Toulouse, Peninsula, Waterloo, Alma, Sevastopol, Lucknow, Tel-el-Kebir, Egypt 1882, Nile 1884-85, Atbara, Khartoum. These names of glory adorn the Regimental Colour.

When the South African War broke out in the autumn of 1899 the 1st Camerons were in Cairo and as the months dragged past they felt somewhat left out. In March 1900, however, there was jubilation – the battalion was placed under orders for active service.

The fighting ebbed and flowed across difficult terrain in the Transvaal and Orange Free State against a tough, crafty and well-armed foe. There were several British reverses at the outset but on reinforcements arriving the Boers lost the initiative and were forced on to the defensive.

The 1st Camerons took part in the advance north from Bloemfontein, forded the Vaal River and entered Pretoria with the enemy in retreat. The battalion was in the Wittebergen operations which hemmed in General Prinsloo's force in the mountains along the border of Basutoland.

The Camerons were in the brisk engagement at Retief's Nek, where 4,000 of the enemy surrendered. But although their two capitals – Bloemfontein and Pretoria – had been captured the highly mobile will o' the wisp Boer commandos fought stubbornly on, and when they later resorted to guerrilla tactics, prior to their surrender, the Camerons fought a series of successful minor actions at widely separated points.

At Nooitgedacht, on December 13, 1900, Sergeant Donald Farmer, serving with a Mounted Infantry detachment, earned the first Victoria Cross to be awarded to a Cameron Highlander. In a surprise enemy attack, with men falling all round him, Sergeant Farmer dashed through heavy close range fire and brought back a badly-wounded officer. Later the regiment was granted the battle honour South Africa 1900-2, which appears on the Regimental Colour.

Meanwhile the 2nd Battalion had experienced tours of duty in Crete, South Africa, North China and India. At the outbreak of World War I the 1st Battalion was stationed in Edinburgh and the 2nd Battalion at Poona, India. Fifty-two battle honours were conferred on the Regiment for its outstanding contribution to victory.

The following ten were selected to appear on the Sovereign's Colour : Marne 1914, '18, Aisne 1914, Yypres 1914, '15, '17, '18, Neuve Chapelle, Loos, Somme 1916, '18, Delville Wood, Arras 1917, '18, Sambre, Macedonia 1915-18.

The other battle honours were : Retreat from Mons, Langemarck 1914, Gheluvelt, Nonne Bosschen, Givenchy 1914, Hill 60, Gravenstafel, St. Julien, Frezenberg, Bellewaarde, Aubers, Festubert 1915, Albert 1916, Bazentin, Pozieres, Flers-Courcelette, Morval, Le Transloy, Ancre Heights, Scarpe 1917, Arleux, Pilckem, Menin Road, Polygon Wood, Poelcappelle, Passchendaele, St. Quentin, Bapaume 1918, Lys, Estaires, Messines 1918, Kemmel, Bethune, Soissonnais-Ourcq, Drocourt-Queant, Hindenburg Line, Epehy, St. Quentin Canal, Courtrai, Selle, France and Flanders 1914-18, Struma.

Practically the entire regimental staff of the 1st Battalion perished in the early days of the war, when on September 25, 1914, the explosion of a cluster of shells brought down the roof of a cave in which they were taking cover. Only four of the entombed H.Q. staff were brought out alive. September 25 was a date of ill-omen for the battalion. A year later, on September 25, 1915, the 1st Camerons entered the Loos holocaust.

The battalion, though at times gravely depleted by casualties, came through the ordeal of trench warfare in France and

Flanders. It fought with distinction, particularly in the Retreat from Mons, the stand in the Cambrai-Le Cateau area, the advance to the Marne and the Aisne, at Loos and in the smashing of the German 1918 spring offensive.

The Victoria Cross was awarded to Private Ross Tollerton of the 1st Camerons for an act of gallantry during the battalion's advance from the Aisne with the 1st Brigade on September 14, 1914. The Camerons were subjected to intense artillery and machine-gun fire and Lieutenant Matheson was severely wounded.

Private Ross Tollerton carried the officer pick-a-back out of action and set him down behind a cornstack. He then returned to the firing line and was twice wounded. When the battalion was ordered to withdraw he rejoined the officer and remained with him for three days with the Germans moving all round them. Both were too weak from loss of blood and hunger to attempt an escape but were saved by the British advance.

The greatest World War I battle of The Queen's Own Cameron Highlanders was Loos, five battalions of the regiment being committed: the 1st, 4th (T.A.), 5th (Lochiel's), 6th and 7th. 'There's nae lads left here. . . . They a' joined the Camerons and the feck o' them fell in an awfu' place called Lowse', says one of John Buchan's characters, 'Mr. Standfast'.

The Germans had established a formidable line backed by artillery and as the country was dotted with miners' cottages and pitheads this impeded manoeuvre and afforded the enemy excellent observation and fields of fire for their batteries and machine-guns. The Germans considered the defences impregnable and manned them with seasoned troops.

On that dark, misty bleak morning of September 25, 1915, the Camerons stood drenched and chattering with cold in the trenches. Each man was laden with extra ammunition and bombs, rifle, bayonet, entrenching tools and other implements of warfare. They were tensed and waiting for the 'off'.

The stalemate on the British front was broken by the guns roaring a raucous overture to an offensive launched over a six mile front between Lens and La Bassée. The pipes screamed as the infantry swarmed over the top and surged through shot and shell to reach the forward enemy positions.

The German line was pierced, the bayonets flashed and

several deep penetrations were made. All Scotland thrilled to the news that her two 'Kitchener's Army' divisions, the 9th and 15th, led the way. The 51st and 52nd Divisions were there too, also the 1st Division which had more than a leaven of Scots.

But soon there was a re-assessment. Some of the successes so dearly won with bomb, bullet and bayonet had not been exploited. In a number of instances units had pressed on too far with the result that the reserves were unable to give adequate support.

The enemy retaliated with a powerful counter-attack and re-captured several strongpoints. When the Battle of Loos ended in mid-October the British line had been pushed forward about two miles on a frontage of 8,000 yards and the casualties totalled in the region of 50,000 dead, wounded and missing.

The 2nd Camerons served in two zones of conflict; on the Western Front and in the Balkans. Coming from the sweltering heat of India in December 1914, the battalion acquitted itself valiantly in the freezing waterlogged trench lines.

The Camerons took part in a ceaseless war of attrition – patrolling, reconnaissance, sniping, raiding and bombing sorties – and braved the lashing barrages of the German artillery. This shell-pocked dismal wilderness, scarred by the crazy network of trenches, was devoid of wild flowers and greenery. An occasional stunted, grotesquely twisted tree broke the horizon. This land the Camerons shared with their foes; and the rats and lice.

The bombardments uncovered the remains of dead and ere the ground ceased quaking under the explosions arms and legs protruded from the walls of dug-outs and trenches and, not infrequently, the fire-steps and parapets were festooned with intestines. The sights and sounds were unnerving and the stench nauseating.

In November 1915, the 2nd Battalion was withdrawn from the Western Front and dispatched to the Balkans where the Highlanders soon had the measure of their adversaries, the Bulgars. The battalion fought with great dash on the Struma and was prominently identified with the resounding Allied victory at Karajaköi.

The Bulgarian Army then entered on a disorderly retreat which ended with overtures for an Armistice. The 2nd Camerons went on to Batum and along tortuous roads with precipitous hairpin bends to enter the deep forest lands of the Caucasus and occupy Tiflis, on the shores of the Caspian Sea. The battalion was in Southern Ireland in 1921 during the 'troubles' and tours of duty followed in Palestine and Egypt.

On the collapse of the German spring offensive in 1918 the 1st Camerons crossed the Rhine and as part of the Army of Occupation entered Cologne. In the post-war period the battalion was in India, Burma and the Sudan. At the outbreak of World War II the 1st Battalion was in the U.K. and the 2nd in Egypt.

Marshal Graziani's 300,000 troops, comprising Regular and 'Blackshirt' divisions, was poised on the Western Frontier of Egypt for the most of 1940. General Wavell faced the Italians with a token force of Empire fighting men, including the 2nd Camerons who were with the seasoned 4th Indian Division.

The position was critical. After the chaos of Dunkirk no reinforcements could be sent to North Africa. But 'Archie' Wavell, a former Black Watch officer, was not dismayed. He decided to attack and so began the highly successful desert campaign of September 1940-February 1941.

Defended towns, villages, airfields, forts, posts and encampments were quickly overrun while the R.A.F. kept Mussolini's air force grounded. At Nibeiwa, a few miles from Sidi Barrani, the 2nd Battalion, on troop-carrying lorries, followed the armour into the Italian positions.

The Highlanders received their final order from a loud-speaker. It was 'Camerons – Go!' Leaping from their carriers they closed with the bayonet, the pipes singing in the thin desert air. Nibeiwa fell and the Camerons were the first infantry to thrust into Sidi Barrani.

The attack swept on past Benghazi to Beda Fomm. And several thousand of the enemy not so fleet of foot as many of their comrades found themselves trudging in long winding columns into captivity. Then the challenge of the 250,000 Italians and their native levies in East Africa was accepted.

The 4th and 5th Indian Divisions were detached from General Wavell's desert army and after crossing Egypt and the Sudan the Indians and Camerons skirmished towards the Keren Hills, driving in enemy outposts en route. They began the difficult ascent and battled the Italians off 1,000 to 1,500 ft. high crags in the face of artillery, mortar, machine-gun and rifle fire. The enemy also showered down grenades and rocks but as the bayonets came winking over the heights they either withdrew or put up their hands.

Though the Italians held the aces the Camerons and Indians took all the 'tricks'. The enemy had superiority in numbers, were well supplied and installed in prepared positions with excellent cover, observations and fields of fire. But the 4th and 5th Divisions were 'excelsior' divisions – up and up, and on and on.

The operations in the Keren Hills lasted several weeks. One of the principal heights wrested from the enemy by the Highlanders was appropriately named 'Cameron Ridge'. The Red Sea port of Massawa was captured and, with the 1st South African Division and the 5th Indian Division crushing Italian resistance in Abyssinia, the East African Campaign was over by the middle of May, 1941. Some called it 'the two months' war'.

Early in June 1942, 'Desert Fox' Rommel launched a powerful attack on the Gazala-Bir Hakeim Line. Enemy pressure increased, Tobruk was isolated, the Luftwaffe joined in and armour burst through the defence perimeter. There was no air cover, help could not be sent by the hard-pressed Eighth Army and Tobruk surrendered on June 22 – but not the 2nd Camerons and a battalion of The Gurkha Rifles.

The Camerons were still hitting back gamely but, running out of ammunition, ringed with tanks and infantry, pounded from the sky and by artillery and utterly exhausted, they too had to give up. But that was 24 hours after the surrender of Tobruk. The battalion formed part of the 11th Indian Brigade then attached to the 2nd South African Division.

While stationed in the Shetlands the 4th Battalion The Queen's Own Cameron Highlanders – originally a Territorial Army formation – was re-numbered to become the 2nd Battalion in mid-December 1942. The 4th had been with 152 Brigade in the 51st (Highland) Division's fighting retiral from the Somme to St. Valery-en-Caux. After the St. Valery disaster early in June 1940, the 4th was reconstituted at Inverness in July of the same year.

The battalion was dispatched to Aruba, in the Dutch West Indies, where it guarded the vital oil refineries until mid-

February 1941. On returning home it was moved to the Shetlands. As the 2nd Battalion it went to Italy early in 1944 and fought with distinction at Cassino. The 2nd Camerons were prominent in the violent actions on both sides of the Appennines and in the piercing of the Gothic Line and other serial defences along the leg of Italy.

The 2nd liberated the mini-republic of San Marino after two days fighting. On October 2 the Camerons came under fire from machine-guns set up in the three castles and among the mountain crags. The enemy at first dominated all movement eastwards towards Rimini.

The battalion countered by bringing up their anti-tank weapons during the night, and from daybreak the gunners made things extremely unpleasant for the marksmen on the heights. Orders were to knock out the gun posts but to spare the town and its castles unnecessary damage.

The fire of the battalion had the maximum effect on the enemy positions and the minimum on the capital of San Marino. On October 3 the Germans moved out and the Camerons entered the picturesque town perched on the mountain top.

After crossing the Rubicon the Camerons were dispatched to preserve order in Greece during the strife between warring political factions in November 1944. Similar employment followed in Trieste – claimed by the Italians and Marshal Tito's Jugoslavs. The 2nd Battalion, after returning to the Highlands, was disbanded at the close of June 1948.

The 1st Camerons arrived in France from Aldershot in October 1939. At first theirs was a watching and waiting role. Then the expected happened – the Germans invaded the Low Countries early in May 1940. The battalion was in the advance to contact across the Belgian frontier.

Enemy superiority in numbers and artillery, weight of armour and the bombing attacks of the Luftwaffe forced a withdrawal, and the Camerons were involved in a series of grim rearguard and holding actions, particularly during the retiral from Tournai to La Bassée towards the end of the month.

Communications and supply lines were in chaos and the roads practically impassable because of the mass exodus of refugees. During the epic fighting retreat to the coast Highlanders from the Isle of Skye, MacLeods and their septs, longed to wave the magic victory-giving Fairy Flag of the clan. But the Isle of Mist and Dunvegan Castle seemed an eternity away.

In the bitter confused fighting near the coast part of the battalion was cut off but the remainder was evacuated from a stretch of beach near Dunkirk. The depleted battalion was re-organised and in April 1942, sailed for India.

In 1943, King George VI – who became the Colonel-in-Chief on his accession – authorised the regimental pipers to wear kilts of the Royal Stewart tartan to commemorate the 150th anniversary of the raising of the regiment.

In March 1944, the 1st Camerons arrived in Burma with the 2nd Division and provided some of the 'teeth' of the 14th Army in halting the Japanese advance on India.

Due to the strict security black-out some time elapsed before Scotland learned that her Cameron Highlanders were engaged in the Far East. Then news was released that the 1st Battalion had distinguished itself around Kohima and Imphal. The scene was now set for the all-out offensive which liberated Burma and in the consequent operations the Camerons were committed to fighting under the most exacting conditions.

On March 7, 1944, Tokyo Radio triumphantly announced 'the march on Delhi has begun'. But less than four months afterwards the diseased, bedraggled demoralised remnants of the Japanese attacking formations were straggling back across the Chindwin leaving a trail of sick, wounded and dying in their wake.

Keypoint of the turning of the tide in Burma was the Battle of Kohima which, according to Lord Mountbatten, was 'one of the greatest battles in history'. Kohima and Imphal were the most crushing defeats ever suffered by the Imperial Japanese Army.

The 1st Camerons were prominent in the operations which forced the road to Kohima. They had a leading role in the dramatic capture of this enemy stronghold, the battalion effecting a turning movement which necessitated a 1,000 ft. climb. This was followed by several violent engagements which relieved Imphal and cleared the Japanese from Tamu.

Imphal had been under siege and all supplies came in by air. The Japanese had advanced to the portals of India and Imphal remained the base and storehouse on which our defences depended. It was defended by three divisions deployed over a vast area of hill and jungle.

It was not a battle in the accepted sense but a long drawn-out killing match; hills taken, re-taken and taken again, ambushes on jungle tracks and a fight to the finish, aggressive patrolling, night assaults, close-quarter melees with grenades, bayonets and Gurkha kukris. No holds were barred. And it lasted four months.

British and Gurkha troops held out in their 'boxes' and when the Japanese finally withdrew they left around 50,000 of their best troops decomposing on the ground, which suggests something of the ferocity of the fighting.

The 2nd Division led the advance on Shwebo over the Chindwin, and after attack and counter-attack among the hills, jungles and swamps the assault-crossing of the Irrawaddy was a feat of arms by this formation. The river was about a mile broad, in spate and the landing craft were indifferent.

Coming out of concealment the 1st Camerons splashed in and the leading company gained the enemy-held bank with light casualties and quickly dug in. Then a storm of shot and shell was unleashed which rendered their position in the small bridgehead precarious.

So violent was Japanese reaction that only a trickle of re-inforcements got through as the river was now hissing, foaming and creaming with exploding shells and grenades and splashing bullets. For three days the Camerons endured this ordeal of fire, wounds and death but maintained their 'finger-hold' on the enemy bank.

As reinforcements continued to percolate there was a gradual build-up which enabled an attack to be put in with sufficient strength to root out the Japanese from their defences. The bridgehead battle won and the Irrawaddy forded, the advance on Mandalay and Rangoon began.

The Camerons on several occasions bore the brunt of the fighting which led to the capture of Chauk, Yenangyaung and Magwe – Burma's largest oil centres. Sweeping down the east bank of the Irrawaddy they wiped out a number of Japanese suicide groups in skirmishes among the derricks and the companies fired their last rounds in clearing the enemy from the slopes of Mount Popa.

Because of its outstanding contribution to victory in the Far East the 1st Battalion was selected to go to Japan as the representative Scottish unit in the British occupation force. The kilted Highlanders paraded through Shiro and Kure and the *pibroch* sounded in the Lands of the Samurai.

World War II battle honours of the Regiment are: Defence of Escaut, ST. OMER-LA BASSÉE CANAL, Somme 1940, St. Valery-en-Caux, Falaise, Falaise Road, La Vie Crossing, Le Havre, Lower Maas, Venlo Pocket, Rhineland, REICHSWALD, Goch, RHINE, North-West Europe 1940, '44-45, Agordat, KEREN, Abyssinia 1941, SIDI BARRANI, Tobruk 1941-42, Gubi II, Carmusa, Gazala, EL ALAMEIN, Mareth, Wadi Zigzaou, AKARIT, Djebel Roumana, North Africa 1940-43, Francofonte, Adrano, Sferro Hills, Sicily 1943, Cassino I, Poggio del Grillo, GOTHIC LINE, Tavoleto, Coriano, Plan di Castello, Monte Reggiano, Rimini Line, San Marino, Italy 1944, KOHIMA, Relief of Kohima, Naga Village, Aradura, Shwebo, MANDALAY, Ava, Irrawaddy, Mr. Popa, Burma 1944-45. (Battle honours printed in capitals are borne on the Queen's Colour.)

During 1947 the 1st Camerons were in Malay co-operating with the police in a difficult danger-fraught internal security role which involved patrolling vast areas of hill, swamp and jungle and 'shadow boxing' with a fleet-footed, elusive and crafty foe; gangs of Communist terrorists and saboteurs. The battalion came home the following year.

After taking part in street and desert skirmishes in the troubled Suez Canal Zone the battalion returned from Egypt in the spring of 1952, and in the autumn departed for service in Germany. The battalion was back in the homeland early in 1955 but a few months later it was ordered to Korea, where it remained for over a year under United Nations Command. A short spell of anti-terrorist operations followed in Malaya in 1956.

The 1st Camerons experienced active service again in 1957 when the battalion arrived in the Aden Protectorate. There was a number of successful actions against Yemeni tribesmen who had crossed the frontier to embark on a campaign of raiding, attacking forts and posts and ambushing convoys in difficult rock and desert country. In the spring of 1958 the battalion 'trooped' for home.

The Queen's Own Highlanders (Seaforth and Camerons) rehearse de-
planing on the flight-deck of the aircraft-carrier H.M.S. Bulwark for the
assault on Seria, December 1962

The epic stand of the 'Thin Red Line' of the 93rd, or Sutherland Regiment, at Balaclava

FARQUAR SHAW

Above: Private Farquhar Shaw o
The Black Watch in an early
uniform of the Regiment. Shaw
was shot in the Tower for his pa
in The Black Watch Mutiny

Opposite: Part of the Pipe Band
the Queen's Own Highlanders

The Raising of The Gordon Highlanders by Jean, Duchess of Gordon, 1794

Argyll and Sutherland Highlanders of the 51st Division crossing the railway at Douchy by the ruins of the blown-up railway bridge, October 23, 1918

A rare photograph of 2nd Battalion Argylls in Malaya, 1941. All the men of the battalion were either lost or captured during the withdrawal to and eventual fall of Singapore

On the amalgamation of the Seaforths and the Camerons in February 1961, to form The Queen's Own Cameron Highlanders the following battle honours were authorised for the new regiment:

Regimental Colour – Sphinx superscribed Egypt, Elephant superscribed Assaye: Carnatic, Hindoostan, Mysore, Egmont-op-Zee, Cape of Good Hope 1806, Maida, Corunna, Busaco, Fuentes d'Onor, Java, Salamanca, Pyrenees, Nivelle, Nive, Toulouse, Peninsula, Waterloo, South Africa 1835, Alma, Sevastopol, Koosh-ab, Persia, Lucknow, Central India, Peiwar Kotal, Charasiah, Kabul 1879, Kandahar 1880, Afghanistan 1878-80, Tel-el-Kebir, Egypt 1882, Nile 1884-85, Chitral, Atbara, Khartoum, Paardeberg, South Africa 1899-1902.

World War I: Le Cateau, Retreat from Mons, MARNE 1914, '18, AISNE 1914, La Bassée 1914, Armentieres 1914, YPRES 1914, '15, '17, '18, Langemarck 1914, Gheluvelt, Nonne Bosschen, Festubert 1914, '15, Givenchy 1914, NEUVE CHAPELLE, Hill 60, Gravenstafel, St. Julien, Frezenberg, Bellewaarde, Aubers, LOOS, SOMME 1916, '18, Albert 1916, Bazentin, DELVILLE WOOD, Pozieres, Flers-Courcelette, Morval, Le Transloy, Ancre Heights, Ancre 1916, ARRAS 1917, '18, VIMY 1917, Scarpe 1917, '18, Arleux, Pilckem, Menin Road, Polygon Wood, Broodseinde, Poelcappelle, Passchendaele, CAMBRAI 1917, '18, St. Quentin, Bapaume 1918, Lys, Estaires, Messines 1918, Hazebrouck, Bailleul, Kemmel, Bethune, Soissonnais-Ourcq, Tardenois, Drocourt-Queant, Hindenberg Line, Epehy, St. Quentin Canal, Courtrai, Selle, VALENCIENNES, SAMBRE, France and Flanders 1914-18, Struma, MACEDONIA 1915-18, Megiddo, Sharon, PALESTINE 1918, Tigris 1916, Kut-el-Amara 1917, BAGHDAD, Mesopotamia 1915-18.

World War II: Defence of Escaut, ST. OMER-LA BASSÉE, Yypres-Comines Canal, Somme 1940, Withdrawal to Seine, ST. VALERY-EN-CAUX, Odon, Cheux, CAEN, Troarn, Mont Pincon, Quarry Hill, Falaise, Falaise Road, Dives Crossing, La Vie Crossing, Lisieux, Nederrijn, Best, Le Havre, Lower Maas, Meijel, Venlo Pocket, Ourthe, RHINELAND, REICHSWALD, Goch, Moyland, RHINE, Uelzen, Artlenberg, North-West Europe 1940, '44-45, Agordat, KEREN, Abyssinia 1941, SIDI BARRANI, Tobruk 1941, '42, Gubi II, Carmusa, Gazala, EL ALAMEIN, Advance on Tripoli, Mareth, Wadi Zigzaou,

AKARIT, Djebel Roumana, North Africa 1940-43, **Landing in Sicily**, Augusta, Francofonte, Adrano, Sferro Hills, SICILY 1943, Garigliano Crossing, ANZIO, Cassino I, Poggio del Grillo, GOTHIC LINE, Tavoleto, Coriano, Plan di Castello, Monte Reggiano, Rimini Line, San Marino, Italy 1943-44, MADAGAS-CAR, Middle East 1942, IMPHAL, Shenam Pass, Litan, KOHIMA, Relief of Kohima, Naga Village, Aradura, Tengnoupal, Shwebo, MANDALAY, Ava, Irrawaddy, Mt. Popa, BURMA 1942-45.

The World War I and World War II battle honours printed in capitals are borne on the Queen's Colour. The complete list represents the outstanding achievements of each of the partners in the union.

Within a few weeks of the amalgamation the 1st Battalion The Queen's Own Highlanders left Edinburgh early in April and sailed from Southampton for Singapore. This was soon to prove an eventful tour of duty during which the new regiment distinguished itself in action.

The Highlanders quickly curbed piracy off the Borneo coast and raids by sea marauders on remote peaceful villages and settlements. Nerve-centre was Sandakan, on the east coast of North Borneo, and here 'Chisel Force' was born.

Detachments went out on motor launches on patrol while other parties operated in sweeps through the jungle. The Royal Navy and the Royal Air Force co-operated closely and the raiders no longer found the Borneo coast a happy hunting ground.

Early in December 1962, The Queen's Own Highlanders were flown from Singapore to Brunei, in North Borneo, to deal with a rising in the Sultanate. The hard core of the insurrection was the oil town of Seria, where over 400 Europeans were being held as hostages.

The Highlanders and Gurkhas swept in from opposite sides and Seria was cleared of the rebels and the majority of their captives liberated. An enemy group held out in a police station they had seized. R.A.F. planes buzzed the building and appeals were made over loud-speakers to the defenders to lay down their arms and surrender.

The time limit expired and the Highlanders rushed in, dis-armed the rebels and set free the last of the European hostages. They brought out the leader under guard and the emergency was soon over. In May 1963, the battalion had another, but less troubled, spell of duty in Brunei.

During February 1964, The Queen's Own Highlanders were air-lifted back to Scotland and at the close of May the battalion departed to join the Rhine Army. While in Germany the unit underwent transition from a jungle infantry role to that of a fully mechanised battalion and in record time the Highlanders, in the language of the clans, were *deas gu cath* – ready for battle.

The battalion spent two years in Berlin where it provided border patrols, furnished guards for Spandau Prison with Rudolf Hess the sole prisoner, and participated in several large-scale manoeuvres and training exercises. The Queen's Own came home early in September 1968, their carrier planes touching down at Turnhouse Airport, Edinburgh.

Next posting was to Sharjah, on the Persian Gulf, where they spent nine sweltering months. The battalion experienced all the problems of existing in the arid waterless deserts and mountains – 'in Hell but not dead' was their summing-up.

Early in February 1970, The Queen's Own Highlanders returned to the Scottish Capital. They took over as public duties battalion in an eventful year which included the Commonwealth Games, brightened throughout by the flash of their tartan and the plangent skirl of the pipes.

The tenth anniversary of the formation of the regiment, on February 7, 1961, was celebrated in Redford Barracks in mid-March 1971. Included were a reunion, march past with affiliated T.A.V.R. and Army Cadet Force units participating, a pipers gathering, military band concert, exhibition football match 1st Battalion Q.O.H. *v.* Hearts Colts, and a display of unarmed combat.

The regiment's impressive array of silver, trophies, cups and other awards were on review, the pipes and drums combined in the Beating of Retreat and an 'at home' was held with parties for serving and former members of the various messes.

But it was 'Hello, Welcome and Cheerio'. For the Brotherhood of the Clans – The Queen's Own Highlanders (Seaforth and Camerons) – departed from the Capital at the close of April for a tour of duty at Osnabruck, Germany.

CHAPTER III

The Gordon Highlanders
A Duchess gave them 'Kiss of Life'

Legend has it in the land of the Sassenach that the
muffled beat of Drake's Drum is heard when England is in
danger. When Scotland is in peril the drums and pipes
of the Gordon Highlanders sound. And in no muffled manner.

No regiment in the British Army, or in any other army, has a more romantic origin. The Gordon Highlanders sprang from the lips of 'Bonnie Jean', wife of the 4th Duke of Gordon. The comely Duchess donned a regimental jacket and Highland bonnet, mounted her horse and, accompanied by several pipers, toured her husband's estates and also country fairs and markets during 1794.

She is reputed to have placed a guinea between her lips and kissed each man who came forward to enlist – and the recruits were numerous. In one village there was a handsome powerful young blacksmith who had been much sought after by the Guards and other regiments. But he could not resist the charm of 'Bonnie Jean' and took the guinea and her kiss.

Then he paid the *ladye fayre* a gallant compliment. To show that it was not the gold that prompted him he tossed the guinea into the crowd. As the Duke's lands stretched from Speymouth to the shores of Loch Eil this recruiting campaign was no mean feat of endurance with travelling conditions as they were in these far-off days. No modern-day recruiter has ever come near to matching her achievement.

The regiment, originally numbered the 100th, was born in a year of crisis, for the French Revolutionary Government had declared war on Britain. In 1794 the Government accepted the offer of the Duke of Gordon – known throughout the Highlands as *Coileach an taobh tuath* (The Cock of the North) – to raise a regiment on his estates.

Among the Highland chiefs and other influential gentlemen who sponsored the regiment were Lochiel, Cluny MacPherson, MacNeill of Barra, MacDonald of Glencoe and Campbell of Barcaldine and practically every clan was represented in the roll.

The Letter of Service, dated February 10, 1794, authorising the Duke to raise the regiment, conferred on his son, the Marquis of Huntly, the commission of Lieutenant-Colonel Commandant. The Marquis, a captain in the 3rd Foot Guards (later The Scots Guards) had also served in The Black Watch. On June 24 the new Highland corps was embodied at Aberdeen and the following day it was inspected by Lieutenant-General Sir Hector Munro.

Sturdy lads from Skye, the Uists and Barra came over to the mainland in open boats and tramped towards Aberdeen. During the voyage they sang the songs of the islands and on landing marched behind their pipers. And Highlanders from Inverness-shire, Banffshire, Caithness, Sutherland, Ross-shire, Moray, Nairn, Perthshire, Stirlingshire, Kincardine and Argyllshire also converged on the Granite City.

At the historic first muster close on 800 men were on parade. And there were 50 Irishmen, over a dozen Englishmen and one Welshman. About 100 recruits were from Aberdeen and county. Three-quarters of the new regiment was composed of High-landers, many of whose forebears had fought in Prince Charlie's ill-fated Army of the White Cockade.

A few days later the 100th marched to Fort George, embarked for Southampton and while encamped on Netley Common was uniformed in the full Highland dress, *breacan-an-feilidh* (plaid and kilt in one), hose were of red and white cloth with scarlet rosettes and garters and buckled shoes.

The distinctive Gordon tartan was worn but of a smaller sett than that resorted to later. This was not the clan tartan, having been designed for the Duke by William Forsythe, of Huntly, Aberdeenshire, for use by the Gordon Fencibles, one of four regiments raised by *Coileach an taobh tuath*. The tartan, however, was afterwards adopted by Clan Gordon.

Headdress consisted of the round bonnet ornamented with ostrich feathers, a diced border of red, white and green, the colours of the hackle identifying the Grenadier, Light and Battalion companies, and black cockade. Officers' sporrans were of badger-skin with a silver rim round the top and six silver-mounted white tassels. Sporrans of other ranks were of grey goatskin with six white tassels.

The sashes carried over the left shoulder by officers and sergeants were crimson and officers had a gilt gorget. Officers and sergeants wore scarlet jackets and other ranks, red, all facings being yellow. Officers had silver epaulettes, having two yellow silk stripes in the centre of the strap with a gold-embroidered thistle and a blue binding round the edge. Officers' waistcoats were scarlet laced with silver, those of the other ranks being white. Buttons were silver or plated bearing the regimental number.

Officers were armed with the Highland sword carried at the back in a buff belt fastened by an oval silver breast-plate with a crown and thistle device surrounded by the words 'Gordon Highlanders'. They also had a silver-mounted dirk. Sergeants were accoutred with the Highland sword and pike and other ranks carried flintlock muskets and bayonets. Knapsacks were of goatskin. Musicians were armed with the Highland sword.

A rumour circulated that Lord Huntly had sold the regiment to the East India Company. The Highlanders assembled, minus their officers, and some were in favour of marching to Scotland as The Black Watch had attempted to do half a century before. Lord Huntly's timeous return from London eased this danger-ous situation. He at once reassured the Highlanders that there was no foundation to their fears and duty was immediately resumed.

At the beginning of September the ten companies embarked at Southampton for Gibraltar. Early in June 1795, the High-landers sailed for Corsica and in mid-May 1796, a formation suppressed an insurrection at Corte. In August 200 Gordons made a sudden and highly successful raid on Porto Ferraio, Elba.

Early in September the 100th Regiment returned to the 'Rock' but owing to lack of information it was not known that Spain had declared war and in an attack by Spanish fighting ships a transport was lost with over fifty Highlanders on board. In the spring of 1798 the regiment landed in Dublin to repel a French invasion.

The enemy and their Irish adherents were routed without the 100th being committed but the Highlanders took part in round-ing up scattered bands of rebels. On October 16 the corps was re-numbered becoming the 92nd, or The Gordon Highlanders.

Towards the close of August 1799, the 92nd participated in an expedition against Holland and a landing was made at Helder Point. The British and their Russian allies captured Bergen but on the Russians being driven out later there was a retiral to Zype. An assault between Bergen and Egmont-op-Zee forced the French and Dutch to withdraw but, while escorting guns along the beach, the 92nd was rushed by several thousand French infantrymen.

Though heavily outnumbered the Highlanders went at them with the bayonet and after four hours of violent close fighting near Alkmaar the enemy was forced back by their charges. Lord Huntly was wounded and there were over 300 casualties in this encounter which proved to be one of the greatest bayonet battles in history. Egmont-op-Zee was the regiment's first battle honour.

On an Armistice being concluded the Anglo-Russian forces left Holland. Early in 1800 it was decided to raise a Rifle Corps on an experimental basis and The Gordon Highlanders provided a kilted contingent. Three companies of riflemen, including the detachment from the 92nd, accompanied an expedition against Ferrol in August of that year and distinguished themselves in two engagements with the Spaniards. The new corps became the 95th or Rifle Regiment from which The Rifle Brigade later took shape.

At the beginning of March 1801, a British fleet sailed into Aboukir Bay. A few days later hundreds of boats laden with troops, including the Gordons, headed shorewards. The campaign to wrest Egypt from Napoleon had begun. As the British leapt ashore they were charged by cavalry, subjected to concentrated artillery fire and there was wild confused fighting and severe casualties before the French were beaten back.

At the Battle of Mandora the regiment was assailed by the French cavalry but their volleys emptied many saddles and turned the charge. The 92nd is one of only two regiments – both Scottish – who list Mandora among their battle honours.

The Gordons advanced across the desert with their Turkish allies, following the course of the Nile. The 92nd was engaged at Ramalieh, where there was an enemy surrender. Cairo was reached in mid-May and capitulated within a week. Alexandria surrendered early in September. Egypt had been freed from the French yoke and for their gallantry and sacrifice The Gordon Highlanders received Royal sanction to bear on their Colours the Sphinx superscribed 'Egypt'.

After a few months in Ireland the regiment arrived at Glasgow in June 1802. A second battalion was raised in Colchester on November 24, 1803, with men from the counties of Aberdeen, Moray, Nairn, Banff, Angus and Inverness. In the autumn of 1804 the 2nd departed for Ireland and proved a valuable 'feeder' for the 1st during the Peninsular Campaign. The 2nd was disbanded in October 1814.

Until July 1807, the corps was styled The 92nd Regiment of Foot or Gordon Highlanders, but soon afterwards the titles in general use were The 92nd (Highland) Regiment of Foot and The 92nd Regiment of Foot.

When it was learned that Napoleon planned to seize the Danish Fleet an expedition – which included the 1st Battalion and over 100 men from the 2nd – was dispatched from Harwich with a naval squadron. The surrender of the Danish Fleet was asked and a guarantee given that it would be returned after the war.

The Danes refused and British troops were landed near Welbeck in mid-August 1807. The 92nd led the attack on the Danish Army at Kioge and after a brief stand the Danes retreated on their capital, which capitulated at the end of September. The British terms were accepted and a number of Gordons helped to man the Danish ships during the voyage to Chatham.

At the close of August 1808, the battalion marched from Lisbon towards Madrid. Unaware that Spain had been defeated, the Highlanders entered Villada on December 24 believing battle was imminent. But that night – Christmas Eve – they began a retreat of over 200 miles, the epic Retreat to Corunna.

Madrid had surrendered and several French columns – one led by Napoleon in person – were racing to trap the comparatively small British force. In a few days the straggling lines of famished troops were reeling with fatigue during the forced marches. Sick and wounded collapsed by the roadside in scores as they toiled on through snow, hail, sleet and freezing rain.

Exhausted men, their feet festering, bleeding and gangrenous, sank to the ground and those who could not be borne had to be left to the mercy of the French – who were not always merciful. The peasantry barricaded their doors and windows and refused to sell food to the ragged, verminous, wild-eyed men. The soldiers ate turnips torn from the fields and raw flesh cut from dead horses.

The French cavalry, operating like wolf packs on the flanks and rear, ruthlessly cut down isolated groups and stragglers. Rearguard actions were almost non-stop.

At Lugo the light of battle once more flared in the eyes of the Highlanders. A determined onfall by the French was broken up by the volleys of the Gordons and they withdrew. Corunna was entered on January 11, 1809, and upon the transport ships arriving the sick and wounded were evacuated.

Meanwhile the French came on with the intention of annihilating the British *canaille*. Their guns were silenced after an artillery duel but waves of infantry overran the forward areas. Under a lashing fire and spirited counter-attack, however, they gave way. Companies of the 92nd repulsed the onslaught after desperate fighting on the left, near the sea.

Embarkation orders were given and the victorious tatterdemalion little army boarded the transports with the French making no attempt to interfere. Men of the 92nd who had been on outpost duty were among the last to be taken off.

Towards the end of July 1809, the 1st Battalion joined an expedition sent against Antwerp. Landing on Walcheren it advanced to take Flushing. But in mid-August another enemy struck – disease.

The entire force was ravaged by 'Walcheren fever' which rendered further progress impossible. The expedition sailed away from the unhealthy Lowlands of Holland early in September with several thousand, sick, wounded and dying.

Disembarking at Lisbon on October 10, 1810, the battalion joined an army assembling for another joust with Napoleon's legions. Action followed at Sobral, Santarem, Pombal and Redhina, and defeat added impetus to the flight of the French from Portugal.

On May 3, 1811, at Fuentes d'Onor the Gordons were set upon by waves of infantry supported by a furious cannonade. There was frenzied close fighting but on receiving reinforcements a stirring bayonet charge hurled back the enemy.

To *brosnachadh* (cheer) the Gordons Pipe-Major Alexander Cameron sent his pipes into full skirl but a bullet pierced the bag which deflated with an unearthly wail. The incensed Gael picked up the musket of a wounded Highlander and shouting *Bheir sinn ceol dannsaidh eile dhaibh!* (We'll give them a different kind of dance music), he fired at the enemy, drew his sword and rushed into the melee.

Two days later, near Poco Velho, though raked by fire, a

detachment frustrated several attempts by cavalry to capture a British battery. At the close of October, after a forced march, the battalion surprised the French in Arroyo dos Molinos. Suddenly 'Hey Johnnie Cope Are Ye Waukin Yet' shrilled on the pipes as the Gordons charged and sent the enemy into headlong flight.

They emerged out of a thick mist and 'first-footed' the French at Almendralejo on January 1, 1812, but the enemy did not wait to exchange pleasantries, and the Highlanders enjoyed Continental cuisine before resuming the march. On the road to Ciudad Rodrigo the battalion was charged by cavalry but their wall of bayonets prevailed.

The French were ejected from Almaraz in mid April. Fort Napoleon and Fort Ragusa were taken and at Alba de Tormes early in November the Gordons stood firm under enfilade fire, and kept the attacking infantry at bay until they were ordered to retire.

On June 21, 1813, at Vittoria, several French battalions began to turn the left of the hard-pressed 71st Highland Light Infantry. Then the pipes of the Gordons skirled as the 92nd poured volley after volley into the close-packed ranks of the enemy and drove them back down the ravine they had been ascending.

The French began a retreat across the Pyrenees and the Highlanders advanced on to the heights of Maya. But here, on July 25, many a Gordon fought his last great battle. The Gallant Ninety-Twa entered the fray about 850 strong and lost over 360 in killed, wounded and missing.

The Highlanders formed part of a force of 2,600 troops who, though raked by a withering fire, engaged for nine hours 11,000 of the enemy. The French assault was sudden and launched in overwhelming strength.

Aware of the sacrifice of the Gordons the General did not include the battalion in his next move. But Pipe-Major Cameron had other ideas. He had been peremptorily ordered on two occasions to desist lest his pipes send the remnants of the formation to certain doom. Now he defied authority and struck up the rousing 'Haughs of Cromdale'.

As one man the Gordons leapt to their feet and surging forward led the reinforcements in an onslaught which drove the

French back at bayonet point. But as the right flank had been turned the magnificent charge on the Col de Maya was in vain.

Within a few days the 92nd inflicted sharp punishment on a strong force of infantry at Buenza and towards the end of July they harried the French retreating through the Pass of Donna Maria. At the Battle of the Nivelle in mid-November the Gordons captured three fortified redoubts and early in December crossed the Nive.

Among the tunes of glory of The Gordon Highlanders is *Cogadh na Sith* (War or Peace). It will ever be associated with the three pipers of St. Pierre who played this *piobaireachd* to the death. When one fell another took it up and when he went down the third continued the air.

On December 13, at St. Pierre, near Bayonne, the French attacked out of a mist. The 92nd met the challenge but the enemy brought up reinforcements and the Gordons were borne back by weight of numbers, though fighting like men possessed.

The 92nd refused to accept defeat. The battalion reformed and advanced, Colours flying, pipes playing and bayonets gleaming as if on parade, and headed straight for the enemy. Then the impossible seemed to happen.

A French officer at the head of the assaulting column reined in on observing the approaching Highlanders. He signalled with his sword and the troops began to retire. This was the turning point. The enemy was driven back in disorder with heavy loss in a battle they almost won but for a few hundred Gordon Highlanders and their pipers.

Arriving at Urt in January 1814, the battalion engaged shipping and gunboats on the Adour, disrupting the French supply line. The enemy retaliated with a morning raid but found the Highlanders were early risers and quickly re-crossed the river.

The advance was resumed in mid-February and the Gordons cleared the enemy from Helette and the heights of Garris. They burst into Arriverete and secured a crossing for the other formations. The Battle of Orthes at the close of February began badly for the British but when the 92nd led its brigade in the seizing of a ford the issue was no longer in doubt.

The battalion drove the French from a ridge near Aire and on April 10 at Toulouse – the last great battle of the Peninsular

Campaign – the Gordons were in the assault which penetrated the forward entrenchments. On entering Villefranche the Highlanders learned that Napoleon had abdicated and the war was over.

At the end of February 1815, Napoleon escaped from Elba and made a triumphal entry into Paris. The 92nd, coming from Cork, entered Brussels at the close of May. A group of Gordons demonstrated the art of Highland dancing at the historic eve of Waterloo ball given by the Duchess of Richmond, daughter of the Duke of Gordon. It was a *danse macabre* for the French were nearing Quatre-Bras, some twenty miles away.

Just after midnight the bugles and pipes sounded through the streets and the battalions, brigades and divisions began to assemble. As the marching columns approached Quatre-Bras Dutch troops were being pressed back by the French.

The 92nd engaged the enemy in wheatfields. The Cuirassiers made several furious charges but the volleys of the Gordons emptied numerous saddles and the French retired. They returned to the attack but the battalion stood firm.

The Gordons went over to the offensive when, covered by artillery, two strong formations of enemy infantry moved into a large house several hundred yards away. The staff of the Regimental Colour was shattered and the officer bearing it killed. The King's Colour was also hit and the Gordons were going down thick and fast as their charge lapped round the two-storey dwelling, bullets streaking from its windows and the surrounding hedge.

Colonel John Cameron of Fassiefern was mortally wounded and fell from his horse. Many of the Highlanders saw their Commanding Officer go down. The pipes screamed the wild notes of 'The Camerons' Gathering' and the avenging Gordons battled the enemy from the hedge and out of the house. Every Highland blade was red – blood red.

The French made determined attempts to recapture the position but they in turn came under a hail of fire and were driven back with heavy loss. The battalion and its 'chieftain' received honourable mention in the Duke of Wellington's dispatches.

The Duke withdrew to a much stronger position, on the slopes of Mont St. Jean, near Waterloo – the 92nd forming the rearguard during this manoeuvre. Here, on June 18, the fate of Europe was decided.

Raked by a concentration of artillery fire and broken by a massed infantry attack, Bylandt's Dutch-Belgian Brigade streamed back from the left centre of the British line at La Haye Sainte. The French poured into the wide gap. The crisis in the battle had come.

The 92nd fired a deadly volley into the cheering infantry as they came on confident of victory. This fusilade silenced the French and as they reeled and wavered the pipes sounded their clarion call, and the flash of the Highlanders' bayonets gleamed through the drifting gun-smoke.

At this moment The Royal Scots Greys came up. As they rode past through openings made for them by the Highlanders many Gordons grasped their stirrups, the shout 'Scotland For Ever!' arose amid the din of battle and both regiments charged together.

The French, in close formation, had no freedom of movement and in a few minutes it was all over. The ground was strewn with enemy infantrymen and littered with discarded weapons and equipment.

The 92nd then took part in the assault which drove the French from the crest of a position at La Haye Sainte. Napoleon fled and it became a general *sauve qui peut*. The charge of The Royal Scots Greys and The Gordon Highlanders inspired Lady Butler's famous painting 'Waterloo'.

The battalion marched into Paris and was employed on occupation duties. It was dispatched to Kingston, Jamaica, early in 1819 and within a few weeks close on 300 succumbed to tropical diseases. Companies sailed north round the coast on reports of an uprising but there were no incidents.

The long peace which followed the Napoleonic Wars was broken by hostilities in the Crimea. There was an urgent call for volunteers and several hundred Gordons responded. Many of them served with the 42nd (The Black Watch) and the 79th (The Queen's Own Cameron Highlanders).

In August 1855, the 92nd was ordered from Gibraltar to the Crimea and the depleted battalion joined The Highland Brigade at Kamara. Though under fire the Gordons were not committed to battle, and when peace was signed in the spring of 1865, *Na Gordanaich* returned to the 'Rock'.

Actions of the Somme Crossings. Gordons in support in an old trench near Nesle, which can be seen in the distance, March 24, 1918

2nd Battalion Gordon Highlanders marching to the trenches along the Becordel-Fricourt Road, October 1916. Colonel Turnbull, D.S.O., on white horse : Drum Major Kenny, V.C., in front of Band.

Roll call of the 1st Black Watch outside their billets at Lapugnoy, April 10, 1918

Men of the Black Watch (15th Division) celebrating New Year's Day in the hutments at Henecourt, 1917

Wellington eludes French cavalry at Quatre Bras by taking shelter
among The Gordons

'The Gay and The Gallant'
Gordon Highlanders of the Waterloo period

THE ARGYLLS IN ADEN

Above: At the wheel, Lt.-Col.
Colin Mitchell in Aden's Crater
district

Opposite: Home from home –
Regimental Headquarters in Aden

UNIFORMS OF THE ARGYLL AND SUTHERLAND HIGHLANDERS
THROUGH THE YEARS

Left: The Pipe Band of the Argyll and Sutherand Highlanders

Right: The four-footed Argyll in his dress uniform – Cruachan II, the
temperamental but popular Shetland pony mascot of the Regiment

The first Gordon Highlander to win the Victoria Cross was Private Thomas Beach, a Forfar man. While serving in the 55th Regiment (Border Regiment) at the Battle of Inkerman, on November 5, 1854, he observed several Russians plundering Lieutenant-Colonel Carpenter, 41st Regiment, who was lying wounded. Private Beach went to his assistance, accounted for two of the enemy and defended the colonel until help arrived.

In May 1857, the Bengal Sepoy Mutiny threatened to engulf India. The 92nd landed at Bombay early in March, 1858, too late to take part in the principal actions against the rebels. Nevertheless the Gordons, operating with mobile columns, rendered invaluable assistance in pursuing, engaging and taking the surrender of bands of mutineers, and hunting down groups who had turned to banditry.

The insurgents took severe punishment near Mungrowlie, Koraie and near Rajpore. Companies of the 92nd cleared the rebels from the jungles of Jhansi and the Bundelkand region, and a detachment astride elephants surprised and rounded up a force of mutineers in their jungle hide-out at Seepree.

The battalion returned to the U.K. in the spring of 1863 but in January 1868, it was again ordered to India. In the early 70's the Stag's Head with the motto *Bydand* (Stand Firm) of the Ducal family of Gordon replaced the Sphinx, superscribed 'Egypt', as the regimental badge.

The murder of the Viceroy's envoy at Kabul in September 1879, triggered off war in the high passes. The 92nd joined an infantry brigade of the Kabul Field Force assembling at Alikhel. In the advance on Kabul the Highlanders had several fierce engagements with the tribesmen.

Working round to the east of Charasiah companies commanded by Major Stuart White engaged the enemy among the trees, hills and ledges on both sides of a gorge. The Afghan leader fired at the officer but missed. Major White's bullet found its target and, their commander killed, the tribesmen began a retiral abandoning their guns.

The pass was cleared and the advance continued. Major White (later Field-Marshal Sir George White) was awarded the Victoria Cross. From a spur on the heights Gordon marksmen drove the Afghans from their guns and Kabul was entered in mid-October. Companies were engaged in further clashes in the Arghandeh Kotal area.

The battalion participated in the assault on Takht-i-Shah, a natural fortress towering 2,500 ft. above the plain. Lieutenant William Henry Dick-Cunyngham rallied a number of breathless Gordons and led them into the defences near the summit and the fanatical hillmen were driven out. For his courage and inspired leadership Lieutenant Dick-Cunyngham was awarded the Victoria Cross.

The enemy went over to the offensive and the force was ordered to retire to Sherpur and in this move the Gordons formed part of the rearguard. Before dawn on December 23 a beacon flared on the Asmai heights – signal for a concerted assault.

The Afghan horde arose and poured towards Sherpur, the main attack developing against the eastern flank held by the Gordons. The crackle of musketry rolled round the perimeter and the thundering artillery felled the tribesmen in heaps. The cavalry then charged driving the enemy back into the hills.

On August 9 General Sir Frederick Roberts set out on his historic march of over 300 miles from Kabul through the hostile Logar Valley to the relief of the garrison at Kandahar – an outstanding feat of endurance in stifling heat and choking duststorms in the arid, rugged, mountainous terrain. It was a long climb as well as a long march.

The brigade columns snaked deep into enemy territory and for about three weeks nothing was heard of them. Because of the nature of the country no wheeled transport was taken and lack of bridges caused problems in getting mules bearing guns across quick-flowing rivers. Kit and supplies were cut to the bare minimum.

General Roberts reached Kandahar on August 31, and on September 1 an attack was launched. Major White led a charge on a band of fanatics rallying round two pieces of artillery and the Gordons burst in among them before they could fire. The enemy camp at Mazra was entered and the hillmen began a slow fighting retiral. Kandahar was the last major engagement in this campaign.

The 92nd arrived at Durban in mid-January 1881. The Boers had rebelled against British annexation and were invading

Natal. Three companies totalling about 180 men were with General Sir George Colley's ill-fated force of 350 men which on February 26 attempted to seize Majuba Hill.

Under cover of darkness the hill was scaled and then things began to go awry. Fire had been opened on the Boers beneath and the element of surprise was lost. The bare exposed summit afforded scant cover for the defenders, while the attackers scrambled up from several angles and were frequently obscured from view.

Marksmen picked off the British troops and when it was considered they were sufficiently thinned out the Boers came on in strength. Though the 92nd suffered severe casualties the companies held on tenaciously, but had to give ground under mounting pressure. About 150 Gordons were making a determined stand when the order to retire was given.

General Sir George Colley, Governor of Natal, was among the fallen. Attaching himself to the 92nd he soldiered it out to the end under the murderous fire. More men were lost as the bullet-swept body-strewn hill was abandoned to the enemy.

On July 1, 1881, the 92nd Regiment and the 75th Regiment were amalgamated. The 75th became the 1st Battalion and the 92nd the 2nd Battalion The Gordon Highlanders.

There was quite naturally a feeling of deep regret in the 75th and 92nd at the loss of their respective numerals but they accepted the inevitable. A humorous epitaph was composed by a soldier of the 75th while the regiment was stationed at Malta. It read:

> Here lies the poor old 75th,
> But under God's protection,
> They'll rise again in kilt and hose
> A glorious resurrection,
> For by the transformatory power
> Of Parliamentary laws,
> We go to bed the 75th
> To rise the Ninety-Twas.

And the 92nd while serving in South Africa held a 'wake'. There was a midnight feast on June 30 and a funeral oration was delivered. A torchlight procession followed the coffin bearing a flag inscribed '92'. It was borne in all solemnity, the officers wearing full Highland dress and led by the band playing the doleful 'Dead March'.

At the graveside three volleys were fired and the pipes wailed a lament. But next morning the 'body' was exhumed. On the flag was the inscription in the doric of the North *'Ninety-Twa no' deid yet'*, and on many of the tents similar flags were flying.

The 75th, raised as a Highland regiment in Stirlingshire and the North by Colonel Robert Abercrombie during 1787, was embodied at Stirling in June 1788, with a strength of 700. Colonel Abercrombie, son of the Laird of Tullibody, gathered round him a number of soldiers who formed the nucleus of the new corps. Most of them had been in a light brigade he commanded during the American War.

The original uniform was red with yellow facings. Officers were armed with sword and dirk. Sergeants wore the distinctive sash and laced shoulder-knots and were accoutred with sword and halberd. Some dubiety exists concerning the tartan, but it is believed that the regiment must have been issued with the 'Government' or 'Universal' tartan.

In the late autumn of 1788 the 75th arrived in India. In 1790 Britain went to the aid of the Rajah of Travancore when Tippoo, Sultan of Mysore, invaded his territory. The 75th and Bombay sepoys captured Chowghaset Fort, defeated the enemy in the jungle near Calicut and seized Ferokabad Fort. There was also fierce fighting around Trevangherry.

The army moved on Seringapatam, the enemy capital, in February 1791, but owing to the late arrival of other formations the assault could not be delivered and the troops retired as the monsoon rains set in. Cavalry harried the withdrawal, the 75th fighting a series of rearguard actions.

The campaign was resumed in November. About 100 men of the regiment and native soldiers cleared the enemy from a grove in front of a redoubt at Seringapatam. The Sultan's guns opened fire and his cavalry and infantry attacked forcing a retiral. Over 2,000 warriors of Tippoo's 'Tiger' Battalion charged but the 75th and their sepoy comrades turned about and closing with the bayonet drove the enemy back. The Sultan's peace overtures followed.

On Republican France declaring war the regiment occupied the fort of Mahe and entered Cochin. In the spring of 1799 the Carnatic Campaign was resumed, the Sultan of Mysore and other rulers having joined the French. Tippoo sent 10,000 men against native troops at Ludasier but their relief was effected by companies of the 75th and other units. The Highlanders also baulked the enemy at Agra.

A concentrated bombardment struck Seringapatam on April 23 and continued with unabated fury for ten days. On May 3 two assault forces moved forward, one including companies of the 75th. Rushing the breaches they closed with their bayonets and soon the British flag was fluttering over the ramparts.

The regiment reduced the hill fort of Jemanlabad and in 1800 operated against the rebellious rulers of Malabar and Canara. It relieved Montana and stormed into Pychee. In 1802 Fort Kerria, Pankera and Brodera fell and in 1803 Pamera was taken. Another success was the regiment's advance through torrential monsoon rains to capture the fort of Soangurh.

The 75th was in all four disastrous assaults on the powerful fortress of Bhurtpore. The operations began early in January 1805, and continued for about four months. On each occasion the storming columns achieved some costly initial success but were decimated by concentrated artillery and rifle fire.

In the spring of 1807 the weak battalion returned to Scotland and while stationed at Dunblane a number of recruits and militiamen joined. Very few of them were from the Highlands and this factor, the intake of English soldiers while the regiment was in India and the compulsory drafting of Highlanders into other units, had the effect of changing for some time the 'nationality' of the 75th.

This is believed to have influenced the order of April 1809, that the regiment discontinue wearing the Highland dress and adopt that of the Infantry of the Line. Thus Abercrombie's Highlanders were de-kilted, removed from the Highland establishment and designated the 75th Regiment of Foot until 'reprieved' in June 1882.

While serving in Sicily the 75th was ferried across the Straits of Messina in mid-February 1813, and with naval co-operation surprised the French garrison at Pietro Nero in a night attack. A number of invasion craft was destroyed and the danger of an enemy landing in Sicily removed. In the summer of the following year the regiment arrived in the Ionian Islands.

It was ordered to South Africa in the spring of 1834 and in April 1835, marched with an expedition sent against the Kaffirs.

At Keiskama Hoek the tribesmen suffered heavy losses and fled abandoning thousands of stolen cattle. Guerrilla warfare ensued and the regiment, based on Fort Cox, took part in punitive operations until the Kaffirs surrendered in September.

On the outbreak of the Indian Mutiny in the early summer of 1857 the regiment, while stationed at Kasauli, sent a company – mounted on elephants – to Kalka. This move is believed to have saved many European families fleeing out of Simla from the savagery of the rebels. The 75th then took its place in the hastily assembled field force for the march on Delhi.

Guns at Badli-ki-Sarai, commanding the main approach road, opened up but a wild Highland charge silenced the battery and the way to Delhi was re-opened. The British established themselves on a ridge overlooking the city and the regiment was prominently identified in the fighting at Flagstaff Picquet, Subzee Mundi, Hindoo Rao's Battery, Metcalfe's Grounds and Ludlow Castle.

The expected reinforcements came up, a prolonged bombardment commenced on September 9 and on the 14th British and Indian troops stormed into the breaches created. The 75th was heavily engaged in the costly assaults on the More Bastion, the Kabul Gate and the Lahore Gate. The Highlanders battled into the rebel defences and on September 20 the British flag again flew over Delhi.

The vehemence of the fighting was reflected in the award of three Victoria Crosses to soldiers of the 75th. On June 8, at Badli-ki-Sarai, Colour-Sergeant Cornelius Coghlan and three others dashed into an enemy post under fire and brought to safety wounded Private Corbett. On July 18, at Subzee Mundi, the colour-sergeant rallied his men, led them in a charge and successfully evacuated the injured in a deadly cross-fire.

During this engagement Ensign Wadeson – who later commanded the regiment – saved Private Michael Farrell when he was attacked by a cavalryman. Ensign Wadeson killed another mounted *sowar* that day in rescuing Private John Barry. At Koodsia Baugh, on September 11, Private Patrick Green tackled several mutineers while saving a wounded comrade.

With a mobile column the 75th set out in pursuit of the mutineers, clearing them from Dadra, Bolandshar, Malagarh, Koel, Akbarabad and elsewhere. As Agra was in imminent danger the force changed direction and made a rapid advance, entering the city on October 9.

Meanwhile the garrison at Lucknow was in dire extremities. Relief forces had broken through only to become themselves besieged on linking up with the defenders. Another relief column, including the 75th, marched out from Agra in mid-October.

The regiment, leading the advance, repulsed an attack at Mahagang and, in mid-November, the relief force began thrusting into the city. The 75th fought with distinction at Fort Jalalabad, the Alambagh, Dungapur, Dilkusha and the Sikanderbagh and in March the rebel stranglehold on Lucknow was broken.

The unit came home in June 1862, and towards the close of that year it was designated the 75th, or Stirlingshire Regiment. Two hundred soldiers of the regiment accompanied the force dispatched from Fort Napier at the end of 1873 to deal with the troublesome Kaffirs who were soon scattered in the Drakensberg Mountains.

In August 1882, the 75th – now the 1st Battalion The Gordon Highlanders – joined The Highland Brigade at Ramleh with Egypt aflame during Colonel Arabi Pasha's revolt. After a rapid approach march from Kassassin by two divisions – The Highland Brigade leading the left division – the rebels were attacked at Tel-el-Kebir as the first streaks of dawn were brightening the horizon on September 13.

The pipes sounded, the bayonets flashed and clicked into the fix, and the Highlanders rushed the entrenchments. And Juno, the regimental dog mascot of the Gordons, charged too – and later wore medals to prove it!

In less than half an hour enemy resistance collapsed and the Egyptians and Soudanese fled across the desert. Cairo was entered on the 14th and Colonel Arabi Pasha surrendered. The Gordon Highlanders marched into the Citadel to the skirl of their pipes.

A holy war was raging in the Sudan and the tribes flocked to the standard of Mahomet Ali who declared himself to be the Mahdi, or Messiah. The holy war became an unholy war – tyranny, terror, torture and massacre. In mid-February 1884, the 1st Gordons advanced with a column to make contact with the enemy at El Teb.

The tribesmen opened up with artillery and small arms fire but their guns were soon silenced by the British batteries. The pipes of the Highlanders sang in the thin desert air as the Mahdi's warriors, erupting in screaming yelling thousands from their entrenchments and waving swords, rifles and spears, charged headlong at the compact squares.

Steady accurate volleys dropped them in hundreds and the frenzied onslaught finally broke against the lines of bristling bayonets. The British force advanced to Tamai to again engage the Mahdi's fanatics.

Masses of tribesmen arose from a dried-up watercourse and though decimated by the artillery they surged forward like a long curling tidal wave. The fire order was given in the infantry squares and the carnage of El Teb was repeated. Early in April the battalion returned to Cairo.

The 1st Gordons were in the expedition dispatched at the beginning of November 1884, to rescue Major-General Charles Gordon trapped in Khartoum. The troops sailed up the Nile and in mid-January 1885, the Army's 'fleet' arrived at Korti. A mobile column set out across the wastes of the Bayuda Desert – the shortest route to Khartoum. Another force, which included the Gordons, ascended the Nile on a punitive mission against disaffected tribes.

The desert column fought several sharp engagements for the possession of vital wells and water-holes, particularly at Abu Klea and Gubat, and about thirty Gordons serving as mounted infantry took part in these actions.

On the night of January 25 an orgy of looting and murder was unleashed at Khartoum and General Gordon was killed. Despite forced marches, hard fighting and a breakthrough the column arrived within sight of its objective 48 hours too late and was ordered to retire.

A company of Gordons with the river column was in the attack which dislodged tribesmen from the rocky heights commanding Kirbekan on February 10 thus ensuring the unmolested passage of the force. After bringing several recalcitrant tribes to heel the river column was ordered back and early in March there was a rendezvous with the desert force at Korti. The battalion descended the Nile and arrived at Alexandria in July.

The 1st Gordons were dispatched to India early in 1893 and when Umra Khan, one of the powerful chiefs on the North-West Frontier, threw down the gauntlet and attacked the fort at Chitral the battalion joined the relief force at the close of March 1895. From Nowshera it advanced with the 2nd Brigade towards the Malakand Pass.

An assault on the heights early in April opened the road into the Jendol Valley – Umra Khan's 'home' territory – and the Chitral Relief Force marched through the snow-capped mountains to find their quarry in flight. Chitral was relieved by a column coming up from Gilgit.

Following attacks on frontier garrisons the 1st Gordons took their place in the Malakand Field Force at the beginning of August 1897. On news being received that Fort Maude was under attack the battalion along with other units raced to its relief and arrived just in time to save the defenders.

When the Tirah Field Force assembled the Gordons were with the 1st Brigade of the 2nd Division and early in October they marched by the Kohat Pass to Shinauri. The tribesmen were dislodged from Dargai but later they infiltrated back on to the heights which dominated the road along which the troops had to pass.

Artillery fire had little effect as the hillmen sheltered in deep clefts among the rocks and behind boulders and several assaults failed. Then came the turn of *Na Gordanaich*. They took cover for a few minutes as the Gunners once more concentrated on the summit.

Lieutenant-Colonel H. H. Mathias addressed his battalion. 'The General says this hill must be taken at all costs. The Gordon Highlanders will take it!'

The pipers struck up and with a cheer they leapt to their feet and charged with levelled bayonets. As the Gordons clambered on to the crest the tribesmen were in retreat down the reverse slopes. The Heights of Dargai – where a brigade had been held up for over three hours – was taken in 40 minutes by the 1st Gordons. And when they came down they brought with them their wounded and those of other formations.

Two Gordon Highlanders won the Victoria Cross at Dargai. Piper George Findlater, though shot through both ankles, propped himself up against a boulder and continued to play with bullets whining all round him. Private Edward Lawson carried Lieutenant K. Dingwall, who was badly wounded, to safety and while performing a similar service for Private Macmillan he was twice hit.

Queen Victoria visited George Findlater in Netley Hospital, in England's 'deep South', to hear his personal account of the charge at Dargai. Though his wounds were still troublesome George attempted to stand up and come to attention but Her Majesty stayed him with the words 'Please don't get up'. Then 'good Queen Vic' pinned the Victoria Cross on his tunic.

Piper Findlater later enjoyed a period of stage fame and toured the country with several celebrities including Sir Harry Lauder and Scott Skinner. Born in Forgue, George Findlater later moved to the Mill of Turriff. For many years he was pipe-major of Turriff Pipe Band and the headstone over his grave in Forglen Churchyard identifies him as one of the heroes of Dargai.

After the charge at Dargai The Gordon Highlanders further enhanced their reputation for toughness and gallantry. No stretcher-bearers were available after the action and the Gordons carried down the wounded. News of the charge circulated quickly and as the exhausted Highlanders neared camp the troops lined up and cheered them in. Many stepped forward to offer the Gordons a 'pull' at their water-bottles – when water was strictly rationed.

The tribesmen were cleared from the passes and some fortified villages before the Tirah Field Force backtracked to base. From Bagh the brigade negotiated the Bara Valley to Barkai with the Gordons dealing with marksmen on the heights and fighting a succession of sharp rearguard actions.

A mixed force of about 450 Gordons, Dorsets, Gurkhas and Punjabis contrived a short cut, but with the enemy closing in they entered a large house and from the tower, roof and loop-holed walls they fought off the hillmen until relieved the following morning. The sturdy defence of 'Fort Downman' – named after Major Downman of the Gordons – became a *vignette* in regimental history.

The brigade arrived in Bara, in the Peshawar area, in mid-December. Towards the close of January 1898, it was engaged in a series of punitive expeditions on the Kajauri Plains and around Guli Khel. Soon the warring tribes sued for peace and the rifles ceased to crack in the high passes. The 1st Gordons returned to the Scottish capital towards the end of the year.

After special training about thirty men of the 2nd Battalion went to Rhodesia in the spring of 1896 and served as mounted infantry during a period of tension. They rejoined the battalion a year later. The 2nd Gordons sailed for Bombay in the autumn of 1898.

The battalion arrived at Durban early in October 1899, on the eve of the South African War. A few days after hostilities broke out a detachment along with other troops scattered a force of Boers on Talana Hill.

Reconnaissance confirmed the Boers were in strength on rough hilly ground at Elandslaagte, about seventeen miles from Ladysmith, and several companies of Gordons were in the advance to contact. After an artillery duel the Highlanders zig-zagged through the shell-bursts towards the enemy-held ridge which was taken in a series of rushes. The bugles and pipes sounded as the Gordons swept over the crest with the Boers in retreat before the lines of bayonets.

Two Victoria Crosses were won at Elandslaagte. Lieutenant Matthew Fontaine Maury Meiklejohn rallied a group of leaderless Gordons during a counter-attack and rushed the enemy under a galling cross-fire. Lieutenant Meiklejohn was wounded four times. Regimental Sergeant-Major William Robertson led several assaults and then headed a charge which seized the Boer camp. The R.S.M. was hit twice. Both received the supreme award for bravery.

As the overall military situation had deteriorated there was a retiral behind the perimeter defences of Ladysmith. At the end of October the Gordons marched out with a force which succeeded in diverting enemy attention from a column retreating from Dundee. The two formations effected a rendezvous and withdrew into Ladysmith.

During the 120 days siege the battalion was in action at Lombard's Kop and a detachment in Nicholson's Nek, after losing its reserve ammunition when mules stampeded, was captured after nine hours stubborn resistance. The Boers made probing attacks on Ladysmith during November but met with such a reception that they returned to the start-line.

The battalion area on the south-west of the defences soon

became known as 'Gordons Kop'. Ladysmith, overflowing with refugees, was closely invested and the enemy guns frequently bombarded the makeshift forts and posts. Bullets droned in the streets like angry bees.

In the early hours of January 6, 1900, several thousand Boers stole through the darkness and by dawn secured a firm hold on the south-west of Wagon Hill and on the plateau at Wagon Point. British reinforcements were sent in and the enemy was driven back under artillery and rifle fire.

Then a new foe reared its ugly head – starvation. Several determined attempts to relieve the garrison failed and the cavalry became infantry; so that their horses could be eaten.

February 13 brought the cheering message from Field-Marshal Lord Roberts that the invasion of the Orange Free State had begun, and expressed his hope for the speedy relief of Lady-smith. A few days later the boom of guns was heard – nearer, louder, more continuous – and on the 19th the crackle of rifle fire was also heard. On the 27th news was received of Cronje's surrender.

On the 28th an extended line of cavalry was seen crossing the plain and loud cheering from the outposts prepared Lady-smith for deliverance. There was a call for volunteers to inter-cept the enemy retreat and close on 600 Gordons marched out with the column. But the Boers were moving fast and after a skirmish at Pepworth Hill the pursuit was called off.

General Sir Redvers Buller and his army entered Ladysmith on March 3, played in by the pipers of the 2nd Gordons. In the consequent advance the battalion was in action at Laing's Nek, Witkopjes, Rooikopjes, Frischgewagd, Belfast and Van Wyk's Vlei.

The Gordons tangled with the rearguard at Machadodorp and found the enemy guns troublesome in the move through Lydenberg, in the thrust to Paardeplaatz summit and the ascent of the Mauchberg. They cleared the rearguard from four kopjes known as the 'Devil's Knuckles' and returned to Lydenberg.

Its mission accomplished, the Natal Field Force was dispersed. The Gordons joined the 8th Brigade and garrison, escort and outpost duties followed. When a train was derailed by the enemy at Naboomspruit and the small escort overwhelmed, the sole wounded survivor was asked why the guard did not surrender. He replied 'Why, man? We are Gordon Highlanders!'

From late August until mid-November 1901, companies operated with veldt columns in rounding up scattered bands of the enemy. From Pretoria the battalion began the first stage of a 'trooping' to India early in 1902.

The 1st Battalion, coming out from Britain, arrived in Cape Town towards the end of November 1899. At Magersfontein, early in December, the Gordons went to the aid of the shattered Highland Brigade pinned down by close-range fire.

The battalion got to within 300 yards of the Boer trenches where it was held up by an uncut wire fence and the enemy riflemen. The Gordons dug in with their bayonets, clasp knives and even their bare hands. When the order to retire was given they came under a deadly fire. The artillery had little effect on the narrow deep Boer entrenchments.

For his heroism on December 11, 1899, at Magersfontein and again at Mount Thaba, on April 30, 1900, Captain Ernest Beachcroft Beckwith Towse was awarded the Victoria Cross. During the retiral at Magersfontein he tended his mortally-wounded commanding officer, Lieutenant-Colonel G. T. F. Downman. He bore him back and was later assisted by Colour-Sergeant Nelson and Lance-Corporal Hodgson in getting the colonel out of range of the Boer riflemen.

Captain Towse led about a dozen men on to the summit of Mount Thaba where they engaged 150 Boers coming over from the other side. The enemy commander called on them to surrender, Captain Towse shouted a refusal and brought him down with a shot. The dauntless dozen opened fire and charged. The Boers gave way but the officer and half his little band became casualties. Captain Towse lost the sight of both eyes.

When the Canadians made the final assault at Paardeberg on February 27 the Gordons gave them effective fire cover. White flags fluttered over the enemy position and Gronje surrendered. The advance on Bloemfontein, capital of the Orange Free State, began early in March.

The Gordons were engaged in the hard fighting at Poplar Grove, Leeukop and Driefontein. Bloemfontein was entered and at the beginning of April the 9th Division moved against a large force which had defeated a British column at Sanna's Post. As it was considered too late to retrieve the guns lost by the column, however, a retiral was ordered.

For the push north the brigade joined the Winburg Column which crossed the Modder River and marched on Israel's Poort where enemy resistance cracked. The thrust beyond Thabanchu found the Boers in considerable strength on kopjes overlooking the wooded pass at Hout Nek.

Key to the enemy position was Mount Thaba and two companies were with the troops which ascended the steep slopes. The Boers, observing this move, did likewise and it became a race for possession. As night fell Boer and Briton lay among the rocks watching and waiting.

A sudden charge broke the stalemate and the enemy rose and ran before the bayonets of the Highlanders. Early in May the Winburg Column crossed the waters of the Zand and fought a brisk action near the Rhenoster River. The Vaal was forded and the Gordons ejected the Boers from positions around Doornkop. In this engagement, on Crow's Nest Hill, Corporal John Frederick Mackay braved the enemy fire to tend wounded and brought one of them back to safety. Corporal Mackay was awarded the Victoria Cross.

Johannesburg surrendered and the advance swept on to Pretoria, capital of the Transvaal. At Six Mile Spruit the battalion cleared a range of hills and with the road to Pretoria open its capitulation soon followed. The battalion was engaged at Diamond Hill and about the middle of July took part in the hard-fought action at Leekoehoek, in the Wolverkranz area.

Two Victoria Crosses were won by Gordons at Leekoehoek for a gallant attempt to save the guns. Captain David Reginald Younger and Captain G. S. Allan succeeded in running a limber behind cover, and Captain William Eagleson Gordon called for volunteers to bring in the guns. He dashed out, attached a drag-rope round the nearest and Captain Younger and his party ran to his assistance.

The Boers observed the bid and their fire increased. While moving the gun Captain Younger was mortally wounded, several others were hit and Captain Allan rushed to their aid. Realising the attempt had failed Captain Gordon ordered everyone back, and having seen the wounded to safety, he too retired.

Corporal F. J. Mackay – who won the V.C. at Doornkop – went out and carried away Captain Younger. Captain Gordon and Captain Younger were both awarded the Victoria Cross, but in the case of the latter it was posthumous.

In August the Gordons took their place in the reconstituted 19th Brigade and leaving Lydenberg early in September marched to Komati Poort, close to the Portuguese border. About midnight on January 7, 1901, the enemy attacked Belfast but after bitter fighting they were repulsed with the Gordons in the thick of the fray.

Guerrilla warfare ensued and the battalion experienced a lengthy spell of escort, lines of communication and blockhouse duties. During the campaign the regiment was well represented in a number of Mounted Infantry units. Peace was signed at the close of May 1902, and towards the end of October the 1st Gordons were sailing up the Clyde.

At the turn of the century the battle honours borne on the Regimental Colour were: Mysore, Seringapatam, Egmont-op-Zee, Mandora, Corunna, Fuentes d'Onor, Almaraz, Vittoria, Pyrenees, Peninsula, Nive, Orthes, Waterloo, South Africa 1835, Delhi, Lucknow, Charasia, Kabul 1879, Kandahar 1880, Afghanistan 1879-80, Tel-el-Kebir, Egypt 1882-84, Nile 1884-85, Chitral, Tirah, Defence of Ladysmith, Paardeberg.

The 1st Gordons, forming part of the 8th Brigade, 3rd Division, 2nd Army Corps, crossed the Channel within a few days of the outbreak of World War I. After forced marches the battalion took up positions on August 22, 1914, along the Mons-Conde Canal and in the Nimy Bridge salient, right in the path of the German advance.

At first light on the 23rd the enemy opened a heavy bombardment, followed by a massed infantry attack which wilted before the rifle and machine-gun fire of the British Expeditionary Force. The assault was renewed and, having suffered severe casualties, the 3rd Division was ordered to retire. The 8th Brigade stood fast until nightfall in covering this movement.

On the 25th, after the longest march in the eight days fighting retreat from Mons, the 2nd Corps made its great stand at Le Cateau, the brigade holding an extended line in front of Audencourt and Caudry under continuous shelling and infantry attack. Only one company of Gordons survived. Orders to withdraw failed to reach the remainder of the battalion which fought on until encirclement forced its surrender, a breakout having failed.

A new line was established on the Marne and here, early in September, the B.E.F. made its supreme effort, checked and hurled back the German onrush and advanced to the Aisne. The company of Gordons, which had been reinforced, was heavily engaged in the Petit Morin area.

At the beginning of October it moved north to Flanders and, in violent fighting, captured Croix Barbee and Pont de Hem, withstood counter-attacks and reached Aubers. Early in November the Gordons arrived in the Ypres salient and in mid-December, at battalion strength once more, took part in an uphill charge through the thick cloying mud in an attempt to seize a spur of Wytschaete Ridge, but they were decimated by machine-gun fire.

For close on a year the battalion fought desperately in the ghastly squelching swamp of the salient and it was grim work with bomb and bayonet during the containment attack at Hooge in late September 1915. Men in scores, sometimes in hundreds, riddled with bullets or frightfully sundered by shells, died as they hung on the wire entanglements in front of the enemy trenches. But this sacrificial assault achieved its purpose – the Germans were so heavily engaged that they could not reinforce their troops at the Battle of Loos.

Trench warfare in appalling conditions continued throughout the winter. At the beginning of March 1916, the battalion took part in an onslaught against 'The Bluff', which was captured in frenzied fighting.

In the British offensive on the Somme, which lasted from July to November, the Gordons were engaged in the ebb and flow of battle in the Longueval-Delville Wood area, and in July cleared the Germans from Angle Wood in mid-August. The First Battle of the Somme ended with a check for the battalion at Seree.

They took the first line of trenches but, cut off by infantry bombing attacks, they had to retire re-crossing a Sargasso Sea of deep mud and waterlogged shell craters into which men stumbled and were seen no more. Artillery bombardments, trench raiding and sniping followed in this quagmire until mid-March 1917, when the Germans began their retreat to the Hindenburg Line defences.

The Battle of Arras in April and May is still claimed as a Scottish victory. The 1st Gordons went in at Monchy-le-Preux, taking four lines of trenches, and pressing on captured Bois-des-Boeufs and Guemappe. In mid-June there was a 'tailpiece' to this onslaught. The Gordons launched a sudden surprise attack which ejected the enemy from Infantry Hill – a position that had defied all previous assaults.

In operations at Passchendaele in late September the Gordons took their objectives near the Ypres-Roulers railway and advanced beyond Zonnebeke. New positions were established along several thousand yards of the main ridge – the key to Passchendaele.

By the spring of 1918 the British successes at Arras, Ypres and Cambrai and the breakthrough in the Hindenburg Line had forced the enemy back with very heavy losses. But, on the defection of Russia, German divisions were moved to the west and unleashed in the early hours of March 21.

This mighty offensive, on a front of over 50 miles between Bullecourt and the River Oise, was intended to drive a deep wedge between the British and French armies and so end the war before American forces could land. The Germans died in battalions but fresh troops came on in shoulder-to-shoulder formation.

The 1st Gordons barred the way with the 3rd Division on the left of the River Sensee and made the area a vast enemy graveyard. The Germans gained less than a thousand yards at prodigal loss.

The enemy assault in this Second Battle of the Somme failed to achieve its purpose and another massed attack was launched on April 9 at the Battle of the Lys, on the Flanders front. The 3rd Division was rushed to Hinges to stem the German flow towards the Lys, and the 1st Gordons made several successful forays and held the ground gained. The German onrush again ended in disaster after making initial progress.

On May 27 the German High Command mounted its last desperate onslaught and though losing several thousand men a day in the Third Battle of the Aisne, the river was crossed and the enemy reached the Marne. But here, at the Second Battle of the Marne, the Allies regained the initiative and the Kaiser's armies were sent reeling to their doom.

In late August, during the push on Bapaume, the 1st Gordons were heavily committed at Courcelles, Gomiecourt and Ecoust. A month later, in the attacks towards Cambrai, the Canal du Nord and the northern defences of the Hindenburg Line, the battalion was prominent around Flesquieres, Rumilly and Seranvillers. Early in October it captured La Targette and during the advance on Valenciennes and Famars the Gordons fought their last major action in World War I.

Coming from Egypt the 2nd Battalion joined the 7th Division in time for the First Battle of Ypres. Within a few weeks Victoria Crosses were won 'for conspicuous bravery' by Drummer William Kenny at Kruseik on October 23 and Lieutenant James Anson Otho Brooke near Gheluvelt on October 29.

In the fighting near Ypres which preceded the First Battle Drummer Kenny in five separate acts of gallantry and under very heavy fire rescued wounded men. Twice he saved machine-guns by carrying them out of action and on a number of occasions he conveyed urgent messages over fire-swept ground.

As dawn was breaking on October 29, 1914, the Germans initiated their offensive at Ypres along the Menin Road. The fury and weight of the assault made some headway but companies of the 2nd Gordons clung to their battered crumbling trenches under a terrific bombardment, and the enemy was checked by wild bayonet charges.

At this crisis Lieutenant Brooke arrived in the Gheluvelt shambles. Quickly appreciating the situation, he collected a number of batmen, cooks and orderlies and led them into action. He was killed in recapturing a trench thus preventing a possible German breakthrough.

A new defence line was organised at Zillebeke and a local counter-attack cleared the enemy from the woods at Zwartelen. The British infantry suffered severe losses in facing odds of six to one and the 7th Division though surrounded on several occasions broke out. The 2nd Gordons were reduced to about company strength but the Germans were fought to a standstill.

In mid-March 1915, at Neuve Chapelle, the battalion twice assailed the dominating feature – Aubers Ridge – through a mud swamp and, when checked by concentrated fire, they consolidated the ground won. Two months later, at Festubert, they overran a line of trenches and stayed put under the pounding of the German guns.

In the Loos bloodbath in late September the depleted formation attacked the trenches around Hussey Redoubt, swept on to cross the Vermelles-Halluch road, capture an artillery battery in Gun Trench and reach the Lens-La-Bassee road. A powerful counter-attack lapped round the flanks but the Gordons fought their way out in the darkness and, returning to Gun Trench, helped to repel the German assault.

At the First Battle of the Somme the Gordons burst into Mametz and a week later took Bazentin-le-Petit which they defended against a counter-attack. Ordered into the assault on High Wood their objectives were two roads. They got astride one but were held up by rifle and machine-gun fire and dug in. In the general advance the battalion recaptured Ginchy but severe casualties ruled out further progress.

In the final phase of the Somme battle, while the fighting raged round Beaumont Hamel, the 7th Division went in to the south of Serre. The weather had deteriorated, the area lay under several feet of mud and the 2nd Gordons sustained crippling losses in front of the enemy trench lines.

There followed several months of trench warfare. Men lived like animals up to the knees, thighs and waists in freezing, waterlogged and mud-filled shell craters. Meals were half-cooked, often raw. There were sudden sallies with bomb, rifle and bayonet, enemy counter-raids and desperate hand-to-hand fighting in the foul-smelling quagmire. Bodies were strung in a crazy pattern along the barbed wire until they were blasted away by the guns. But particles of uniform remained flapping in the icy wind.

Thundering bombardments lasted for hours, sometimes days and nights, great waterspouts erupting where the shells burst. Each barrage unearthed the dead – hands, arms, legs and feet protruded from the walls of dug-outs and parapets. The machine-guns rattled at intervals invariably followed by rifle fire and the cries of the wounded and dying – and the drowning.

When the artillery ceased there was an uneasy silence usually broken by the sharp echoing crack of a sniper's rifle – and the splash of a falling body. Rats scampered along the trenches and over the fire-steps, their eyes glowing red at night. And there were the lice. . . .

When relief came men had to be pulled from the sucking mud-traps. Some were found to be minus their reason, others suffering from frostbite, shell-shock or trench feet -- or dead. This was the no man's land of the Somme – where the chirp of birds was never heard, no wild flowers grew and grotesque blackened trees raised their shattered branches like protesting arms to the heavens. . . .

The 1917 German retreat to the Hindenburg Line began towards the middle of March and in the follow-up the 2nd Gordons made a successful attack early in April on Longatte and established themselves on a stretch of road between the village and Noreuil. Now they were bumping the outer strongpoints of the formidable enemy defence system.

In the Battle of Arras the battalion was in a night assault on Bullecourt, took its objectives and at the beginning of October it participated in the third advance during the Battle of Passchendaele. The Gordons fought their last action on this front in the salient near Gheluvelt towards the end of the month.

In mid-November the 2nd Battalion with its division left for Italy and in January 1918, the Gordons were in the trenches along the bank of the Piave. They raided the Austrian lines on several occasions and early in August the battalion took part in the 7th Division's attack on Cavaletto.

At the Battle of the Piave, towards the close of October, the division established itself on Grave di Papadopoli; the Gordons crossed to this island and then forded the river under enfilade fire. The Austrians were driven back and the battalion entered Torre.

The battalion crossed the Tagliamento with the enemy in rout and suing for peace. Hostilities in Italy ended on November 4, 1918 – a few days before the Armistice in Germany. The 2nd Gordons were in Aberdeen before the end of March, 1919.

Battle honours awarded to the Regiment were: MONS, Retreat from Mons, LE CATEAU, MARNE 1914, 1918, Aisne 1914, La Bassée 1914, Messines 1914, Armentieres 1914, YPRES 1914, '15, '17, Langemarck 1914, Gheluveet, Nonne Boschen, Neuve Chapelle, Frezenberg, Bellewaarde, Aubers, Hindenburg Line, Canal du Nord, Selle, Festubert 1915, Hooge 1915, LOOS,

SOMME 1916, '18, Albert 1916, '18, Bazentin, Delville Wood, Pozieres, Guillemont, Flers-Courcelette, Le Transloy, ANCRE 1916, ARRAS 1917, '18, Vimy 1917, Scarpe 1917, '18, Arleux, Sambre, France and Flanders 1914-18, Bullecourt, Pilckem, Menin Road, Polygon Wood, Broodseinde, Poelcappelle, Passchendaele, CAMBRAI 1917, '18, St. Quentin, Bapaume 1918, Rosieres, Lys, Estaires, Hazebrouck, Bethune, Soissonais-Ourcq, Tardenois, Piave, VITTORIO VENETO, Italy 1917-18. (The ten printed in capitals appear on the Colours.)

After serving in the Army of Occupation the 1st Battalion returned from Cologne in May 1919. Early in April 1920, it arrived in Constantinople where there was tension following a Greek invasion of Asia Minor. While serving in the Army of the Black Sea – an Allied force – the Gordons manned a defence line on the Ismid peninsula and a mounted detachment was sent to Derindje.

Two companies came under fire in mid-June while going to the aid of Indian troops in a forward area and another unit operated against bandits. Early in September there was a reconnaissance to Armasha, in Anatolia. The mounted detachment moved to Biyud Dere. In the summer of 1921 the British contingent was reduced, the Gordons going to Malta in late November.

In the autumn of 1922, however, the battalion was again in Turkey. To prevent the conflict spreading the Allies set up a bridgehead at Chanak, on the Asiatic side of the Dardanelles. The Gordons crossed from Chanak to Rodesto and acted as a buffer between the opposing armies. Later the battalion was stationed near Constantinople and returned to Malta at the end of August 1923. Duty followed in Egypt, India and Palestine and early in 1935 the 1st Gordons came home.

In mid-1919 the 2nd Battalion was in Dublin and at the ready during the strife prior to partition. The Gordons experienced another tour of duty in Ireland, in the North, and in October 1934, the battalion disembarked at Alexandria. After a few weeks in Egypt it returned to the 'Rock'. In March 1937, the 2nd Gordons were ordered to Singapore.

The 1st Battalion arrived at Aldershot in the spring of 1938 and joined 2 Brigade of the 1st Division. After the outbreak of war the Gordons moved to Southampton in mid-September

1939, and crossed to Cherbourg. From Neuville the battalion was dispatched with its divison to the south-east of Lille where the British Expeditionary Force took over part of the field defences skirting the Franco-Belgian frontier from the western end of the Maginot Line to the sea.

Early in March 1940, the 6th Gordons (T.A.) was switched from 153 Brigade of the 51st (Highland) Division to 2 Brigade, 1st Division. Its place in 153 was taken by the 1st Battalion which was brigaded with the 4th Black Watch (T.A.) and the 5th Gordons (T.A.).

Towards the close of the month the Highland Division relieved the French in the Armentieres-Bailleul area, the Gordons being positioned at Nieppe. About the middle of April the division entered a sector of the defences in front of the Maginot Line between the Moselle and the Nied, on the Saar 'front'.

Companies of Gordons took post in the *ligne de contact* and platoons were established in the Grössenwald, Betting, Wölschler, Petit Wölschler and Heydwald. During the first week of May, German patrols were observed but these withdrew when fire was opened on them.

With the collapse of Denmark and Norway, German armour, infantry and air power massed beyond the frontiers of the Low Countries. Early on May 10 concentrated bombing attacks were made on Allied airfields and three days later an artillery bombardment crashed down on the divisional area.

The Gordons were in the *ligne de receuil* manning positions commanding the approaches to the Maginot Line. The enemy came on at first light and after being repulsed renewed the attacks and made some progress. On the 15th the division was ordered to withdraw in conformity with the French defence plan and moved via Metz to Etain and Varennes.

By this time German armour had burst through the French lines and was operating between the 51st and the other B.E.F. formations. The Highland Division was on the anvil of disaster and soon the hammer blows were destined to fall.

Holland and Belgium had capitulated, the B.E.F. was reeling back to Dunkirk, the enemy had established two bridgeheads on the Somme, and Paris was threatened. The 51st took over a defence line stretching from Bray to the sea, 153 Brigade holding the centre.

Preceded by an artillery 'stonk' the Highland Division and French tanks and infantry assaulted the enemy bridgehead on the Somme at Abbeville early on June 4. The Gordons successfully dealt with machine-gun posts in the Grand Bois, but several tanks were lost in a minefield, others were hit and the attack failed. There were no reserves, and as several units were in exposed positions with uncovered flanks, the order was given to retire.

On June 5 a powerful enemy counter-attack on a fifty mile frontage overran forward posts and the battalion made a fighting withdrawal to the Abbeville-Le Treport road; then it moved on to high ground near the River Bresle, north-west of Gamaches. Next day the Germans came sweeping on but were checked by the brens, anti-tank guns and rifles of the Gordons.

Extended from Oisemont to near Woincourt the Highland Division, with some French formations, had succeeded in temporarily taking the edge from the enemy thrust. Losses were severe, no reinforcements were forthcoming and the troops were exhausted. The position was critical and another retiral was decided upon.

The brigade took post on the Gamaches-Monchaux line but the Germans, fording the river at Ponts-et-Marais and Eu, penetrated the weak left flank. French resistance crumbled in the south and German armour turned the Bresle line. The Highland Division moved back to the River Bethune.

Meanwhile the Royal Navy was planning to embark the 51st at Le Havre and General Fortune co-operated by assembling at Arques-la-Bataille a formation styled 'Ark Force' which he dispatched westward at night on June 9 to cover the withdrawal of the division.

'Ark Force' – which included the remnants of the 7th and 8th Argylls, the 4th Black Watch, Gunners and Corps troops – reached Le Havre but as the rapidly advancing Germans had closed the road and held the crossings of the River Durdent from Cany to Veulettes, on the coast, this composite formation embarked, otherwise it would have been trapped.

General Fortune then retired his battle-weary division on the small fishing port of St. Valery-en-Caux and organised a defensive perimeter to keep the enemy at bay while evacuation proceeded. Considerably reduced in numbers, ammunition low and short of rations the 51st began digging in early on June 11. The Gordons were positioned in the Neville area and placed under command of 152 Brigade.

Enemy air activity increased and in the afternoon their tanks rumbled and clanked across the battalion front. The 1st Gordons and the 2nd Seaforths opened up with machine-guns, light anti-tank guns and anti-tank rifles but these weapons proved of no avail.

The armour sliced through the 7th Norfolk Pioneers and broke into the positions of the Seaforths near Le Tot. The tanks got on to high ground on the coast but failed to penetrate the inner defences round St. Valery. Dive-bombers were active and the Gordons also came under artillery fire.

Early that evening a directive on embarkation – timed for 1.30 p.m. – was issued and hopes again rose. Artillery fire and air attacks forced the evacuation ships out to sea and as darkness fell a heavy rain-mist enveloped the coast and they were unable to come in. The Highland Division was doomed, but the Navy succeeded in embarking several thousand French and British fighting men at Veules-les-Roses.

About 10 p.m. the battalion was subjected to intense machine-gun and mortar fire. Several posts were overrun. The Germans got in between and behind the forward companies and all communication and cohesion ceased. It was the beginning of the end.

The hopeless battle against heavy odds by the drenched, weary and famished units went on with unabating fury until they were overwhelmed; for surrender does not come easily to a Gordon Highlander. The remaining combatant French troops capitulated at 8 a.m. on the 12th.

General Fortune – though under French command – delayed his surrender for another two hours until he realised evacuation was impossible and further resistance useless. Only then did this lionheart reluctantly order the remnants of his dying division to lay down their arms. Scotland's sorrow was matched by her pride in this sacrifice to uphold the Auld Alliance with France.

The ghastly ordeal of the fighting retreat was over and the survivors of the Highland Division began the long march across northern France, Belgium and Holland into Germany. It ended behind the barbed wire maze of prisoner-of-war compounds, but the magnificent *esprit de corps* of the Scottish regiments endured five years of captivity and their faith in ultimate victory never wavered.

When North *loons* and Heilin' *callants* foregathered at camp concerts there was a bothy nicht-cum-ceilidh – and 'The Bonnie Lass o' Fyvie' soon found German admirers! 'The Skye Boat Song', 'The Barnyards o' Delgaty' and 'The Ball o' Kirriemuir' also set Nazi feet a-tapping, and the singing of the old Scots psalms caused many a sentry to pause and listen as he paced his rounds.

On December 8, 1941 – the day after the U.S. Pacific Fleet was crippled by the Japanese air attack on Pearl Harbour – Singapore was heavily bombed. The 2nd Battalion The Gordon Highlanders in the 2nd Malaya Brigade – forming part of the garrison – was then at Pengerang.

The enemy had mastery of the sea and sky, numerical superiority and better equipment. Towards the close of January 1942, in the British retiral to Johore Baru and across the causeway linking Singapore Island, the 2nd Gordons reinforced the 27th Australian Brigade on the main road running south-east from Ayer Hitam.

Companies took up positions in a rubber estate, other units being in semi-jungle country. Action came suddenly. An enemy air attack was followed by an infantry assault but the mortar and automatic fire of the Gordons quickly thinned the Japanese ranks.

As darkness closed in the battalion was ordered to withdraw about two miles. A Japanese formation which had the temerity to approach on bicycles had more than their tyres punctured! The battalion entered the bridgehead to hold stretches of the Skudai Road but there was no enemy interference. When the last troops had crossed the causeway it went up in a series of rumbling explosions.

Singapore was jam-packed with refugees, the pipe line carrying the water supply was cut; the R.A.F. was withdrawn, only a small force of Hurricanes remaining at Kallang; the naval base was evacuated; air attacks caused chaos and havoc at the docks and Service personnel took over; and ships bearing much-needed guns and supplies were sunk in bombing raids.

About 75,000 troops – U.K., Australian and Indian – were

strained and exhausted, casualties were severe and reinforcements in many instances had no battle experience and were ill-equipped; soon ammunition was limited, with petrol too in short supply; enemy air attacks and artillery bombardments were intensified; the streets became a shambles of corpses and blood-splashed debris and the stench was overpowering; food and medicines began to give out.

Singapore was dying in agony. General Tomoyuki Yamashita – 'Tiger of Malaya' – was its torturer and executioner. The Japanese crossed the Johore Strait in spite of desperate resistance by the Australians and control of the causeway was lost. When an Indian hospital at Tyersall Park was bombed parties of Gordons toiled among the rubble to extricate and bear to safety scores of wounded.

In mid-February the battalion moved into positions between Racecourse Village and the railway and engaged the oncoming infantry. The Japanese, employing light tanks, captured Bukit Timah and the Australians and Gordons were ordered back to the Singapore defence perimeter. The battalion took over in the Farrar Road-Holland Road salient with artillery pounding the area. The destruction of equipment was an indication that the end was near.

A breakdown in essential supplies and the privations and carnage suffered by the civilian population precipitated General Gordon Bennett's request for an armistice. He hoped clemency would be shown to non-combatants and the numerous casualties, civilian and military.

Pending a reply the fighting continued. The Japanese, like the Assyrian, 'came down like a wolf on the fold' and breaking into the Alexandra Military Hospital they committed a train of frightful atrocities.

Suddenly the enemy guns ceased to fire and an eerie silence fell across the battlefront. It was broken by discordant high-pitched yells of triumph from the Japanese lines. In October the battalion – what was left of it – was transported to Siam and, along with thousands of other unfortunates, was set to constructing the Death Railway.

Hundreds sickened and died – they had lost the will to live; others collapsed in the stifling heat and when comrades went to their aid they were stopped by the bayonets of the guards;

once strong men wasted away to a rickle of bones – skeletons but not quite dead; the sick who could walk were forced to work; beatings were an everyday occurrence; it was mental and physical torture and semi-starvation.

Few were without sores and dysentery; malaria, fever and other diseases took their daily toll in the filthy insanitary compounds; there was an accute shortage of medical supplies and equipment which the Japanese did nothing to remedy; escape into the jungle was just another form of death; there was no mail from home and Red Cross parcels seldom got through.

The Bridge on the River Kwai ! The 2nd Gordons built several – and found devious means of sabotaging them as they took shape. The construction of the Death Railway cost untold horror, misery, suffering and over 125,000 lives. But the bearing and discipline of the Gordons born of fierce pride of race and regiment, earned for *Na Gordanaich* the grudging respect of a barbaric foe. Deliverance did not come until the eventful summer of 1945.

When the 1st Gordons marched into captivity at St. Valery in June 1940, the battalion was reconstituted at Aberdeen before the end of the month. The nucleus was formed by over 100 soldiers at the Depot, a number belonging to the original battalion. The reconstituted unit took its rightful place in 153 Brigade of the new 51st (Highland) Division.

There was further evidence of the resilience of the Regiment after the loss of Singapore when the 11th Gordons – formed from the 50th Holding Battalion – became the 2nd Battalion in May 1942. This formation joined 227 (Highland) Brigade of the 15th (Scottish) Division.

At El Alamein on October 23, 1942, the reconstituted Highland Division entered the lists against the General who took the surrender at St. Valery – Erwin Rommel. That night the clan chiefs of yore must have made merry in their Valhalla as their kith and kin charged across the moonlit desert straight at the throat of the enemy, pipes shrilling through the reverberating booming roar of the massed artillery.

Kilted pipers led their battalions out of the slit trenches into battle with the wild stirring bitter-sweet music of loch, glen and mountain fastness, of heroes and their deeds. 'Monty' made

Rommel dance to his tune. They said in the North it was the Highland Fling!

Each battalion was allotted objectives named after towns or villages in their regimental areas and it fell to the Gordons to capture 'Kintore', 'Braemar', and 'Aberdeen'. They crossed the 'Devil's Gardens' – minefields – and 'Kintore' and 'Braemar' were overun. 'Aberdeen' was carried with armour in support and other features, including Kidney Ridge, were wrested from the enemy.

In mid-November the pursuit rolled across the desert wastes to El Agheila and early in January 1943, while moving rapidly along the coast road, 153 Brigade came upon the Germans ensconced on a ridge at Buerat behind a minefield. Flail tanks, sappers and artillery co-operated and it was a 'little Alamein' – the Gordons advancing in bright moonlight with the pipes at full skirl. The enemy did not wait and the Eighth Army raced towards Tripoli.

The battalion was represented in 'Hammerforce' – a flying column of tanks, guns, engineers and infantry – which set out on January 21, bridged rivers, filled in gaping bomb and shell craters yawning across roads, and crashed over or through scores of obstacles to reach Tripoli in the early hours of the 23rd. Mounted on tanks the Gordons were the first infantry to enter.

The division approached the Mareth Line and 153 Brigade took up positions behind Wadi Zessar. Early in March, after a bout of shelling, German tanks and infantry struck at Medenine but were hurled back. The Gordons took several important features and the Germans vacated the Mareth Line.

The Highland Division headed for Sfax but an obstacle had to be cleared en route – the Gabes Gap – a bottleneck pass. Here at the Wadi Akarit a minefield and an anti-tank ditch provided a formidable defence and the enemy made the most of it.

Early in April, 153 Brigade established a firm base and gave supporting fire for the attack of 152 Brigade on Roumana Ridge and for 154 Brigade in its assault on Wadi Akarit. The British barrage crashed down but the German artillery, mortars and machine-guns remained active and there was bitter confused fighting and heavy casualties ere the enemy was ejected.

With armour co-operating the battalion led the consequent

advance and tangled with the rearguard at Wadi Cheffar. Early in April a company entered the battered seaport of Sfax – which could be smelt long before it was sighted. The 51st took over a stretch of the fire-swept front between the Garci Hills and Enfidaville.

The enemy guns and mortars joined in a raucous chorus night and day but it was the swansong of the Axis in North Africa – Tunis and Bizerta had fallen. The colourful spectacle of the massed pipes and drums of the Highland Division stole the show at the Allied Victory Parade in Tunis.

The 1st Gordons were detached from 153 Brigade to form an independent battle group which came under command of 154 Brigade. This formation embarked at Sfax at the beginning of July – destination Sicily.

On the 10th, several hours before daybreak off Cape Passero Island, they climbed down from the ships into assault craft and made the run in. The companies met weak resistance and the island was soon cleared of the enemy. The landing on the Sicilian mainland was also accomplished without difficulty.

The fishing village of Portopalo was taken, the eastern end of Goal Ridge – dominating the vital 'Amber Beach' landing area – secured, and Pachino entered. The battalion returned to 153 Brigade and by the middle of the month it was advancing on the hilltop town of Vizzini. With artillery support the Gordons assaulted up the terraced slopes and Vizzini changed hands.

Carriers of the battalion crossed the River Monaci and moved up the mountain road. On Ramacca being taken by 154 Brigade, 153 secured the Catania road. When 152 Brigade ran into trouble setting up a bridgehead over the River Dittaino carriers and anti-tank guns of the battalion assisted the brigade to accomplish its mission.

The 1st Battalion and two companies of the 5/7 Battalion launched a midnight assault on Sferro with artillery support. The enemy guns retaliated but the Gordons kept going. The 1st cleared the railway station while the 5/7 companies burst into the village. The Germans mounted a counter-attack which the Gordons fought to a standstill and, as a troop of Shermans nosed forward, the enemy made a fade-out.

The 1st Gordons descended the northern face of Monte

Turcisi and established themselves on Monte Guzzarano. Centuripe and Adrano fell early in August and about this time the Highland Division left 30 Corps to join 13 Corps and operate along the coast. From the hills the Gordons had their first glimpse of Italy across the narows.

U.S. troops entered Messina on the 12th and next day the '39 days war' in Sicily was over. The capitulation of Italy followed on September 8. After brief stays in Messina and Syracuse the battalion boarded troopships at Augusta in mid-November. The Highland Division was homeward bound.

After several months hard training with new weapons and equipment in England the Highland Division joined 1 Corps. On the afternoon of June 6, 1944 – D Day – the 1st Gordons landed on the Normandy beaches. They splashed ashore at Courseulles under intermittent shelling and bombing and concentrated at Banville.

On the 10th 153 Brigade went into action east of the River Orne, the Gordons being engaged near Touffreville and Escoville. Recovering from the shock of the landing the Germans fought back vigorously but were repulsed on the Breville road.

The brigade suffered severe casualties in the bitterly disputed area which became known as the Triangle. On July 9 the Gordons raided into Colombelles with artillery support and encountered stubborn resistance and a brigade attack with the Gunners again co-operating fared no better.

A week later, however, 8 Corps burst out of the containment area and headed for Caen. The Gordons took over a sector near Cagny and early in August the 51st Division, under command of 2 Canadian Corps, was in the thrust along the fire-swept Falaise road.

The battalion captured Secqueville-la-Campagne, skirmished through Fierville to reach Pierre-en-Auge, and crossing the River Dives at the Bretteville bridgehead took Doux Marais, Ste. Marie-aux-Anglais and St. Maclou. It went over the River Vie under a galling fire and pressed on to La Forge Vallee in the wake of the retreating Germans.

The enemy contrived a stand at Lisieux but their resistance again broke and towards the end of the month the Gordons arrived at Barneville-sur-Seine, where they were harrassed by mortaring and moved into the Forêt de Mauny. In clearing the loop of the river here the count of prisoners was considerably augmented.

After engagements with the rearguard the Seine was forded at Duclair and Mauny. Rouen was entered and at the beginning of September the Highland Division raced for St. Valery. There were flags, flowers, wine, kisses, cheers, singing and dancing, the drums beat and the pipes skirled. St. Valery was *en fête* celebrating the liberation and welcoming back the 51st.

But this pleasant interlude was interrupted by the challenge of Le Havre, isolated by the Allied advance. Following bombardments from sea, land and air the 1st Gordons led their brigade in clearing the Forêt de Montgeon. The northern defences breached, the fort surrendered in mid-September.

Towards the close of the month the division moved to the Maas front and was deployed between Eindhoven and Nijmegen, 153 Brigade being located from St. Oedenrode, on the River Dommel, to Fratershof. Operations were confined to patrolling and raiding.

In mid-October the brigade struck north and the Gordons went through Schijndel to round up groups of 'paras'. They attacked towards Oisterwijk and participated in the thrust north-westward through Loon-op-Zand, to enter Sprang at the end of the month.

Early in November 152 and 153 Brigades made an assault-crossing of the Aftwaterings Canal, the objective of the Gordons being the western end of Nieuwkuijk, which they took with the assistance of flame-belching 'Crocodile' tanks. After its succession of canal crossings in a bleak, foggy partially-flooded wilderness the division literally dried out at Vught.

In the mid-November offensive to drive the enemy over the Maas the 51st made an assault-crossing of the Nederweert-Wessem Canal from the east of Weert. The enemy retired and the Gordons, mounted on 'Kangaroos', entered Roggel and Vlaas and forded the Zig Canal.

Towards the close of the month the 51st was in the Nijmegen bridgehead. The area between the lower Rhine and the River Waal became known as 'The Island' and here the division had a mud-bath lasting over a week – sometimes under bombardment. The Waal was in flood, the water began to rise, and when the Germans blew a wide gap in the dykes the immediate evacuation of civilians from farms and villages was ordered.

The Gordons crossed the Vaal south of Andelst in assault craft to arrive near Veghel, in the s'Hertogenbosch area. Hitler launched his last desperate offensive in the Ardennes in mid-December and 30 Corps, which included the Highland Division, was dispatched hurriedly south.

Early in January 1945, while in the Marche area, the division went into the attack. Led by the 1st Gordons, 153 Brigade, skirmished along the slopes of the Ourthe Valley to Verdenne with the country in the grip of an Arctic-type winter. The battalion secured Lignieres and, moving through Laroche, forward elements arrived at Hubermont and scattered the enemy.

It entered Nisramont and patrols reached the banks of the Ourthe. About the middle of the month, a few miles east of Nisramont, two American armies met and, the 'snowman's war' over, the Highland Division returned to the Maas.

In the onslaught to drive the Germans back over the Rhine 30 Corps came under command of the Canadian 1st Army. The 1st Gordons crossed the Maas at Mook to skirmish along the fringe of the Reichswald and occupy St. Martensberg and Graf-wagen. After an artillery and mortar 'stonk' a bayonet charge ended the resistance of an enemy 'pocket' holding out in the woods beyond De Hel.

The battalion crosed the racing flood waters of the River Niers in assault craft and cleared the Germans out of Gennep. In mid-February the brigade's assault on Goch, a bastion of the Siegfried Line, went in from the north-west with the object of securing the region south of the river.

Determined opposition was met and, because of the rubble-blocked streets, the use of tanks was limited. The battalion suffered severely in several days of desperate house-to-house fighting, particularly at Thomashof.

The Allied Armies advanced to line up for the crossing of the Rhine. On March 23 the massed artillery pounded the eastern bank and at night the 1st Battalion went over in 'Buffaloes' to land near Rees. Some shelling and mortaring was experienced but the battalion lost no time in traversing the open country to reach the Rees-Speldrop road and attack into Rees.

The town was held by paratroops who put up fanatical

resistance from behind debris and ruined buildings, but they were overwhelmed after an all-night battle. From near Empel the Gordons attacked under cover of darkness and occupied a factory area. Königshof and several small villages were entered, then Isselburg, and the battalion crossed the Ems and Weser mopping up 'pockets' en route.

At the beginning of May the companies were heavily engaged around Hoskensburg and Brettorf. A formation of Panzer Grenadiers was holding Orel and the Gordons, taking up the challenge, fought their way through. One unit moving on Barchel, about a mile distant, drove back a counter-attack and in this area the battalion fought its last action of the campaign.

Bremerhaven was occupied on the 8th – VE Day – and on the 12th the Highland Division with its massed pipes and drums staged a victory parade through the town. Lieutenant-General B. G. Horrocks, C.B., D.S.O., M.C., commanding 30 Corps, took the salute. The battalion later arrived in Neustadt and in August the 51st (Highland) Division became part of the British Army of the Rhine.

After strenuous training in the South of England the 2nd Battalion embarked on landing craft with 227 (Highland) Infantry Brigade of the 15th (Scottish) Division at Newhaven on June 18, 1944. The Gordons went ashore near Arromanches on the 20th and their first action was in the biggest assault launched from the beachhead.

Caen was the objective and 227 Brigade – 10th Highland Light Infantry, 2nd Gordon Highlanders and 2nd Argyll and Sutherland Highlanders – had the task of securing the crossings of the River Odon to facilitate the advance of the armour. The Gordons, with tanks co-operating, passed through the ruins of Cheux to the thunder of the guns pulverising the German defences.

At the approaches to Colleville and Tourville they encountered stubborn opposition principally from dug-in tanks and machine-guns firing from behind high hedges. On the 28th British armour crossed the Odon at Tourmauville and the division now held a precarious salient some three miles long by about a mile broad. Next day the enemy sent in a powerful counter-attack on its western line, the Gordons were withdrawn to Colleville under non-stop mortaring, and the tanks had to retire over the river.

On the 30th the battalion attempted to cross and hold the Monchaux bridgehead but made no progress because of a prolonged bombardment. Nevertheless the 'Scottish Corridor' was held in the teeth of violent assaults by seasoned German troops. The untried 15th (Scottish) Division had proved itself.

After the fall of Caen and the crossing of the Odon the battalion was shelled and mortared at Baron. Objective was high ground overlooking Evrecy and the attack went in with the aid of 'artificial moonlight' – employed for the first time. Searchlights were beamed on the clouds so that the 'throwback' illuminated the operational zone.

Aircraft machine-gunned the Gordons' positions and artillery and mortars kept up a continuous bombardment. With the assistance of a gun-battery several assaults were repulsed and conditions eased when another brigade arrived on the scene. The two Odon battles over, the division was dispatched to the pastoral Caumont area.

On July 30 it attacked south-west into the hills around le Beny Bocage, 227 (Highland) Brigade leading. With armour in close support the 2nd Gordons cleared the Germans from Lieu Mondant and Lutain Wood. Early in August the Gordons, in troop-carriers, spearheaded the brigade drive through St. Martin des Besaces and Montcharivel to Au Cornu.

On approaching Estry, however, the battalion was soon pinned down by a hail of fire. In determined attempts to break in the brigade sustained severe losses and a number of tanks was destroyed. The Germans had turned Estry into a formidable strongpoint and it was not entered until they pulled out a few days later.

The Gordons launched a crossing of the Seine near Le Mesnil Ande but, as the leading company neared the opposite bank, machine-guns sprayed a pattern of death. Those who managed to scramble ashore from the bullet-riddled assault craft were made prisoners.

The battalion went two miles downstream to St. Pierre du Vauvray and made a night crossing. In widening the bridgehead they overcame resistance around Le Mesnil Ande, Muids and Fretteville and in clearing this loop of the Seine, most of the Gordons taken prisoner in the earlier attempt regained their freedom.

The advance into Belgium and Holland followed and by mid-September the 15th (Scottish) Division was in the Gheel bridgehead beyond the Albert Canal. A crossing of the Schelde-Maas Canal near Donck by the 2nd Gordons failed, the companies coming under intense machine-gun fire. The battalion next operated in the Aart bridgehead, some three miles to the north, enduring a 48-hour bombardment and fighting off furious attacks.

A few days afterwards the battalion crossed the Schelde-Maas Canal and reached Eindhoven. By this time the division had set up a bridgehead over the Wilhelmina Canal at Best, and the Gordons were given the unenviable task of breaking out of the containment area over flat coverless ground to secure a firm base for the assault on Naastbest by the remainder of 227 Brigade.

The Germans, well dug-in along the railway, opened up a deadly fire forcing the battalion to withdraw at night. Towards the close of the month the Gordons were immersed in crumbling waterlogged slit trenches on the fringe of an enemy-held wood near Steenweg under a cloudburst downpour.

Despite the enfilade fire of the German guns the 51st (Highland) Division duly effected the relief of the 15th (Scottish) Division. But the drenched mud-caked Gordons still retained their sense of humour and there were shouts of 'Fit wey tae the pier, Mac?' and 'Hiv ye seen the tartan-funnelled leave boat, Jock?'

In mid-October the battalion moved with its brigade up to the line of the Boxtel-Best railway and the division entered Tilburg at the end of the month. When the German offensive on the east of the Nijmegen salient forced back the Americans 27 Brigade was rushed to Asten.

There was sporadic skirmishing around Meijel and early in November the Germans began a general withdrawal. The brigade then headed east for the Maas. As the enemy retreated they left burning villages in their wake and there were engagements, particularly at Sevenum, Brockhuizenvorst and Lottum, ere Swolgen by the Maas was reached.

At the end of January 1945, the 2nd Battalion left the Maas to enter the Battle of the Rhineland, the 15th (Scottish) Division's assignment being to breach the Siegfried Line north of the Reichswald. The Gordons advanced from Kranenburg through Nutterden and Donsbruggen to clear hilly wooded country on the road to Cleve, which was entered on February 11.

While the battle raged for Goch, another Siegfried Line bastion, the Gordons drove the Germans from the woods around Schloss Calbeck, captured Plessenhoff and secured the area up to the Cock-Udem railway. By the middle of March the great build-up for the crossing of the Rhine was completed. The battalion assembled on the eastern fringe of the Hochwald.

About midnight on the 23rd they stood by their assault-craft as the flashing, reverberating barrage pulverised the enemy. A platoon crossed with the 10th H.L.I. opposite Wolffskath, one company went over opposite Hübsch but the remainder of the battalion landed south-west of Haffen under mortaring.

Companies cleared Haffen and Hoverhof and mopped up the surrounding country. On the 28th the Gordons moved quickly north, attacked through Sonsfeld Forest and got on to high ground on its eastern edge beyond the Wessel-Haldern road. The division was poised for the drive deep into the Third Reich.

Early in April, from Lengerich, the battalion advanced via Osnabrück and Stolzenau to Celle. At Uelzen the Germans made a determined stand which temporarily checked progress. The Gordons passed through its smoking ruins to enter Barum and Tespe and were on the banks of the Elbe on the 20th.

The battalion went over at Artlenburg under artillery fire and the companies fanned north-westward. extending the bridgehead, cleared the main road through Grünhof Forest and secured Tesperhude and Hamwerde. Resistance was crumbling along the entire front and formations were surrendering practically en masse.

On May 2 the brigade set out for Hamburg, the 2nd Gordons arriving on the following day as Field-Marshal Montgomery was taking the unconditional surrender of the German forces at Lüneburg Heath. Early in June, 227 Brigade moved to Lübeck. A draft of over 100 left the 2nd Battalion for the Far East but the war with Japan was terminated within a few weeks of its departure.

The battle honours awarded to The Gordon Highlanders were: Withdrawal to Escaut. Ypres-Comines Canal, Dunkirk 1940, Somme 1940, St. Valery-en-Caux, ODON, La Vie Crossing,

Lower Maas, Venlo Pocket, Rhineland, REICHSWALD, Cleve, GOCH, RHINE, NORTH WEST EUROPE 1940, '44, '45, EL ALAMEIN, Advance on Tripoli, MARETH, Medjez Plain, NORTH AFRICA 1942-43, Landing in Sicily, SFERRO, Sicily 1943, ANZIO, Rome, Italy 1944-45. (The ten in capitals appear on the Queen's Colour.)

The 1st and 2nd Battalions formed part of the Army of Occupation, but the 2nd was detached for a tour of duty in Tripoli. When Regular Army infantry regiments – except the Guards – were 'pruned' to one battalion each in 1947 the 2nd was absorbed in the 1st at Essen, Germany, early in July 1948.

The 1st Battalion returned to the U.K. in mid-December 1950, and strength was considerably reduced by the excellent response to the call for volunteers to serve in Korea with the United Nations forces. Within a few weeks of arrival in the homeland the Gordons were under orders for Malaya and in March 1951, they relieved The Seaforth Highlanders.

In three years of 'jungle-bashing' in Pahang, Perak, Negri Sembilan and Malacca the battalion patrolled over 2,500 square miles of territory in sweltering heat and plagued by myriads of flies and insects. Detachments operated among arid hills and rocks, through prickly scrub and dense tangled undergrowth, and crossed foul-smelling mangrove swamps and rushing mountain torrents.

Supplies and mail were air-dropped into small clearings hacked out of the jungle and helicopters set down patrols in these 'pancakes'. They moved out with Iban trackers to stalk and ambush terrorist gangs. In an encounter in Kuantan Pahang in May 1951, four Gordons took on about twenty 'jungle cats' and accounted for several before the enemy made a run for it, bearing their wounded.

Early in January 1953, a patrol operating in the Jasin area surprised a group and killed an important leader. In this clash they also wounded three and captured arms, ammunition and food. There were scores of similar sharp, sudden actions and over 70 terrorists fell for the loss of 19 Gordons.

The battalion came home in April 1954. In October the following year it was flown to Cyprus, then racked by disturbances organised by Greek Cypriots to achieve union with Greece. The Gordons provided guards for Government buildings, police stations and strategic points, furnished anti-riot squads, dispatched patrols along the rugged northern coast to co-operate with the Navy in countering gun-running, and formed escorts for convoys passing through danger zones. It was round-the-clock duty.

Soon after their arrival they quelled a riot and attack on a police post at Morphou. Their vigilance foiled an attempt to steal explosives from mines about thirty miles from Nicosia, the island's capital. Detachments went after trigger-men, bomb-slingers and saboteurs, and set up road blocks.

With pine-clad mountains and gleaming white villages nestling on the slopes and dreaming in the sun, bells tinkling across verdant valleys, the island seemed idyllic, tranquil and set gem-like in the 'wine dark deep'. But here there was only hate and violence.

Pretty girls drew their fingers across their throats when soldiers passed. As military vehicles negotiated hairpin bends hidden marksmen had them in their sights. At any moment the windscreen might be patterned with a machine-gun burst or spatter of rifle fire. There were occasions too when their crews were catapulted onto the road and villagers hurried past and left them to bleed in the high, bright sun.

There was no let-up in Nicosia and its 'Murder Mile', in Larnaca, Famagusta, Limassol – or in the grim fastness of the Troodos Mountains. Houses, villages, monasteries and churches were entered in the never-ending search for arms and ammunition, wanted men and suspects. For months the order was 'Cordon and search!' And thus it came about that the battalion was dubbed the 'Cordon Highlanders!'

In the chase after the Greek Cypriot leader, General Grivas, in the Paphos area the Gordons are believed to have come very near to capturing him. They discovered a glass jar containing some of his diaries and letters.

In this region in mid-June 1956, while still on the trail of this will o' the wisp, a sudden forest fire swept downwind on the pursuing Gordons and other troops. Petrol and ammunition exploded in burning vehicles and over a score of soldiers were trapped in the dense choking smoke-pall and rushing, leaping wall of flame.

During the battalion's tour of duty in Cyprus only three

Gordons were killed on operations, but thirteen lost their lives in this inferno. In a thankless danger-fraught internal security role the tact, firmness and steady bearing of the 1st Gordons in spite of great provocation earned the respect of the populace.

The battalion returned to the 'Northern Lights' in January 1957, and departed for Celle, Germany, in the autumn of 1958. It joined the 7th Armoured Brigade – successors of the 'Desert Rats' – and was employed on a new role, that of armoured infantry, the rifle companies being transported in armoured personnel carriers, or 'Saracens'.

The Gordons left the Rhine Army early in October 1961, and after a few weeks in Scotland they were preparing for service in Kenya. The battalion sailed in mid-December and joined the 24th Infantry Brigade – forming part of the Strategic Reserve – at Gilgil, about 75 miles from Nairobi.

At the beginning of May 1962, companies reinforced the police in Zanzibar during the unrest which preceded the island gaining independence. In mid-June 1963, the battalion was airlifted to Swaziland where a politically-inspired strike accompanied by violence was paralysing the country. Following swoops by police and detachments of Gordons in Mbabane, the capital, and elsewhere, the emergency was soon over.

Towards the close of January 1964, there was disaffection among African troops in Uganda, Tanganyika and Kenya and the Gordons were rushed to strategic points. The situation was quickly brought under control and in March the battalion was flown to Essex. By the end of the year, while stationed in Edinburgh, the battalion was under orders for another 'flashpoint' – Malaysia.

The Gordons were transported by aircraft and in mid-February 1965, began 'driving' the green hell of the North Borneo jungles in operations along Malaysia's 1,000-mile frontier with Indonesia which was menaced by infiltrators. Like wraiths the Gordons ghosted through the shadows. Tracks were avoided as they may have been booby-trapped or led to an ambush on some well-chosen killing ground.

An unusual noise and a patrol would 'freeze' or, at a signal, melt into the greenery. Occasionally the krump of mortars would be heard. 'Theirs – or ours?'

There was the incessant squawking and fluttering of birds

and the buzz, whirr and drone of insects – or the hiss of monsoon rains. After the deluge the jungle glittered – a masterpiece of Mother Nature's artistry – in watercolour! Then the noise with a difference – enemy movement. Eyes strained, rifles were gripped, thumbs ready to ease forward the safety catch, trigger fingers curved. . . .

And in Malaysia there were 'Jock Tars' – full cousins of the Jack Tars! For the battalion had its own 'navy'. Using fast assault craft the Gordons formed an amphibious group off Tawau, Sabah. In the bow of each were a machine-gunner and rifleman. The Jock Tars patrolled among clusters of islands, steered their craft through creeks, narrows and shallows and sailed into inlets and quiet sinister backwaters.

Twenty-foot long vessels were stationed a few hundred yards from the sea boundary separating Malaysia and Indonesian Borneo and powerful binoculars were constantly trained on enemy gun positions, living quarters and movements. The Jock Tars and other jungle patrols were the eyes, ears and teeth of the British and Malaysian forces in the hide-and-seek confrontation campaign.

Early in September the Gordons were in action on the Sabah-Indonesian border. An ambush detachment put to flight a band of about twelve infiltrators, killing one and probably wounding several. Three Gordons received minor injuries from grenade fragments.

As 1965 drew to a close the battalion was in a 'tizzy' preparing to return home. The advance party alighted near Edinburgh a few days before Christmas and the remainder followed through in the early spring. The ubiquitous 'Regiment of the North' left the Scottish capital towards the end of March 1967 – destination Minden, Germany, for service with the British Army of the Rhine.

The Gordons took part in several major training exercises and manoeuvres in which their enthusiasm and physique were tested to the full. They 'graduated with honour', in the regimental traditions of the 'Gallant Ninety-Twa'.

The 1st Gordons featured prominently in the Dino de Laurentis-Mosfilm production of *Waterloo*, under the direction of Russia's Sergei Bondarchuk, of *War and Peace* renown. In this Russian-Italian masterpiece 20,000 soldiers of the

Soviet Union, including an entire cavalry brigade, were employed.

Waterloo required several years of planning and cost in the region of £12,000,000. Appropriately the premiere was presented in the Odeon Theatre, Leicester Square, London, on October 26, 1970, and the proceeds were devoted to a Services charity.

In this memorable film 45 Gordons added colour, animation and spectacle to the eve of the battle ball held in Brussels by the Duchess of Richmond. At Waterloo the battalion portrays the 92nd standing firm under the lashing bombardment of Napoleon's massed cannon and the thundering charges of his cavalry.

Then, kilts and sporrans swinging over bare knees, bayonets gleaming and pipes screaming above the booming roar of the guns and crackling musketry fire, they are shown in the fury of the Highland attack, the red uniforms contrasting with rolling green fields. Depicted too are the muddied bloodied bodies of men and horses and artillerymen frenziedly toiling at their guns – or lying around them in death.

A few years previously another outstanding historical film – *Khartoum* – featured a detachment of the 1st Gordons crossing the desert with a column in early November 1884, in an attempt to rescue General Charles Gordon.

Their four years tour of duty in West Germany over, the advance party of the 1st Battalion was flown into Turnhouse Airport, Edinburgh, at the beginning of December 1970. The remainder touched down by 'instalments' at R.N.A.S. Lossiemouth during the middle of January 1971. After leave the Gordons re-assembled at Fort George.

The companies were soon deployed on rigorous training throughout the North, with some emphasis on bandit-hunting techniques. A welcome 'break' from this activity was the battalion's march through Aberdeen on February 24, in bright sunshine – in sharp contrast to the downpour experienced at the farewell parade in Minden.

In April they were airlifted to Cyprus where their Glengarries and kilts were replaced by the blue berets and khaki drills of the United Nations Force. In prospect was a six months term with this peacekeeping organisation.

Cyprus was an island of unhappy memories for the battalion which, from autumn 1955 to the beginning of 1957 had lost sixteen soldiers in operations against extremists. But, in the spring of 1971, they expected a reasonably peaceful vigil. Several old-timers, however, kept their fingers crossed.

Since the Junta of Generals seized power in Greece in April 1967, the Greek Cypriots who clamoured for *enosis* – union with Greece – had been lying low. Nevertheless Cyprus was known to be a slumbering volcano of tension and an occasional wisp of smoke in the way of sporadic incidents served to keep the United Nations Force on the island at the ready – and the Gordons were taking no chances.

Its Colours are the soul of a regiment. The Colours of The Gordon Highlanders are scarred – but these scars are emblazoned in gold. For each one of them is a proud battle honour. In this Highland corps are blended tradition, enthusiasm and magnificent fighting qualities. Here sons and grandsons follow in the footsteps of their ancestors.

On peaceful Sunday mornings when Buchan's own lovely old hymn tune 'Crimond' echoes over the green pastures, brown ploughlands and gleaming rivers of the Gordon country – and in lands 'far across the faem' – we remember so many of them.

CHAPTER IV

The 'Thin Red Line': Balaclava to Aden Saga of the Argyll and Sutherland Highlanders

THERE IS NO RETREAT FROM HERE! YOU MUST DIE WHERE YOU STAND!

These might have been the words of the Spartan commander at the Pass of Thermopylae in 480 B.C., when several hundred of his warriors prepared to sacrifice themselves to delay the advancing hosts of King Xerxes of Persia.

The spirit of Thermopylae was abroad when about 500 men of the 93rd, or Sutherland Regiment (which later became the 2nd Battalion The Argyll and Sutherland Highlanders) stood firm at Balaclava as a mass of Russian cavalry thundered towards them.

Major-General Sir Colin Campbell, veteran commander of The Highland Brigade, rode down their ranks and gave the historic order, 'There is no retreat from here! You must die where you stand!'

Bayonets glinted, three volleys crashed out, and nine squadrons of the Czar's cavalry faltered and reeled in confusion. Saddles emptied, horses plunged, reared and collided with each other, and the enemy turned and galloped from the field. The British base at Balaclava was saved.

That was on October 25, 1854, on a cannon and bullet-swept ridge in the Crimea – the magnificent episode of The Thin Red Line. Less than a century later, in Korea, about *THIRTY* men, all that was left of two companies of the 1st Battalion The Argyll and Sutherland Highlanders, held the blazing crest of a hill against overwhelming odds after being bombed in error by the Americans. The Thin Khaki Line too glows on the pages of history.

And the first Victoria Cross awarded for valour in this campaign was won by an officer of the regiment, but it was, unfortunately, posthumous. Thus the Argylls of 1950 kept faith with The Thin Red Line of 1854 – *Cuimhnich gaisge agus treuntas ar sinnsear* (Remember the deeds of your ancestors).

The Argyll and Sutherland Highlanders was formed by the union of the 91st (Princess Louise's) Argyllshire Highlanders and the 93rd, or Sutherland Highlanders, in 1881. The 91st became the 1st Battalion and the 93rd the 2nd Battalion of the regiment.

The 91st was raised as the 98th Regiment of Foot. A Letter of Service, dated February 1794, was sent by King George III to John, fifth Duke of Argyll, authorising him to raise a regiment for foreign service. As the Duke was in ill health, he delegated this duty to his kinsman, Duncan Campbell of Lochnell, Argyllshire, a captain in the 1st Foot Guards.

With the assistance of several other Highland gentlemen, Duncan Campbell, who became Lieutenant-Colonel Commandant of the new corps, organised recruiting. About half of the regiment was composed of Highlanders and the majority of the officers came from Argyllshire. Clan Campbell was strongly represented.

Lowlanders were also enrolled, principally from Glasgow and Edinburgh, and recruits were added from Ireland, Somerset, Wiltshire, Gloucestershire and Warwickshire. The 98th was embodied, inspected and passed as efficient and fit for service by Lord Adam Gordon after a parade at Stirling in May 1794. Fully accoutred as a Highland corps it arrived in England the following month. For some time the new formation was known as The Argyle Regiment.

Originally the men wore the Highland military garb, with short coat or jacket faced with yellow, belt and plaid. The Tartan was the 'Military' or 'Government tartan' – the same tartan worn by some of the Independent Companies which regimented as The Black Watch.

In 1795 the 98th was ordered to South Africa and after some sporadic skirmishing the Cape of Good Hope was seized from the Dutch. In 1798 the regiment was re-numbered, becoming the 91st.

It returned to the U.K. in two contingents, the first arriving towards the close of 1802 and the second about three months later after taking part in the ceremony of handing back the Cape of Good Hope to the Dutch, in compliance with the Treaty of Amiens.

While serving at the 'Cape' white trousers replaced the kilt and on the regiment's homecoming the only part of the Highland dress which was resumed was the feather bonnet. When supplies of tartan cloth arrived it was made into trousers.

Worse was to follow. In 1809, during the Peninsular War,

the 91st and certain other Highland regiments were ordered to adopt the uniform of the Infantry of the Line. The 91st had also to discard its county title of 'Argyllshire' and the appellation 'Highlanders' and was merely designated the 91st Regiment of Foot. But the officers were not long in securing that the pipers at least should march in the Garb of Old Gaul.

When Britain went to the aid of her ancient enemy Spain in her struggle against Napoleon, the Duke of Wellington landed his forces at the Mondego River in August 1808. He soundly defeated the French at Rolica and Vimiera; the earliest battle honours of the 91st.

In the second phase of the Peninsular War, General Sir John Moore advanced into Spain with four divisions intending to join up with the Spaniards and attack the French. The 91st was in this force which began the march on Madrid, but near Salamanca Sir John learned that his allies had been decisively defeated and that several strong enemy columns – one commanded by Napoleon in person – were converging on him from different directions.

Heavily outnumbered, his supply base and lines of communication threatened, Sir John gave the order to retreat north-westwards to the sea, and on Christmas Eve, 1808, there began one of the British Army's greatest rearguard actions – the epic Retreat to Corunna – which ended on January 11, 1809.

The 91st was in the Reserve Division, which fought an almost non-stop engagement with the enemy's advanced troops. The route involved a 200 mile march, the crossing of the Cantabrian Mountains and barren, desolate inhospitable country where supplies were impossible to obtain. The troops were soon famished and in sodden rags, many staggering barefoot over jagged rocks through blinding snowstorms, deep mud, freezing slush and icy rain into the teeth of howling blizzards.

There was no rest or shelter and the cold was intense. Animals and men collapsed through lack of food and heavy wagons and equipment had to be abandoned in the drifting white hell of the passes.

Again and again the 91st clashed with the French and held them at bay. On reaching Corunna no evacuation ships were waiting. With the enemy coming up in strength General Sir John Moore faced about his weak starving army and inflicted a punishing defeat on his pursuers, the Reserve Division smashing the French left wing.

The transports arrived and the British trooped on board bearing their numerous sick and wounded with the French spectating – at a safe distance. Corunna is another golden name on the Colours.

In 1809 the 91st was included in the disastrous expedition to Walcheren, on the low-lying Dutch coast. About 40,000 strong, this force was intended for an attack on Antwerp but it was soon ravaged by sickness. Several thousand succumbed and the survivors, with about 11,000 sick, were evacuated after eight weeks.

Rejoining the 'Iron Duke' in Spain the regiment took part in the fighting advance north into France, and men coming out of hospital formed a Service Company which participated in the victory at Talavera in 1809. The battle honours Pyrenees, Nivelle, Nive, Orthes and Toulouse were purchased with blood, privation and sacrifice.

The French made a determined stand at Toulouse. The 91st charged with The Highland Brigade, which was twice beaten back by the intensity of the enemy fire. The brigade reformed and charged again, carrying its objective on the crest of a hill at bayonet point, but once more casualties were severe.

The 91st was in the force dispatched to Holland in 1814 and was in action at Bergen-op Zoom. The regiment was not committed at Waterloo, being with a flanking brigade. Nevertheless it took part in the pursuit of the shattered French Army and was engaged at the siege of Cambrai.

A drummer boy of the 91st, William Ballantine, bearing a flag of truce, led the Allied Armies into Paris to begin the occupation of the French capital. And at St. Helena in 1840 a detachment from the regiment was present at the disinterment of Napoleon's body, which was taken to France for re-burial.

In 1820 the county title was restored and the regiment was designated the 91st (Argyleshire) Regiment of Foot. It is evident that there was some confusion over the spelling of the regimental title and this continued for many years. About 1824 the 91st was offered the Highland uniform, but with trews instead of the kilt. This offer, however, was declined.

A Reserve Battalion, formed in 1842 from depot companies,

served in South Africa with the regiment and was employed on mobile operations and outpost duties against the plundering Kaffirs in the 'War of the Axe' from 1846 to 1847. There was also sporadic trouble with the disgruntled Dutch settlers, the Boers.

There were long arduous marches through difficult bush and mountain country, frequently on short rations, and the troops had to contend with torrential rain, mud and heat. Uniforms and boots suffered severely – but not the discipline of the 91st. After the 91st left for home in 1848 the Reserve Battalion was engaged in further punitive forays from 1851 until 1853, and South Africa 1846-47; 1851-2-3 was later emblazoned on the Colours.

While bound for South Africa in 1842 officers and other ranks of the Reserve Battalion saved the families of soldiers when, on August 27, the transport *Abercrombie Robinson* was driven ashore in a hurricane and wrecked in Table Bay. Only one boat was available for rescue operations, but the 460 Reservists, commanded by Captain Murray Gordon, ferried all the women and children through the thundering surf to safety, before the ship began to break up. After serving in South Africa the Reserve Battalion returned to the U.K. in 1855 and reverted to depot company establishment.

Discipline was again the common denominator in another drama of the sea. Reinforcements for the 91st and other regiments were on the ill-fated troopship *Birkenhead*, bound from Cork to the Cape, when she struck a submerged reef near Simonstown on February 26, 1852.

The ship began to sink, and as the number of lifeboats was quite inadequate for the 631 on board, all troops not engaged along with the sailors in assisting women and children into the boats were assembled on deck. They were told that if any more were taken off the lifeboats would capsize.

The lifeboats got safely away and the remainder of the troops joined their comrades lined up on both sides of the quarter-deck. They stood fast in silence as the *Birkenhead* slid under them. Then only did a number of soldiers strike out for the shore, but most of the troops went down with the ship.

A total of 438 officers and other ranks were lost, but as a result of their splendid discipline and sacrifice all the women and children – the families of soldiers – were saved. Among the survivors were Captain Wright and eight men of the 91st, who were in a draft of 60 sent out from the regiment to the Reserve Battalion which was on active service against the Kaffirs.

This saga of gallantry so impressed Her Majesty Queen Victoria that she erected a memorial at Chelsea Hospital. The King of Prussia raised a monument in Berlin and ordered an account of the sinking of the *Birkenhead* to be read out at the head of every regiment in his army on three parades.

In 1864 the regiment was styled the 91st Argyllshire Highlanders and permission was soon forthcoming to wear trews of the Campbell tartan, but with a red stripe added to the sett. A diced shako replaced the feather bonnet. The Kilmarnock bonnet was worn for 'walking out'.

In March 1871, on the occasion of the wedding of H.R.H. Princess Louise to the Marquis of Lorne, son of the Duke of Argyll – whose ancestor had done so much to raise the regiment – the 91st furnished a Guard of Honour, band and pipers. To commemorate this Royal event Her Majesty Queen Victoria ordered in 1872 that in future the regiment should be designated The 91st (Princess Louise's) Argyllshire Highlanders and always march past in quick time to the pipes.

The 91st returned to South Africa in 1879 as reinforcements in the short, sharp campaign against Chief Cetawayo and his massed Zulu 'impis' in Eastern Natal. The regiment's principal engagement was at Ginghinlovo, where the ferocious black warriors were severely punished for their reign of terror on the frontier. In the Zulu War the 91st carried its Colours into action for the last time. The battle honour South Africa 1879 was later awarded.

Under the sweeping Army reforms of 1881 the 91st became the 1st Battalion Princes Louise's Sutherland and Argyll Highlanders, but a year later the title was amended to the 1st Battalion Princes Louise's Argyll and Sutherland Highlanders.

Princess Louise, who later became Colonel-in-Chief of the Regiment, devised the plaid brooch (the only one in the British Army of Celtic design) also the sporran, the pattern for officers and sergeants being unique; badger skin with the head of the animal forming the flap top. The badge included the Boar's Head of the Campbells with the motto *Ne Obliviscaris* (Do Not

Forget) within a wreath of myrtle and the Wild Cat of the Sutherlands and the motto *Sans Peur* (Fearless) within a wreath of broom.

The Coronet of Princess Louise and the crossed and entwined 'L's' symbolise Her Royal Highness's wedding to the Marquis of Lorne. The tartan of the 93rd was adopted, also a special diced border on the bonnet. 'The Campbells Are Coming' became the Regimental March of the 1st Battalion and 'Hielin' Laddie' that of the 2nd Battalion.

The 93rd was raised under the patronage of the Sutherland family. The Letter of Service, dated March 1799, was sent by King George III to Major-General William Wemyss of Wemyss, a nephew of the Earl of Sutherland, authorising him to recruit a regiment in the county.

This formation was not raised in the usual way, but by a form of conscription. A census was taken of the able-bodied sons of tenants on the estates of the Countess. General Wemyss visited the various parishes in turn and they were lined up for his inspection. He passed along the ranks, his snuff 'mull' in his hand, and behind him came a servant bearing a goodly supply of *uisge-beatha* (whisky).

Each man he selected for service stepped forward, was offered a pinch of *snaoisean* (snuff) and a dram. His name was entered on the roll and he received the King's bounty money. The men then dispersed to resume their occupations, principally on farms and crofts and other rural industries, to await the embodiment order.

In August 1800, they were summoned, by notices displayed on the parish churches, to join the regiment as proof of their loyalty to the King and to their Chief. This is believed to have been the last exercise of feudal power in the Highlands on a large scale, and not a man was absent when The Sutherland Regiment held its first muster at Strathnaver.

Close on 650 strong, the new corps marched to Inverness where it was pronounced fit for service after an inspection by Major-General Leith Hay. In October it was numbered the 93rd. The Sutherland Regiment in its early days was also known as Major-General Wemyss' Regiment of Foot, and, considered to be more Highland than any other Scottish corps, it soon earned the nickname of 'The Rories'.

In addition to men from the Sutherland estates recruits were enrolled from other northern counties, Ross-shire being well represented. General Wemyss had previously raised two regiments of Sutherland Fencibles for home service, and as one of these formations was disbanded just before the Regular regiment was formed, a number of Fencibles joined the 93rd. The full Highland uniform was worn, with feather bonnet and kilt and plaid of the 'Military' or 'Government tartan' – the same tartan as the 42nd (The Black Watch) – and the facings of the red coat were yellow.

Right from its inception there was an unbreakable 'esprit de corps' in the 93rd. This probably sprang from the fact that originally the units represented districts or parishes. All the officers and other ranks knew each other or were related, and there was a complete absence of crime and a healthy rivalry between the various companies.

The Sutherland Highlanders first experienced active service in South Africa. With the 71st (H.L.I.) and 72nd (Seaforths) the regiment formed a Highland Brigade. After a difficult and opposed landing the enemy was defeated on the Blaauberg, or Blue Mountains. In a brief campaign the Highland regiments were instrumental in forcing the capitulation of the Dutch (then allies of the French) and Cape Colony came under British control.

The Cape was of great strategic importance as it stood on the route to India. Cape of Good Hope (1806) was the earliest battle honour of The Sutherland Highlanders. While serving in South Africa the 93rd inaugurated a regimental kirk. Elders were appointed and, by voluntary subscriptions from their meagre pay, the Highlanders maintained a Presbyterian chaplain.

In the war with the United States from 1812 to 1814 Britain sent a fleet bearing an expedition, which included the 93rd, into the Gulf of Mexico with the object of capturing New Orleans. In early January 1815, an ill-conceived assault on the strongly entrenched Americans failed and the force was withdrawn. The 93rd lost over 500 in casualties.

The Americans, commanded by General Jackson, held a strong position behind a rampart mounted with artillery and below was a canal. As the Highlanders advanced across open coverless ground their front and flanks were subjected to the maximum effect of the fire and they were decimated.

Paul Wellman, General Jackson's biographer, described the battle:

To the very edge of the canal before the rampart the few that were left of the kilted regiment marched, then halted there. The men who had been detailed to bring scaling ladders and fascines had failed to come up. They were unable to go forward, too proud to retreat, although the regiments behind them had all fallen back.

At length a mere handful of what had been the magnificent regiment slowly retired, still in unbroken order, still turning to face the foe. From the rampart the Americans cheered them wildly. All rifle-fire ceased.

And this shambles at New Orleans was all so much needless waste of life. Peace had been made some three weeks previously but the soldiers in the field were not informed that the war was over.

Serving in Canada in 1838, the 93rd was involved in the political strife of the period and clashed with armed mobs and bands of trouble-makers. The disorders, however, were quickly and effectively dealt with and the ringleaders rounded up. In 1845 the 93rd arrived in the Crimea and joined The Highland Brigade, commanded by Major-General Sir Colin Campbell, who was later to become Colonel of the Regiment.

During the advance on Sevastopol there was stiff fighting on the Alma and in the hills beyond. The Highland Brigade (formed by the 93rd, 42nd (Black Watch) and 79th (Camerons)) waded waist-deep through the fast-flowing treacherous river and attacked up the steep slope into a devastating fire to capture the enemy positions. The bullets and bayonets of the Highlanders drove back the Russians and shattered their counter-attack at its outset.

The enemy retired on the fortress, arsenal and docks at Sevastopol and the dysentery and cholera-ridden British Army marched southwards to the coast at Balaclava, which, with its small but useful harbour, soon fell. A base was then established for the landing of reinforcements, guns, munitions and supplies.

The Battle of the Alma was a spectacular achievement by a young battalion which had experienced no active service for close on half a century. But another and even greater glory day for the 93rd dawned on October 25. The Sutherland Regiment remained at the base to furnish fatigue parties for the unloading of ships and other duties, and it looked as though it would take no further part in the fighting for some time.

But on October 25 General Menschikov dispatched 25 battalions of infantry, 34 squadrons of cavalry and 78 guns to destroy the British base at Balaclava. General Sir Colin Campbell faced this formidable array with the Heavy and Light Cavalry Brigades, the 93rd Highlanders ('The Rories'), three battalions of Turkish troops, 800 Royal Marines, several score soldiers of The Rifle Brigade and an assortment of troops recovering from wounds or sickness.

One Turkish battalion held some hastily prepared positions on a ridge known as the Causeway Heights at the head of the Balaclava valley, along which ran the road into Sevastopol. The Turks on this exposed hilltop were subjected to a concentrated bombardment and suffered severe losses. The unnerved men abandoned their shattered redoubts and streamed towards the base, and soon several thousand Russians were in possession of the heights.

General Sir Colin Campbell lined up the 93rd, with a battalion of Turks on each flank, along the crest of a hill, possibly intending to counter-attack and restore the position. With the enemy gunfire mounting in ferocity and causing a number of casualties, however, he retired them a little way down the reverse slope.

As nine enemy cavalry squadrons detached, wheeled away from the main body and entered the valley for a charge into Balaclava, the General again advanced his line to the top of the hill. The heaving press of Russian horse came thundering on through the British artillery fire, and, after loosing off a confused, useless volley at 800 yards, the Turks broke and fled. All that stood between the massed galloping squadrons were two lines of kilted Highlanders.

Lightning flashed along the ridge as the bayonets were fixed. General Sir Colin Campbell rode down their front and gave the order that rang through history: 'There is no retreat from here! You must die where you stand!' And the men of the 93rd roared back their pledge to do just that – probably in their native Gaelic.

The avalanche of Russian cavalry, bristling with waving swords and levelled lances, gathered impetus as it swept over the grassy downland. The Highlanders stood silent, motionless, resolute, awaiting the next command. It came from the General, and two volleys – one at 500 yards and the other at 200 yards – crashed into the charging Russians.

The enemy was thrown into confusion. Falling men and rearing plunging riderless horses checked the surge of the charge, and the mass of cavalry reined in and wheeled away, men still toppling from their mounts. The Russians reformed, canter became gallop, gallop became charge, and the cavalry hurtled towards the right flank bared by the flight of the Turks. The Grenadier Company of the 93rd quickly formed line to meet them. At close range another volley rang out.

Hundreds of horses and men sank to the ground. Frenzied wounded animals cannoned into each other and fell over bodies strewn in their path, and once more the galloping cavalry was halted. The reeling, shot-riddled and confused squadrons continued the charge, but in the opposite direction, away from the lines of death-spitting rifles. The Balaclava lifeline was saved. The Thin Red Line of The Sutherland Regiment had triumphed over the Czar's cavalry.

The 93rd was the only infantry regiment allowed to commemorate Balaclava on its Colours; one of the proudest battle honours in the British Army. It is kept evergreen too by the stirring march 'The Thin Red Line' and by the famous painting by Robert Gibb, R.S.A.

The regiment experienced several tours of duty in the trenches before Sevastopol in the grim winter of 1854-55. There was a shortage of food and water, boots and clothing could not be replaced, and there was practically no shelter from the winds and intense cold in the muddy waterlogged trenches.

No water was available for washing and the undernourished troops were clad in verminous rags. Conditions worsened as the winter progressed and snow-drifts frequently blocked the entrenchments. And to the Russians, dysentery and cholera a new enemy was added; that of frostbite. The sickness and casualty figures were high and the medical services could not cope.

Two unsuccessful assaults were launched on the formidable Redan Redoubt in the summer of 1855 and the 93rd was selected for a third attempt. On the eve of the attack, however, an officer of The Sutherland Regiment was the first to discover that the Redan was unoccupied.

A party comprising men from the 93rd and 72nd (Seaforths) was about to enter and investigate when the redoubt was rent asunder by a terrific explosion. The Russians were abandoning Sevastopol and systematically destroying the defenceworks. The end of the war was at last in sight. In addition to Balaclava the 93rd gained two other battle honours – Alma and Sevastopol.

In the Crimean War the tall bearded fighting men of The Highland Brigade, their feather bonnets waving, kilts and sporrans swinging above bare knees, advancing out of drifting battle-smoke, shouting wild clan war cries in Gaelic, rifles and bayonets levelled and gleaming, and pipes skirling eerily through the rumble of cannon and crackling roll of musketry, struck terror into the hearts of the illiterate superstitious peasant soldiers of the Czar. They thought they were beset by a legion of hairy demons in red coats dripping with gore, who marched to the shriek and wail of souls in the torment of Hell.

General Sir Colin Campbell coined another famous phrase in the heat of battle during one of the violent onslaughts to relieve Lucknow during the dark days of the Indian Mutiny. In mid-November 1857, about 2,000 sepoy rebels holding the Sikander-bagh, a tall strongly fortified building enclosing a spacious court-yard, poured a withering fire from embrasures and loopholes into the assaulting 4th Punjab Rifles.

The General, now Commander-in-Chief, India, on witnessing the execution among the loyal Punjabis, gave the dramatic order *'BRING ON THE TARTAN!'* The 93rd was 'the tartan'. With a rousing cheer The Sutherland Regiment rushed through the murderous fire and fought its way into a breach created by the gunners. In four hours of mad fury with rifle and bayonet they cleared the mutineers from the Sikanderbagh.

Another key position in the Sikanderbagh – the Shah Nujjef – was also captured. Under a rain of bullets a 12-year old boy, Drummer Ross, climbed to the top of a minaret by the main gate and, assisted by Lieutenant/Adjutant William McBean and Sergeant Hutchison, unfurled the Regimental Colour of the 93rd – surmounted by a Highland feather bonnet.

The hastily assembled relief force, led by Sir Colin, had

marched with all possible speed from Cawnpore to Lucknow, where several hundred British women and children were being defended, by a small garrison in the battered Residency, against thousands of mutineers and their adherents.

The column dealt ruthlessly with bands of rebels encountered en route, and, on reaching Lucknow, found the mutineers in great strength holding palaces, domes, minarets, archways, gardens, bazaars, public buildings, and native dwellings along narrow, winding evil-smelling labyrinths of alleys. Every possible vantage point was loopholed and fortified.

The Highlanders battled on towards the besieged Residency, and after several days of desperate hand-to-hand fighting, in which the garrison co-operated to the fullest, all the women and children were saved from a massacre similar to that at Cawnpore.

At Lucknow on November 16 six Victoria Crosses were won by officers, N.C.O.s and privates of the 93rd. Those who received this supreme award for heroism were: Captain W. G. D. Stewart, Colour-Sergeant J. Munro, Sergeant J. Paton, Lance-Corporal J. Dunley and Privates P. Grant and D. MacKay.

General Sir Colin Campbell realised that he was not strong enough to completely clear Lucknow of mutineers and hold the town. A division was left in the Alambagh to keep the rebels occupied and he marched for Cawnpore with a force which included the 93rd. With it went 600 women and children and over 1,000 sick and wounded under heavy escort. This large convoy was well clear of the town before the mutineers were aware of its departure.

En route Sir Colin received intelligence that Cawnpore was under attack. The 93rd was ordered to make a forced march to reach a bridge of boats before nightfall, so that the convoy could cross the Ganges. Though exhausted by fighting and marching, the Highlanders covered the 47 miles in 30 hours and went over under fire to rout the mutineers on the other bank. The convoy followed in safety and headed for Allahabad.

The 93rd continued the march on Cawnpore, and with the 42nd (Black Watch), severely punished over 25,000 rebels from Gwalior who had surrounded the small British force in the town. In March 1858, with considerably augmented numbers, totalling about 30,000, Sir Colin retraced his steps to relieve the heavily outnumbered division he had left in the Alambagh at Lucknow.

The mutineers, however, were also strongly reinforced, numbering in the region of 120,000. They constructed three formidable lines of ramparts, but the British came in from a different direction and their guns fired on the rear of these defenceworks with deadly effect.

General Sir Colin Campbell's second assault was practically a repetition of his previous onslaught. The Sutherland Highlanders and The Black Watch decimated the mutineers in the courtyard of the Begum Kothi, and the garrison – which included the 79th (Camerons) – moved out from the Alambagh and joined in the fray.

The 93rd burst into the building and rushed at the trapped sepoys who had barricaded themselves in a maze of corridors and balconies. Bags of gunpowder with lighted fuses were thrown in among them and the Highlanders followed through with the bayonet. Lieutenant/Adjutant McBean entered a room and single-handed accounted for two N.C.O.s and nine other mutineers. Throughout the wild fighting Pipe-Major John McLeod marched up and down the corridors playing his stirring battle music.

Lieutenant/Adjutant McBean, who joined the 93rd as a private in 1835 and was commissioned in the Crimea, was awarded the Victoria Cross. When the medal was pinned on his tunic and he was complimented on 'a good day's work', the modest William McBean replied, 'Tuts, Tuts, it didna tak me tweenty meenits.' This stalwart Highlander later commanded the regiment. And just before the capture of Lucknow the Queen appointed General Sir Colin Campbell Colonel of the 93rd.

When organised resistance broke, the 93rd was employed in a series of mopping-up activities. The Highlanders scoured the country in mobile columns and pursued and rounded up scattered bands of mutineers who had not surrendered.

There were forced marches and a number of sharp clashes with formations of sepoys who sought refuge in the jungle or took to the hills and became brigands. These pacification duties continued well into the autumn of 1859 before peace was restored to strife-torn India. Lucknow was later added to the 93rd's battle honours.

During the next decade the 93rd remained on duty in India,

peace being broken only for a brief period when a small punitive expedition was organised to deal with the disaffected Yusufzai tribesmen. Service followed in the U.K. and at Gibraltar and, on its return from 'The Rock' in 1881, the formation became the 2nd Battalion The Argyll and Sutherland Highlanders under the Cardwell Reorganisation.

The battalion returned to India in 1891 and in 1897-8 was engaged in operations against the troublesome tribes of the Tochi Valley, on the rugged mountainous North-West Frontier – for so long the great training ground of the British Army.

By this time the following battle honours adorned the Regimental Colour: Cape of Good Hope 1806, Rolica, Vimiera, Corunna, Pyrenees, Nivelle, Nive, Orthes, Toulouse, Peninsula, South Africa 1846-47, 1851-2-3, Alma, Balaclava, Sevastopol, Lucknow, South Africa 1879.

Just before the turn of the century friction between the Transvaal and Orange Free State Boers and the British once more flared into open hostility. At the outset of the South African War the Boers had superiority of numbers and at once took the initiative, besieging Kimberley, Ladysmith and Mafeking.

Of sturdy Dutch stock they were tough, wily and resourceful fighters, well-led and equipped and excellent marksmen expert in guerrilla warfare, raiding and defensive tactics. Organised in highly mobile columns and unhampered by lines of communication problems they operated over the rolling scrub-covered 'veldt' and the innumerable 'kopjes', or hills. The latter provided natural vantage points and formidable strongholds.

Within about twelve months of landing at Cape Town the 1st Battalion The Argyll and Sutherland Highlanders – formerly the 91st – was heavily committed in three major engagements: the passage of the Modder River, Magersfontein and Paardeberg. In this gruelling campaign the battalion fought with its traditional dash and fortitude and enhanced its reputation for marching, covering over 3,500 miles in difficult terrain under disconcerting climatic conditions.

The Modder River battle, fought during the bid to relieve Kimberley, lasted all day when a strong British force, including the 1st Battalion – serving with the 9th Brigade – advanced in the open under a withering fire from the Boer trenches. The attacking troops lost heavily and were driven to earth and with their bayonets they scooped up little mounds for cover.

Some further headway was made at the cost of mounting casualties. They were now in a crescent-shaped bend of the river, some three miles wide, with several thousand concealed Boer riflemen and gunners pouring a well-directed concentrated fire into them. There was little opportunity to hit back at the unseen marksmen.

Various diversions failed to improve the situation, but a company of the 1st Battalion succeeded in crossing by means of a dam on the far left. As darkness fell, however, the entire force was ordered to withdraw. At first light it was discovered that Commandant Cronje had also retired during the night.

A fortnight later the battalion, now with The Highland Brigade, participated in the disastrous attack on Magersfontein Hill. After a difficult approach march at night in a thunderstorm the brigade, unaware if was only a few hundred yards from the Boer positions, deployed from quarter column as the first light of dawn was breaking. The enemy suddenly opened up a murderous fire at close range throwing the front lines back in confusion on the supports.

A second attack was shattered practically at its outset for lack of sufficient covering fire, and the Highlanders and scores of their wounded and dying lay for over ten hours on the open corpse-strewn ground in sweltering heat, bullets whining and whistling over and among them. The decimated Highland Brigade was finally extricated from this death-trap with the help of the artillery.

The 1st Argylls were prominent in the Battle of Paardeberg, which immediately followed the relief of Kimberley. Here the enemy took heavy punishment. Their entrenchments were assaulted and overrun and, completely out-fought. Commandant Cronje surrendered with several thousand of his dejected 'Burghers'. At Paardeberg the reorganised Highland Brigade avenged the carnage at Magersfontein.

The battalion was engaged in a succession of minor actions and mopping-up operations until the close of the war. The battle honours Modder River, Paardeberg and South Africa 1899-1902 symbolises the sacrifice and gallantry of the Argylls on 'veldt' and 'kopje'.

From India the 1st Battalion, with the 81st Brigade, 27th Division, arrived in France towards the close of 1914 and took over a sector in the bitterly-disputed Ypres salient. Though there was no major engagement between mid-January and the end of March 1915, the war of attrition in the blood-spattered, muddy and waterlogged trenches went on with unabated fury.

The battalion was in the desperate fighting at the Second Battle of Ypres from May 8 to 13, and the stubborn resistance of isolated companies prevented a large-scale German breakthrough. The Argylls were in the line or in close support for over a month without relief. Artillery fire was weak as shells were rationed owing to an acute shortage of 'ammo'.

The 27th Division moved to Armentieres and here the 1st and 2nd Battalions were aligned in the trenches. The 1st experienced a welcome lull during the summer and on the Somme before the division was placed under orders for Salonika in November 1915.

When the Bulgarians invaded Macedonia in August 1916, the 81st Brigade advanced into the Struma Valley, taking up positions on the hills to the south. The brigade moved forward to establish a bridgehead on the Struma, which necessitated the capture of two villages.

One village was taken with comparative ease but the second, an objective of the 1st Argylls, proved a tough proposition. Two companies were pinned down by intense enfilade fire and the other two were not strong enough to dislodge the Bulgars from their well entrenched positions.

With artillery support the reserve battalion of the brigade entered the fray, and the village was finally taken after stiff fighting and held for three days against several determined counter-attacks. The remainder of the year was spent in the plain north of the river, principal employment being in reconnaissance and aggressive patrolling.

In the summer of 1917 the battalion was plagued with malaria, and considerably reduced in effectiveness, withdrew from the plain to an outpost line in the foothills. Early in 1918, Greece having joined the allies and taken over the Struma front. the 27th Division moved westwards to the Vardar River, relieving the French, and at once initiated intensive patrol activity.

In the autumn of 1918 a powerful offensive was sprung on the Bulgars. The role of the 27th Division was to hold the enemy on the Vardar, while troops on the left launched an all-out attack to break through the enemy line. The Bulgar outposts were assaulted and overrun by two companies of the 1st Argylls in early September, and held for several days though subjected to heavy shellfire.

About the middle of the month the French and Serbians burst into the Bulgarian front line and threatened their lines of communication and supply. It was the beginning of the end, and within a few days the enemy was streaming back in disorder.

The 81st Brigade marched north-eastwards to engage the Turks, but as the Turkish Army had been pushed back from the Egyptian frontier and routed during a long pursuit across the desert and into Palestine, Turkey sued for peace. The brigade then returned to Salonika. The battle honour Doiran 1917-18 was later awarded to The Argyll and Sutherland Highlanders for their outstanding service in the Balkans.

The 2nd Battalion was the first British Expeditionary Force unit to land in France in mid-August 1914. The strident notes of their pipes and the rattle of their drums in Boulogne cheered the French, whose armies were being pressed back on Paris by the invading German hordes.

Kaiser Wilhelm referred to the British Expeditionary Force as the 'Contemptible Little Army'. Originally it consisted of only four divisions, but it took on and eventually halted the advancing masses of German infantry during the fighting retreat from Mons to the Cambrai-Le Cateu line. Although exhausted by days and nights of marching and combat, the B.E.F. attacked and hurled the enemy back from the Marne to beyond the Aisne.

Moving into battle the 2nd Argylls, with the 19th Brigade, moved north and, on the left of the French, closed with the Germans at Mons. The battalion was heavily engaged during the consequent retreat and was represented in the epic stand at Le Cateau.

The B.E.F. fought a classic rearguard action which completely upset the enemy's time schedule. With deadly, concentrated and rapid fire the British infantry levelled long lines of close-packed advancing field grey, but the Germans continued to come on, shoulder-to-shoulder, elbowing for a place in their gunsights.

After nine hours of continuous bombardment and desperate in-fighting, a half-company of the 2nd Argylls and a contingent of The Suffolk Regiment were rushed fom the rear and were overwhelmed after battling to the end against impossible odds.

During the retreat there was ghastly non-stop, confused, close fighting, and, when magazines were empty, clubbed rifles, bayonets, spades, entrenching tools – and bare fists – came into play. And not a few Prussians went down before stout army boots.

Encirclement was avoided and the line successfully reformed. The survivors of the 2nd Battalion were reunited early in September and entered the crucial Battle of the Marne and advanced to the Aisne, the B.E.F. crossing in the wake of the retreating Germans.

In trench warfare during the winter of 1914-15 there was bitter fighting; particularly at Le Mesnil and Ploegsteert Wood in October and November. A few months later the battalion experienced a comparatively quiet spell around Armentieres. In the autumn the Argylls moved into the Bethune area and the battalion was heavily committed at the Battle of Loos.

A change of wind blew gas back on the British trenches, delaying the attack by the 2nd Argylls and 1st Middlesex Regiment. When they went over the top they were at once swept by machine- gun and rifle fire, and, suffering heavy casualties, were held up by the intact wire entanglements ranging along the German front line. A gap cut by artillery fire had been repaired during the night.

The supports fared no better. The Argylls brought forward machine-guns but were unable to silence the concealed marksmen. The brigadier ordered a withdrawal to the original trenches and there were further casualties as the Argylls and 'Middies' retired through the crazy pattern of shell craters.

After the Loos debacle trench warfare was resumed and throughout the winter of 1915-16 there was intensive mining activity by both sides. The 2nd Battalion was now serving with the 98th Brigade, 33rd Division, and in the spring raiding was stepped up and continued until the eve of the Battle of the Somme.

From July until the end of November the Somme holocaust dragged on, the 2nd Argylls being prominently identified at High Wood, Delville Wood and Les Boeufs. In mid-August at High Wood – where nothing went right – one company succeeded in getting into the enemy line and there it remained until ammunition was expended. At Delville Wood a successful attack was made on an enemy strongpoint.

'Piece de resistance' of the Argylls on the Somme was at Les Boeufs. A ridge overlooking Le Transloy, which had defied attempts by three divisions to capture it, fell to two companies with the 1st Queen's Regiment operating on their right flank.

After wintering on the Somme the 33rd Division was withdrawn to undergo hard training for the attack near Arras in the Battle of the Scarpe. The onslaught of the 2nd Argylls on April 23, 1917, provided one of the highlights in the saga of the regiment.

The attack went in at 4.45 a.m. and at 6.30 a.m. the 'final objective carried' intelligence came in. But it was not over yet. The Germans recovered and counter-attacked in great force, driving back the troops on the battalion's flanks, leaving companies of Argylls isolated and surrounded.

At 6 p.m. two companies of The Royal Welsh Fusiliers, with what was left of the support companies of the Argylls, attacked to restore the position. This attempt failed and at 7.30 a.m. on the 24th the remnants of the battalion was withdrawn. But the relieving formation, on sending out patrols, discovered that survivors of the companies which had attacked on the previous day were still holding out.

Nor were they lying low. For twenty-four hours they had made the Germans acutely aware of their presence and successfully stalked those who came out to hunt them. Their positions were ringed with enemy dead and wounded.

Second-Lieutenant (Acting-Captain) Arthur Henderson, M.C., in command of one of the companies, was awarded a posthumous Victoria Cross for his heroism and leadership at Fontaine-les-Croisilles. Second-Lieutenant Henderson, of the 4th Argylls, was attached to the 2nd Battalion.

The 2nd Battalion was in violent action during September, taking a prominent role in the attack along the Menin Road. At night on September 24 the brigade was concentrating with the Second Army for an assault on Polygon Wood, but early the following morning the enemy hurled an entire division against it, supporting with a powerful barrage which lasted for about fourteen hours.

The Germans made some penetration of the brigade front, but this was quickly dealt with in a counter-attack by two companies of the 2nd Battalion. The Argylls on retaking the lost ground advanced for a mile beyond, and, though both flanks were uncovered, they dug in and held on with the enemy operating behind them. The Second Army's attack on the 26th was completely successful, and, on the advancing troops coming up, the two companies rejoined the battalion.

In March 1918, the German High Command launched its final mighty offensive on the Western Front, with the object of smashing through between the British and French armies and capturing the Channel ports. All available reinforcements and reserves were poured in, but the German infantry suffered frightful execution and by the end of April the offensive had ground to a halt.

American troops were now in France, and in the autumn the Allies initiated an equally massive general attack which sent the shattered German formations reeling back into a disastrous retreat. Disturbances had broken out in the Fatherland and the enemy sued for peace in November.

During the last victorious advance the 2nd Argylls were in three notable engagements. They captured Villers Guislain after a sharp action, but, as the relieving troops were driven back, the battalion was called upon to give a repeat performance. The Argylls obliged with an encore, which necessitated two attacks and the repelling of an enemy counterblow.

The tempo of the advance quickened and there was much open fighting and brisk skirmishing in the push to the Selle. The battalion's final major action was in fording the river north of Le Cateau.

The impressive list of battle honours awarded to The Argyll and Sutherland Highlanders for gallantry and sacrifice in World War I are: MONS, LE CATEAU, Retreat from Mons, MARNE 1914, '18, Aisne 1914, La Bassée 1914, Messines 1914, '18, Armentières 1914, YPRES 1915, '17, '18, Gravenstafel, St. Julien, Frezenberg, Bellewaarde, Festubert 1915, LOOS, SOMME 1916, '18, Albert 1916, '18, Bazentin, Delville Wood, Pozières, Flers-Courcelette, Morval, Le Transloy, Ancre Heights, Ancre 1916, ARRAS 1917, '18, Scarpe 1917, '18, Arleux, Pilckem, Menin Road, Polygon Wood, Broodseinde, Poelcappelle, Passchendaele,

CAMBRAI 1917, '18, St. Quentin, Bapaume 1918, Rosières, Lys, Estaires, Hazebrouck, Bailleul. Kemmel, Bethune, Soissonnais-Ourcq, Tardenois, Amiens, Hindenburg Line. Epéhy, Canal du Nord, St. Quentin Canal, Beaurevoir, Courtrai, Selle, Sambre, France and Flanders 1914-18, Italy 1917-18, Struma, DOIRAN 1917, '18, Macedonia 1915-18, Gallipoli 1915-16, Rumani, Egypt 1916, GAZA, El Mughar, Nebi Samwil, Jaffa, Palestine 1917-18. (The ten in capitals appear on the Queen's Colour.)

On a tour of duty in India the 1st Argylls maintained order during the Bombay strikes of 1920. While serving in Egypt in 1924 the battalion was rushed to Khartoum in August as there was serious political tension. It was split up into detachments which served in various parts of the Sudan.

Two months later a mutiny of the native troops broke out in Khartoum, where H.Q., two half-companies and a machine-gun platoon of the 1st Battalion were stationed. The Argylls engaged the mutineers and after several hours of sharp skirmishing peace was restored, the firm handling of the situation by the Highland battalion probably averting a general insurrection in the Sudan.

After the Munich crisis passed the 1st Argylls were dispatched to Palestine, then in the throes of an Arab rising. Arriving early in May 1939, the battalion joined the 14th Infantry Brigade of the 8th Division.

Day and night, mobile groups carried out sweeps and exhausting cross-country marches in the Jenin area. There were snap searches of villages suspected of harbouring terrorists or secreting arms and in December two company actions practically ended the emergency period.

On the 5th a band of 'oozles' was run to earth near the Wadi Shubash and on the 17th another gang was destroyed at Umm al Fahm with troops of The Royal Dragoons and a detachment of the Palestine Police co-operating. In mid-January 1940, the battalion joined the 16th Infantry Brigade at Jericho.

Intensive training was carried out but this was suddenly interrupted at the beginning of March. The Argylls were rushed to the Jaffa-Tel Aviv area where the Jews were making trouble as a result of the Government's refusal to allow unrestricted immigration.

One company came upon a party of Jews in the act of sabotage. Out flashed the bayonets and the Argylls chased them through Tel Aviv. The battalion resumed its training programme with the 16th Brigade. This brigade was now part of the 6th Division, earmarked for service in the Western Desert.

While the sweating dust-engrained 'Agile and Suffering Highlanders' were bandit-hunting in Palestine the Monocled Ones at the War Office sent an interesting 'Christmas parcel' to the battalion. Contents – pink panties – sleek, soft silky creations. They were 'on appro' for wearing under the kilt to protect the wearer from the effects of gas warfare.

The Whitehall Warriors were evidently quite unaware that the Arabs did not employ gas, though many of them undoubtedly had B.O. Their best friends did not tell them as probably they suffered similarly.

Reaction in the battalion was a mixture of shock, disbelief, exasperation and shafts of Rabelaisian humour that gave the heat-haze rather a bluish hue. And there were suggestions that 'Jock's box' should be returned to sender with the comment that it was a 'Jessie's box'. The Argylls, of course, were asked to report, no doubt in quadruplicate. They did, and the content of that report is probably better imagined than chronicled.

But the 'Chairborne Division', being much the senior formation, had the last word. It ordered that the kilt would no longer be worn during war service and that no further stocks were to be issued, though kilts in the battalion could be used for ceremonial occasions and walking out. There was a reorganisation of the battalion's 'wardrobe' and kilts were put on a 'care and maintenance' basis. Thus, throughout the war, the 'Garb of Old Gaul' graced many a parade.

The 2nd Battalion was on duty in Ireland from 1920 until 1922 during the 'troubles', and early in 1932 joined the International Force in Shanghai, taking part in guarding the perimeter of the Settlement while the Sino-Japanese War was raging. While serving in the Far East the Argylls sailed with the Royal Navy in anti-piracy patrols on the Yangtse and along the coast to safeguard shipping.

In 1933 the battalion arrived in India and was stationed at 'Pindi'. The 2nd trained in mountain warfare at Jhelum, 'graduating' with first-class honours. These hardy soldiers, many of them from Scotland's hills and glens, learned quickly. To them mountain warfare was 'doin' what comes naturally'.

They experienced the real thing on the North-West Frontier in 1935 during the Mohmand operations, and again in 1937 in clashes with the Mahsud Wazir tribesmen. In August 1939, the 2nd Battalion arrived in Malaya with the 12th (Indian) Infantry Brigade.

Early in September 1940, the 1st Argylls with the 16th Brigade joined the 4th Indian Division in the Western Desert. The brigade was set to preparing the defences of the Baggush 'Box'. Action was not long delayed.

General Sir 'Archie' Wavell, C.-in-C., Middle East, launched his daring offensive across the sands in early December. The 4th Indian Division overran the Italian strongpoints at Nibiewa, Tummar and Point 90. The British attack was made in a wide sweep south of the enemy positions, the 4th Indian 'Div' hitting the Italians hard from the flank and rear.

The 16th Brigade advanced from Sanyet Awlad Ali to Ilwet Matrud, with the 1st Battalion of the Argylls leading. The Scots assaulted the strongly fortified defences between Ilwet Matrud and Alam el Dab, their final objective being the cutting of the strategic Sidi Barrani-Buq Buq road. In a blinding snowstorm and under intense shelling the companies debussed around Beit Ait Hassan, took up a defensive position, then, without artillery cover, they rose up and rushed the range of low hills ahead.

Machine-guns chattered incessantly from the enemy strong-points and casualties began to mount as the companies surged on to capture the defended mounds about Bir Sayid Kayim – an exposed area which was soon swept by a concentrated fire and only held with great difficulty.

The attack was vigorously renewed and Hill X cleared. The reserve companies entered the melee, Graves Hill, Hill 51 and the important Alam el Dab objective were stormed and carried. Argyll bayonets cut the Sidi Barrani-Buq Buq road.

Resistance collapsed and retaliation was confined to long-range shelling – 'spite fire'. Prisoners streamed in by the hundred. The onslaught by the 1st Argylls had struck right into the nerve centre of the Italian defence system and the enemy made a run for it into the hills beyond.

The Italians fought well from a distance, but once the

bayonets began to close in they became cross-country runners – or put their hands up. The reaction of the triumphant, sweating sand-covered Argylls was amusing : 'Must have been Mussolini's Coldcream Guards, that lot'. . . . 'Think we could get some of them to run for us at the sports, Sergeant?' . . . 'Gie them ice-cream freezers then we'll a' be happy.'

After the Battle of Sidi Barrani the battalion manned the defences near Abar Yusef where scores of dejected Italian infantrymen were herded back, the number being considerably augmented in the 'mop up' of enemy pockets between the main road and the coast. In mid-December the brigade moved into the front line facing Italian-held Bardia, with the 1st Argylls in reserve overlooking Halfaya Wadi – otherwise known as 'Hellfire Pass'.

In mid-May 1941, when the brigade landed at Tymbaki, Crete, companies moved up to near Phaistos, Moiras and Ayioi Dheka. They were soon spotted by the enemy and on the 20th Moiras was bombed. The Argylls were unscathed but para-troops landing in the Heraklion area seized the road to Ayioi Dheka, cutting the battalion off from the 14th Infantry Brigade.

One company advanced along the Gournes-Kaireti Farm road and made good headway in spite of two low-flying attacks by Stukas, but when the enemy dropped a strong force of para-troops in the rear of their objective the initiative was lost. Having sustained a number of casualties the company with-drew to near the start point.

Reinforced by other companies the attack was renewed. Some initial progress was made and a platoon got through to the outskirts of Heraklion. One unit attacking the enemy right flank from the rear was heavily bombed and soon afterwards scores of airborne troops were dropped behind it. This company was trapped between two fires and a few survivors straggled back at dusk. Another unit suffered a similar fate.

Orders reached the battalion to disengage and join the 14th Brigade in defending Heraklion, and, led by Cretan guides, the Argylls crossed the hills and took up station on the perimeter on the 25th. Enemy air activity continued and there were further drops of paratroops around Heraklion.

At dawn on the 26th a powerful enemy attack came in over-running the forward posts of one company, but a furious counter-attack by two companies of the Leicesters restored the situation. When German paratroops gave up waves of Stukas came over and the Heraklion defences shuddered, rocked and crumbled under the crash of bombs.

The enemy had unchallenged mastery in the air and could land troops practically anywhere on the island. The western end of Crete was firmly in their hands and Heraklion was becoming untenable. On the 28th the defences were subjected to their most intensive bombing and several hundred paratroops were observed dropping outside the perimeter indicating the build-up for an all-out assault.

Evacuation plans had already been completed. At midnight the garrison began withdrawing and finally the forward posts were abandoned. Embarkation was rapid and orderly and the Germans made no attempt to follow up.

The ships quickly got under way, but at daylight the Luftwaffe spotted the convoy and there was heavy loss of life on the troop-laden ships when the Stukas rained down their bombs. Several naval vessels were sunk, and others reduced to a mass of twisted tangled metal littered with charred broken bodies, limped across the Mediterranean to Alexandria.

Less than 350 Argylls assembled at Sidi Bishr. In the next few weeks, however, small parties of men believed to be dead, wounded, prisoners or missing succeeded in eluding the Germans and, after crossing the sea on fishing boats and other small craft, rejoining the battalion. Each had his own Odyssey to tell.

So it was that a new Minotaur came to Crete. But another Theseus was soon to arise and free this misty mountainous islet of lore and legend. And then did the Gods of Ancient Greece rejoice.

Replacements were soon forthcoming and the reorganised and re-equipped battalion left the 16th Brigade and arrived at Asmara in time to take part in the final phase of the Abyssinian Campaign – the capture of Gondar. The 1st Argylls were now under the control of the 12th African Division.

At the beginning of August the Scots made the Italians at Debivar, Wolchefit and Debarech acutely aware of their presence and they soon surrendered. At the beginning of October a company was detached from the battalion and dispatched to Kufra Oasis in the far distant north-west, where it remained in a garrison role for about nine months.

In mid-November the Scots sent the Italians at Venticinque their visiting cards – about three dozen mortar bombs. A few days afterwards, preceded by an air and artillery 'stonk', the Argylls paid their call and took possession.

At the close of the month the 12th African Division launched its assault on Gondar. Lines of white were seen fluttering all over the enemy positions and it was thought it must be the Italians' washing day. As the troops closed in, however, it was observed they were surrender flags. More time was spent in rounding up and counting the prisoners than in the actual attack.

Only Ambazzo held out and a company of Argylls along with a company of The King's African Rifles were ordered to deal with this last enemy outpost. The artillery served a noisy eviction notice, the Italian gunners protested, then suddenly white flags indicated they had given up the tenancy. Next day the Argylls marched into captured Gondar.

The 'Foreign Legion' company from Kufra Oasis rejoined at Cairo in mid-May 1942. Early in July a detachment was flown into the desert behind enemy lines. This mission was top secret; the setting up of a makeshift landing ground and petrol re-fuelling station for R.A.F. bombers engaged in long-range raiding. The Argylls quickly got to work and were later flown back to rendezvous with the battalion.

By the end of the month the battalion was again in the desert and for some time was shunted to and fro between the 4th, 5th and 10th Indian Divisions in the Eighth Army. The Argylls moved into positions on Ruweisat Ridge at El Alamein, and soon after the take-over there was a 'stand-to' along the entire front. A strong attack came rolling in with the object of breaking through to Egypt but the enemy was completely foiled.

During September the battalion was employed in patrolling and improving the defences. One company, however, had been detached for a seaborne raid on Tobruk. There were inter-communication difficulties, heavy bombing and frequent machine-gunning and the unit, which suffered some casualties, did not land.

The thunder of the guns on October 23 opened the Battle of

Alamein with the 1st Argylls having to stay put in reserve after an attack role had been countermanded. Six days later the battalion got the 'Go Go' while located in the South African Division's territory. The Argylls swept forward hoping to be in at the kill, but again the move was called off – there were no more enemy positions to assault.

It was all very exasperating. After a grandstand view of the 'fireworks' the Argylls had the 'Alamein itch' to get into the fight alongside the other Scottish regiments. When the impatient Scots were at last unleashed the Germans and Italians were dustclouds disappearing over the horizon.

In the spring of 1943, near Hadera, Palestine, the battalion became the nucleus of No. 33 (1st A. & S. H.) Beach Brick. This 'brick' was formed to work with the 17th Brigade of the British 5th Division. No. 33 Beach Brick concentrated at Port Said and its first operation was under way in July; the Allied landing in Sicily.

On July 10 the 17th Brigade and its Beach Brick quickly established themselves at Fontane Bianche, some ten miles south of Syracuse. They toiled in the shallows and on shore under a blazing sun and, in spite of several air raids, the Beach Brick accomplished its first complicated assignment in this new role without outstanding success. A record 'tonnage' of muscle and metal was landed. Syracuse fell within a few hours and the troops began to battle their way inland.

At the end of the month there was startling news. The 1st Argylls were to be relieved of their Beach Brick duties and join the 51st (Highland) Division, then on the banks of the Dittaino facing the enemy-held Sferro Hills. The 7th Argylls (T.A.) were undergoing reorganisation at Ramacca and their place in 154 Brigade had been allotted to the 1st Battalion. Also in 154 were the 1st and 7th Battalions The Black Watch and the 1/7th Battalion The Middlesex Regiment.

The Highland Division's next objective was the Sferro-Catenanuova road so that the artillery could move up and give Adrano a plastering. The division attacked on July 31, and after hard fighting, drove the enemy off the hills. The 154 Brigade was on its left, with the 1st Argylls in reserve. The battalion guarded the start point and flanks until relieved by the arrival of the reorganised 7th Argylls.

In mid-August the battalion was withdrawn from its perch in the hills and reluctantly severed its memorable five-day association with The Highland Division. The 1st Argylls were sent to rejoin the 17th Brigade. The campaign in Sicily was drawing to a close and No. 33 Beach Brick was re-assembling for an 'encore' performance, this time on the Italian mainland.

On September 2 the 17th Brigade and 33 Beach Brick crossed the Straits of Messina to set up their operational zone near Gallico Marina, in the 'toe' of Italy. The 5th Division went for the San Giovanni-Cannitello area while the 1st Canadian Division assaulted Reggio. There were only half-hearted attempts by enemy planes to disrupt embarkation and disembarkation.

Everything went according to plan and there was an ear-splitting naval, artillery and air bombardment. From positions in the hills on the east coast of Sicily the artillery fired across the straits. It was a field day for the Gunners and they were invariably 'on target'.

Disembarkation continued non-stop for four days and the troops pushed rapidly inland. Then Italy threw in the towel. Another job of work well done, the 1st Argylls were signalled to revert to infantry again and the battalion concentrated at Taranto. At the close of October they were back in 'Alex'.

The battalion provided the guard for Mr. Winston Churchill, President Roosevelt and Generalissimo Chiangkaishek at the Mena Conference, near Cairo. The bearing, sparkle and precision of the Scots in kilts and shirt sleeve order created a wonderful impression. After the conference ended the battalion joined the 4th British Division near Suez early in January 1944.

At the beginning of February it crossed to Taranto and became part of the 19th Indian Infantry Brigade of the 8th Indian Division. The Argylls moved to the hill-top village of Castelfrentano within sight of enemy-held Orsogna. The German gunners gave the Argylls a noisy welcome and the whistle of the winter winds merged at times with the whine of shells.

With the 'bahadurs' of the 8th Indian Division the 'Jocks' were committed to several bloody battles in the bitterly-contested advance up the leg of Italy, to final victory in the Po Valley in May 1945. The battalion went over the bullet-swept towering mountain masses of the Apennines, fought through deep snow, in freezing sleet and rain-squalls, along shell-torn bomb-pocked roads, which in the spring turned to a series of mud-filled craters, and skirmished into the gaunt gaping ruins of shattered towns and villages.

The Argylls forded fast-flowing treacherous rivers under fire and assaulted and pierced the enemy's strongly-held serial defence lines. In the summer heat haze they battled through orchards, olive groves, gardens, vineyards and farm country. The roads, some of them little better than cart tracks, climbed; twined and spiralled crazily upward.

At the beginning of March 1944, the 1st Battalion moved into the Poggiofiorito-Arielli area. Here the enemy artillery mortars, and machine-guns on higher ground made life at times rather hectic and there were several patrol clashes. Towards the end of April the Argylls were at Zupparielli during the build-up for the Battle of the Rapido, launched in mid-May.

To secure the San Angelo 'horseshoe' in this offensive against the Gustav Line, the 8th Division's 17th and 19th Brigades were sent in, the 1st Argylls being the left assault battalion of the 19th. A powerful barrage preceded the attack, but things did not go well for the Scots.

There were too few boats and in the night crossing under a vicious fire several were holed and others swept away by the current. The Germans laid down a smoke screen which made the finding and bringing forward of further assault craft impossible. On the far bank three companies, while in full view of the enemy defences, ran into barbed wire in an area that had suffered little from the British barrage. The lashing mortar and machine-gun fire drove them to earth.

On the near side, two other units were also badly shot up and had to seek cover in the irrigation ditches. And for a time radio communication with the brigade blacked out. One platoon, however, got through a gap in the wire and fought alongside the Punjabis throughout the battle.

Only tanks could save the situation, and, on radio contact being restored, brigade was informed of the battalion's plight. The Canadians succeeded in getting a small force of armour across a 'Bailey' at a bridgehead established and gallantly held by the Indians.

At this critical juncture the Germans were observed preparing to launch a counter-attack, but the eloquence of the artillery

THE ARGYLL AND SUTHERLAND HIGHLANDERS

soon persuaded them to change their minds. After about thirty-six hours of desperate combat the companies were ordered to withdraw and the Argylls crossed the Bailey bridge bearing numerous wounded.

The next round went to the Argylls. After a short rest the battalion trooped across the bridge, swung left, and, with tank support, cleared the Liri 'appendix' and took some prisoners. Moving round on Panaccione, which had fallen to the Frontier Force Rifles, the Argylls advanced to and held the Masso Tiscoe-Conte Murro line in co-operation with Canadian armour.

The 'bahadurs' took Pignataro and soon the San Angelo horseshoe changed hands. The 8th Indian Division had carried all its objectives and the Germans were pulling back at speed. The long pursuit to the Arno got under way, a patrol of Argylls being the first troops to reach the banks at the end of July.

About a fortnight later, in the Roccasecca area, paratroops were located. The Argylls with a few tanks moved up to engage, but the Germans did not wait. San Giovanni was taken, but they ran into heavy shelling at Fontana Liri and Lucinette towards the end of May. The British guns retaliated and, on closing in, the Argylls found that the enemy had again pulled back.

A company co-operating with the Frontier Force Rifles took part in the successful attack on Veroli. Early in June, the battalion, in moving through the hills, came under some troublesome shelling north of Subiaco during the push for Arsoli. The British guns were soon on target and the Argylls found the town had been hastily evacuated.

The Scots entered historic Assisi under enemy bombardment. By this time there had been a break-out from the Anzio beachhead, Rome had been liberated and the Germans were in retreat throughout Italy. The battalion resumed the chase, but a sudden break in the weather slowed down the tempo of the advance. Previously the Germans had sought to delay the pursuit by artillery fire, mortaring, demolitions, blown bridges and sniping, but now their rearguard resistance showed signs of stiffening.

This was evident north-east of Castiglione Fiorentino, on the mountain slopes overlooking the road to Arezzo. The Germans in Empoli were made painfully aware of the presence of the Argylls by a lightning raid in which a troop of tanks and some machine-gunners fired into their flank.

At the beginning of August the Scots moved into the Florence area only to find that the German guns could still 'reach'. Here the advance of 220 miles in three months ended, and the 8th Indian Division prepared to cross the Arno for the assault on the Gothic Line.

Monte Abetino, Monte Cavallara, Monte Cerere, and Senio . . . these names are spoken with the thrill of Highland pride in pub, club, factory, work-bench, round the ingle-neuk or in shepherd's sheiling in the western hills. If you hear them mentioned you are in good company – among men of the 1st Argylls. And not one of them but treasures the memory of some comrades who shed their lifeblood in the heather and scrub-covered Italian mountains, where wounds or death lurked in each ridge, fold and cranny.

Sunny Italy ! – but not in the dread winter of 1944-45. Grey leaden skies, snow, hail, sleet and freezing torrential rain lanced through the rolling mists; sodden clothing, clinging, caking squelching mud, waterlogged slit trenches, monotony of diet, the stuttering chatter of enemy automatic fire, the krump of mortars, the whistle, crash and erupting muddy spray from bursting shells, the whine of bullets, the gasp of the stricken, the howling mountain winds their requiem. . .

Towards the end of August the Argylls crossed the Arno, passed through the Punjabis, and advanced into the Decima area without encountering opposition. B Company began the difficult ascent of Monte Abetino but the German guns opened up around Doccio and its H.Q. was practically wiped out. The unit quickly reformed and joined D Company lower down the slope under accurate mortar and spandau fire.

A Company passed through Battalion H.Q. at Baronci in an attempt to find a covered approach to the other side of the valley, as any move along the road from Doccio would be suicidal. This company fared no better and after sustaining a number of casualties linked up with D.

An attack on Monte Abertino was launched on September 2. Enemy reaction was immediate and formidable and B and D Companies were driven to earth. Another attempt was decided upon and B Company made for the farmstead of Fontasenzo, on open ground on the east of the 'monte' and about 300 ft. from its summit.

D Company crawled up through the thick scrub and two platoons reached the top in the face of intense cross-fire. Shouts of 'Tik hai, Johnny' greeted the Argylls, and thinking they had stumbled among their Indian comrades there was some confusion. It was an enemy 'ruse de guerre', an old one, but it came off. Before the Argylls recovered they were surrounded.

The reserve platoon extricated itself along with Company H.Q. and some survivors of the two attacking units, but only after a wild confused rearguard action down the body-strewn slope. A Company made a determined bid for the heights of Ripagfieri but was badly shot up. B Company, moving on Fontasenzo, came under a pattern of mortar and small arms fire. The enemy withdrew later and Fontasenzo, the key to the summit of Monte Abetino, was occupied by the Indians.

Moving from Florence in mid-September the Argylls viewed the towering frowning peaks of the Appenines from positions at Borgo San Lorenzo. These were interwoven into the German defence system of the Gothic Line.

The 8th Indian Division attacked across the Sieve with the 19th Brigade, which included the Argylls, in reserve. The ferocity of the assault and the prolonged concentrated bombardments smashed enemy resistance and this section of the Gothic Line ceased to exist.

The Scottish battalion, with its brigade, trekked across the hills from San Godenzo to San Benedetti and Marradi, and about the end of the month units were located on Monte Susinelli, Monte Bruno, Monte del Becco, Monte Cerro and at the mouth of the Tramazzo Gorge. For some time torrential rain bogged down all activity.

The Argylls had a 'dry-out' at Botteghette before going north into further rugged mountain terrain and taking over a long ridge which ran into Monte Cavallara. The Germans were jittery and loosed off sporadic small arms fire, while the artillery tried to boost their morale with some noisy but ineffective shelling.

The battalion was ordered to capture the 'monte' at all costs. Artillery and mortar fire and smoke were laid on and A Company rose from its wooded position and closed with the enemy. There was violent bayonet fighting and the Germans were finally blasted out with grenades. But Argyll casualties were high in the assault on this strongly defended feature known as Point 744.

On capture it became the target of the enemy artillery and B Company was sent in. Only about 300 yards separated the Argylls on Cavallara from the enemy's reserve position – Point 685. After mortars patterned it two platoons from B Company rushed through a concentration of fire which laid many of them low.

This desperate charge carried Point 685 but the Germans soon counter-attacked in strength and the remaining Argylls were forced to give ground and withdrew in the gathering dusk. On the reverse slope, however, a few wounded Scots fought the enemy to a standstill though their platoon had ceased to exist. They were found by one of their dawn patrols. Point 685 had been held all night by these wounded 'Jocks'.

The battalion's hard-won success on Monte Cavallara and the capture of Monte Casalina by the Indians forced the Germans to pull back so quickly that there was no contact for several days. At the end of the month the Argylls took over a stretch of the line, companies being positioned at Fontecchio and Malanca and on Monte Colombo and Monte Giro. Climatic conditions worsened, particularly for those living in holes in the ground which became veritable freezing mud-baths.

The battalion afterwards was in positions at Loiana, San Cassiano, Castelvecchia, Monte Bassana and Boesima. Information came in that the Germans had withdrawn from their defences ranging from San Cassiano to Monte Tesoto and the Argylls moved forward.

They manned the strategic ridge running from Monte Grande through Monte Cerere. In the Frassineto-Casa Nuova-Trebio area the Scots encountered foes worthy of their steel; a battalion of the 1st Regiment of the 1st Parachute Division which was one of Kesselring's elite formations. The 19th Brigade was now under orders of the 1st British Division.

In mid-December, after an artillery and mortar 'stonk', the Germans attacked strongly out of the morning mist and drove in forward posts of the Argylls and Indians. Casa Nuova fell, but an assault on Frassineto wilted before the defensive fire of artillery, mortars and small arms.

A concentration of fire was poured into the German wedge and a sharp platoon counter-attack was delivered against Casa Nuova, which caught the enemy in the act of withdrawing. The

Argylls re-captured their forward positions and the Indians also re-established themselves. The threat to Monte Cerere was over. And Kesselring's Parachute Regiment was licking its wounds.

Returning to the bleak Borgo San Lorenzo Valley the battalion was switched west to Lucca and moved into the Serchio Valley where an enemy attack was building up. When launched it bit deep into the positions of an American negro division but the Germans penetrated no further on tangling with forward elements of the Scots and their Indian comrades. The enemy then began pulling back – a charming German compliment to the reputation of the 8th Indian Division!

In mid-February the division was under orders to relieve the Canadians in the Po Valley. The 1st Argylls arrived in Russi and by the middle of March they were on the banks of the Senio preparing for an assault crossing.

The enemy had occupied the reverse slope of the near bank and there were numerous bouts of grenade-throwing – not without some 'googly' bowling, much to the discomfiture of the German 'fielders' in this Test Match by the Senio! Had there been an English unit present the Scots would no doubt have derived much encouragement from shouts of 'Well bowled, sir' and 'Howzat!'

The 19th Brigade was on the right of the division during the assault on April 9. Allied aircraft bombed the enemy strong-points, the artillery added to the thundering crescendo of doom and 'wasp' and 'crocodile' tanks sprayed the banks with flame.

The dazed Germans were still keeping their heads down when the Argylls made their rush and, in a matter of minutes, the Senio defence line in this sector was overrun with few casualties to the attackers. Enemy tanks and infantry attempted to retaliate but this move was smashed back with gunfire.

Companies with the aid of several tanks pushed on, C reaching the Canale di Lugo and clearing Casa Grandi en route. The advance swept on to Scolo Arginello and Casa Visani was occupied. In the three-day Battle of the Senio the battalion made a two-mile advance and protected the right flank of the Indian Division. About a week later the Argylls fought the enemy out of Ferrara and the populace turned out in force to hear the pipes and drums. 'Grazie Signor MacJock!'

Towards the end of April the battalion crossed the River Po on amphibious tanks to resume the pursuit of the fleeing Germans. It concentrated at Costa di Rovigo and prepared to move on Venice. But on May 2 the Germans put up their hands; unconditional surrender in Italy.

The Scots and Indians of the 'Chupatti Division' – blood-brothers all – ate and drank and entertained each other in the square. By fiercely glowing bonfires the drums rolled and rattled, the pipes droned and skirled and the Indians leaped and whirled in the wild abandon of their tribal dances.

The Argylls marched and counter-marched, the tartan flashed, they reeled and hooched, and dances were invented on the spot in which 'Jock' and 'Johnny' joined with enthusiasm till their breath failed them. They did not know it then but soon they were to be parted – but never in their memories.

The 1st Battalion was selected for service against the Japanese and returned to the U.K. at the close of June. With victory in the Far East, however, the battalion was sent to strife-torn Palestine, where it was deployed in maintaining order during the Mandate tension and outbreaks of violence by Arab and Jewish extremist factions.

The battalion served in turn with the 6th Airborne Division, 3rd Infantry Division and 1st Infantry Division. It was a strenuous, danger-fraught thankless role which kept the Argylls on their toes practically night and day until they sailed for home in 1948.

When the 2nd Battalion arrived in the Far East in the autumn of 1939 the Argylls carried out intensive jungle combat training which was later to stand them in good stead against the Japanese. With its brigade, the 12th (Indian), the 2nd was mobile reserve for Malaya.

After shattering the principal units of the U.S. Pacific Fleet in heavy air attacks on Pearl Harbour during December 7/8, 1941, the Japanese invaded Malaya across its northern frontier. They seized Singora and the airfields of Southern Siam and also landed at Kota Baru, in Kelantan. Singapore was subjected to concentrated and frequent bombing.

Within a week of the invasion being launched the 2nd Argylls were sent 500 miles north of Singapore to cover the withdrawal of British and Indian troops from a number of threatened posts on the Thai frontier. The Argylls fought a series of skilful delaying actions and on several occasions checked the enemy advance. But inevitably they had to retire either by order or before mounting Japanese pressure and infiltration.

Another grievous blow was the loss of the battleship *Prince of Wales* and the battle-cruiser *Repulse*. Now the Japanese held all the aces; mastery of the sea and the sky and on land superiority of numbers, equipment and weight of armour.

The enemy advanced rapidly down the west coast, the State of Perlis was overrun, then came the determined but unavailing stands at Jitra and Gurun, which sealed the fate of Kedah. Penang was evacuated and there was a withdrawal behind the Perak river. On the east coast Kelantan was abandoned and the struggle to hold the airfield of Central Malaya also failed.

The parched and exhausted British troops, bearing or assisting hundreds of sick and wounded, retreated. They fought back gamely, and, though units became intermingled, order and discipline prevailed. Machine-guns, mortars, rifles, bayonets and grenades took heavy toll of the enemy, but the Japanese sent in waves of fresh troops who came at them through the jungle, rubber estates and paddy fields.

When the enemy infiltrated into front, flanks or rear it became a hellish 'sauve qui peut' in which Scots, Australians and Indian bayonets drank deeply of Jap lifeblood. But it was sheer barbaric butchery in the sun when the enemy came upon wounded or took prisoners, and there were many heroic rescue sallies.

Disaster overtook the 2nd Argylls in the Slim River battle early in January. They were attacked by armour and infantry and, having no effective weapons against tanks, casualties were very heavy. Nevertheless large parties of survivors grouped together and, though famished, fever and dysentery-ridden, succeeded in threading their way through the enemy advance sometimes by stealth and on other occasions by force.

Kuantan and its airfield were abandoned, then Selangor, Negri Sembilan and Malacca. The Japanese continued their sweep down the west coast and defence was concentrated in Johore State; the outer bastion of Singapore Island. But the enemy put the remaining airfields in Johore out of action, the new defence line began to crumble before powerful thrusts, and a general withdrawal to Singapore was ordered.

After the Slim River shambles the 2nd Argylls, numbering less than 100 of all ranks, arrived on the 'Island' in mid-January. Here they received a welcome reinforcement of 200 Royal Marines from the *Prince of Wales* and *Repulse*. They blended well and the composite battalion soon became known unofficially, and semi-officially, as 'The Plymouth Argylls'.

The formation was also augmented by every sick or wounded Service-man who could walk out of hospital and use a rifle. At the close of the month the battalion was back on the mainland, holding the bridgehead and covering the withdrawal of the last troops across the mile-long Causeway from Johore to Singapore Island.

This operation was completed without loss and the Argylls marched over the Causeway in extended order led by their two surviving pipers in 'full blaw'. Minutes later the Causeway went up in a roaring explosion. During the first week in February the Japanese landed on the 'Island' and the Argylls went into action alongside their 'Aussie' comrades.

About two days later the companies were battling well in front of the British lines. Enemy tanks and infantry attacked in strength and for a time the Argylls were cut off and suffered very heavy losses. There were further casualties in a fighting cross-country withdrawal at first light but, within a few hours, the survivors were on the march to another threatened area. En route, however, an order was received to return to base camp.

Enemy air raids on refugee-packed Singapore increased, also artillery bombardments, and there were appalling casualties. Many of the streets were blocked with debris and parts of bodies protruded from the charred smoking rubble. The hospitals were overflowing, the vital water pipe-line was out of commission and food, petrol and medical supplies were running low. The morale of civilian labourers at the docks cracked under the strain and the Services took over. In mid-February General Gordon Bennett made the fateful decision to surrender.

Singapore was the St. Valery of the Far East, but the enthralling epic of the 2nd Argylls in Malaya kindled the fuse that was to explode the Japanese super-man myth. And even in the years of captivity they were not humbled and maintained their splendid esprit de corps and discipline. With unflinching courage and fortitude they endured inhuman treatment from a ruthless foe and even earned their grudging respect and admiration.

Tog suas an t-athainne! (Lift up the torch) was the cry from West Highland hearts. And it did not long go unanswered. On May 28, 1942, His Majesty King George VI ordered that the 15th Battalion stationed in Orkney be re-constituted as the 2nd Battalion. This formation proudly lifted up the torch and history chronicles how gallantly it was borne from the Normandy beachheads to the banks of the Elbe.

In July 1943, the 227th (Highland) Infantry Brigade – which included the 10th Highland Light Infantry, 2nd Gordon Highlanders and the re-constituted 2nd Argyll and Sutherland Highlanders – came under command of the 15th (Scottish) Division. A few weeks afterwards the brigade was integrated in the 'Scottish Lion' Division and entered upon a rigorous training progamme in Yorkshire.

In the spring of 1944 the 15th (Scottish) Division moved to a concentration zone in Sussex under the able leadership of Major-General G. H. A. MacMillan. From Southampton, Newhaven and the Port of London the division made the Channel crossing in mid-June, landing on the eastern beaches between 'Rodger' and 'Queen'.

On June 26 a thundering massed artillery barrage presaged the attack of the 15th (Scottish) Division to seize the strategic Odon bridges. The following day, in a downpour, the 227th (Highland) Infantry Brigade moved towards the river from the north of Cheux. According to humorists in the Argylls they were already in it! And others, in the Glasgow doric, commented 'Greenock wiz nivir like this!'

Cheux, a ruin and jam-packed with traffic, was populated by snipers but the battalion went through to its objective – Tourmauville Bridge – disposing of enemy opposition in Colleville after house to house skirmishing. It pushed on to Mondrainville and Tourville, where the Argylls again chased out the Germans, fought off several armoured cars and knocked out one or two tanks.

Three companies advanced on Tourmauville. One attacked and captured the Odon bridge intact and a small bridgehead was quickly established and a company was installed at Tourville. Thus the 2nd Argylls had carried the division's main objective; the assault and seizure of a bridge across the river for the passage of armour.

Reinforcements arrived and tanks went over to exploit the high ground beyond. Leaving the bridgehead the Argylls turned their attention to the two bridges at Gavrus. about a mile upstream. They were undamaged and unguarded and three companies dug in south of the river with H.Q. and one unit on the north bank.

Next day a sudden but not unexpected German counterattack came in against the three companies in the Gavrus bridgehead and for over five hours there was non-stop bitter confused fighting on the south bank, with the enemy artillery and mortars active throughout. To shorten the front the companies joined up in a wood dominating the bridges and the Germans, after taking a deal of punishment, drew off leaving the Argylls still in possession but with many casualties to be evacuated under mortaring.

Within twenty-four hours an even heavier assault was delivered. The companies in the wood and on the north bank were subjected to an intense artillery and mortar barrage. Casualties were again severe and most of the transport was destroyed. The Argylls were ordered to withdraw under cover of tanks.

The highly successful five day battle of the Odon was over. Until then the 15th (Scottish) Division was untried in World War II, but now it had undergone the supreme test and acquitted itself valiantly. The Scottish Lion had more than ruffled the feathers of the German Eagle!

In the Second Battle of the Odon, during the advance on Evrecy, the 2nd Argylls received a plastering from artillery and mortars while forming up in the Baron-Gourney area. They dug in hoping to retaliate but the attack was called off and the battalion dispatched to Tourmauville and Les Vilains before concentrating with the brigade at Le Mesnil Patry.

About a week later the division was suddenly switched west into the Caumont sector, a green and pleasant land which had suffered little from the blight of war. Then the silence of the 'bocage' was shattered by the snarling crackling roll of musketry, the chatter of machine-guns and the reverberating earth-shaking roar of artillery.

In the British offensive to break out from Caumont the 2nd Argylls advanced from the ridge after a concentrated aerial bombardment of the enemy positions. The battalion was soon subjected to artillery, mortar and machine-gun fire and, because of a chaotic pile-up of transport in the difficult terrain, the Argylls in attempting to by-pass Lutain Wood ran into an anti-personnel minefield near Le Bourg.

In the wake of tanks the Scots took a number of prisoners, cleared Les Loges and occupied the important Hill 226 feature. This brought down on the battalion a mortar barrage and later several German self-propelled guns suddenly emerged from a wood, came barging uphill and through the position to destroy about a dozen tanks. But this did not dislodge the Argylls.

The division was poised to break through in the direction of Lassy and established a firm base for the drive on Estry. From Mancelliere, on the southern slopes of Quarry Hill, the Argylls, mounted on tanks, drove to a bridge near La Caverie without encountering the enemy.

With tank support they attacked south, the objective being a hill overlooking Canteloup. The road was mined and though met by machine-gun fire and mortaring, dug-in tanks and self-propelled guns on the high ground the Argylls succeeded in clearing most of the near side of Hill 208 and consolidated within a few hundred yards of the top.

A dawn attempt to clear the Germans off the crest failed and there were heavy losses. For two days the depleted Argylls held their fire-swept precarious positions until brought down to seal a gap between two units on the road between La Caverie and Estry. After stubborn resistance the enemy pulled out of Estry in mid-August.

The 'Scottish Lion' Division, operating across difficult country, had broken though the German defence line south of Caumont, rolled back powerful counter-attacks and opened the way for the armoured divisions. Soon the Scots were threading their way among the wrecked transport and burnt-out tanks which littered the Falaise 'killing ground'. The push was on to reach the Seine.

The 227th (Highland) Infantry Brigade assaulted the centre

of the Seine 'loop' at St. Pierre du Vauvray, with the 2nd Argylls in reserve. The battalion took up positions across the 'loop' between Le Mesnil Ande and Ande.

The brigade cleared out the enemy and enlarged the bridge-head, encountering only scattered resistance. The Argylls occupied some high ground dominated by a château and had exchanges of fire with the Germans on the reverse slopes. The bridgehead secured, the armour began to cross.

The great advance into Belgium began. On September 2 the battalion made a dramatic 120-mile dash on carriers and took over the Somme crossings at Bernaville two days later. The Argylls moved on to St. Pol where it awaited the arrival of the brigade. On coming up the 227th passed through Lille, Tourcoing and Rubaix to cross the frontier at Moscrun and from the Kerkhove-Bossuyt area it pushed on to just south of Ghent.

In the rapid pursuit-advance the 15th (Scottish) Division accounted for several hundred prisoners. Riding on tanks the Argylls entered the Gheel bridgehead but, on finding the important road bridge at Donck had been blown, the battalion dug in. The Germans flooded an adjoining sector and their artillery, mortars and machine-guns made a shambles of attempts to cross by other units.

The 227th took over positions between the Gheel-Rethy and Gheel-Turnhout roads and effected the relief of two battalions in the Aart bridgehead, north of Gheel. The Argylls got across unscathed in assault craft to join up with the sadly depleted 44th Brigade.

Though frequently pounded by the vengeful German guns the Aart bridgehead on the Junction Canal was extended though at considerable sacrifice. The enemy having lost the initiative began a general withdrawal and the division crossed the Wilhelmina Canal.

The Germans maintained their hold on Best and a move to by-pass the town was initiated. The 227th Brigade attacked over thick scrub towards Liemde Woods meeting light opposition and taking scores of prisoners. On entering the woods, however, casualties began to mount, particularly among the Argylls.

Meanwhile the enemy had conceded Best and the 15th reached the line of the River Dommel. The division was soon casting its net for Tilburg. Booby-traps, mines and demolitions delayed the brigade's advance to Moergestel and as the division neared Tilburg the noise which greeted it was not the thunder of guns and the rattle of automatic weapons but the din of revelry. The German Eagle was again in flight.

By the end of the month the brigade was located at Asten now menaced by a powerful enemy attack against the American 'front'. The 227th was ordered southwards towards Meijel and the 2nd Argylls straddled the road to Heusden.

The Germans occupying the opposite bank of the Deurne Canal rained artillery and mortar fire into the division at the approaches to Meijel. The country was a problem – flat boggy marshland intersected by ditches and all the roads, tracks and pull-ins liberally planted with mines. And to complicate matters St. Swithin had taken over weather duties. He sent rain, more rain and still more rain and this bleak cheerless desolation became a misty squelching morass.

Fighting reminiscent of Normandy developed as the German infantry broke cover and came on with tanks and self-propelled guns. They collided head-on with the 15th (Scottish) Division – and recoiled. The 227th Brigade in a defensive role south-east of Heusden blocked several infiltration attempts through the trees.

Two companies, with tank support, cleared the woods. The armour found the going almost impossible and when the infantry turned to come back the enemy followed up. One unit fought a spirited rearguard action which kept the Germans at bay. While in the sodden quagmire that was Ospel the battalion came under heavy shelling.

In mid-November the Germans withdrew from the battered ruins of Meijel and the battalion took over guard of the bridge at Roggelsche from the 51st (Highland) Division. In the advance to the Maas the 15th (Scottish) Division cleared the area around Helenaveen and Sevenum.

At night the sky reflected the red fiery glare of burning farms and villages as the Germans applied scorched earth tactics during their retreat. A dejected stream of refugees laden with what goods and chattels they could carry trudged wearily through the rain and at times there was complete traffic chaos.

Along roads melting into mud, past brimming shell craters and over the remains of blown bridges went the Scots in the push for the Maas, encountering, at times, stubborn resistance from enemy 'pockets'. On reaching the line of the river the division settled down to a seven week's mid-winter vigil along twenty miles of the bank.

The 15th was launched against the well-defended bastions at the northern end of the Siegfried Line on February 8, 1945. Powerful support was forthcoming from artillery, tanks and bomber aircraft and the men of the 'Scottish Lion' Division over-ran their objectives after overcoming determined opposition.

From Hoogeshof the 2nd Argylls led the brigade attack into a withering fire and battled forward to reach the Dutch-German frontier. Then the tide of war thundered into the Third Reich. A company seized Elsenhof and Hettsteeghof and sent back close on 100 prisoners. This unit also captured a battery of 88 mm. guns.

The Argylls continued their pressure into mounting resistance and furious mortaring, particularly around Kranenburg Station. There was desperate house-to-house fighting in the northern part of Galgensteeg, a 'spur' of the Frasselt defences. The battalion carried objectives extending from the northern area of Bucholt to Bremershof. Over 200 prisoners were taken and within 48 hours the 2nd Argylls entered Goch.

The intricate formidable German defence system at Frasselt, Nutterden, Donsbreuggen, Materborn, Goch, Cleve and in the Reichswald had been pulverised. The claws of the Scottish Lion had rent the Siegfried Line. And there are those who claim that 'Scotland's Army' – the 15th (Scottish) Division, the 51st (Highland) Division and the 52nd (Lowland) Division – won the war when it crossed the Rhine. They gave dissenters short shrift.

The dramatic assault-crossing of the Rhine in amphibious carriers on March 24 was an all-Scottish operation. The near bank was held by the 52nd (Lowland) Division, while attacking formations were the 15th (Scottish) Division and the 51st (Highland) Division.

Over 700 guns of the divisional artillery group sounded an ear-splitting 'fanfare' half an hour from midnight on March 23. Additional fireworks were provided by the ack-ack batteries and anti-tank and machine-gun tracer. Comparatively the enemy reply was a faint mutter scarcely heard amid the crashing, reverberating pulsing roar of the Scottish guns.

As the vivid flickering flashes and streaks variegated the waters of the Rhine the 'Jocks' of the assault brigades preparing to shove off shielded their eyes or turned away and there were some choice comments: 'Ma Goad, Wullie, it's better than the Blackpool Illuminations!'

The 15th Division's crossing was led by the tough battle-hardened 44th and 227th brigades. Things went well for the 44th but the 227th had to fight a succession of sharp costly actions.

Several carriers could not land at the eastern tip of an inlet and the troops clambered ashore on the west side. One company had to march a mile round the inlet to put in its attack on Hübsch and on arriving was hotly engaged by paratroops. Another company came up and Hübsch was mopped-up but casualties were high.

Two other units headed north and after a hard fight the enemy was ejected from Hoverhof. A company lying to the east beat back a counter-attack and the units in Hübsch came under heavy fire from the Germans in Lohr.

The attack on Lohr had to go in across open fields without artillery support as an airborne 'op' was imminent. One company cleared the bund (or weather dyke) after bitter fighting. Another unit assaulted Lohr but was pinned down in some houses a few hundred yards short of the objective.

Enemy resistance began to crumble and their paratroops were observed withdrawing in the direction of Haffen. A number surrendered in Lohr along with a detachment of women snipers.

In a bid to capture the vital bridge over the Bellinghoven Meer the Argylls marched several miles eastwards round the southern end of the Lange Renne. In the rapid advance through wooded country interspersed with defences enemy reaction was quickly overcome.

The bridge was secured 'on the double' but it was so badly damaged that it could not take wheeled traffic, and the vehicles of the Argylls had to re-join their units by the circuitous route south of the Lange Renne. The Argylls were on the alert at Kapenhof, about a mile to the north-east, and when the Germans attempted a night attack they were chased back into the woods.

Within a few days the Scots swept through the Wittenhorst Woods and reached the lateral road, where they dug in, without contacting the enemy. The Battle of the Rhine won, the victorious advance into the heart of Germany was soon under way.

Coming out of the Rhine bridgehead early in April the division began its rapid push to the Elbe, passing north of Minden to enter Celle and cross the Aller. The 227th (Highland) Infantry Brigade, moving up from Ibbenburen, advanced on Celle through Neustadt, Mellendorf and Fuhrberg. Progress was slow because of blown bridges, cratered roads, enemy resistance and the trudging columns of displaced persons who ignored stay put orders and left their camps as soon as the Germans withdrew.

The brigade led the division towards Uelzen and, to by-pass demolitions and other trouble-spots, a detour was made through the woods and the formation came back on to the main road at Eschede, some ten miles out of Celle. Craters, S.P. guns and small arms fire necessitated another diversion and the brigade, mounted on tanks, raced in darkness along a track through the dense woods hoping to surprise the enemy.

The column raced through a string of villages shooting up enemy military traffic on the way but on approaching Holdenstedt, two miles from Uelzen, there was a burst of fire. Many of the vehicles were destroyed or damaged and German infantry began infiltrating from the woods. The 2nd Argylls skirmished forward to clear the wood on the right flank.

It was obvious that the enemy was making a stand around Uelzen in order to gain time for the preparation of a defence line on the Elbe. After the town fell the 227th Brigade headed by the Argylls, entered on the last lap of the advance to the river, via Hittbergen.

The 15th (Scottish) Division's long fighting trek from the shell-pitted beaches of Normandy across France, through Belgium, Holland, into Germany and across the Rhine was nearing an end. But the knock-out 'punch' had still to be delivered on the reeling German Colossus.

The division spearheaded the assault of the 8th Corps across the Elbe in the Lauenburg area and in the breakout north-eastwards from the bridgehead to take Lübeck. The massed artillery began a deafening bombardment at midnight on April 28 and at 1 a.m. next day the Gunners made it 'same again'.

About 3.30 the 2nd Argylls 'shoved off'. The crossing was successfully accomplished but while forming up three companies were blasted by long-range fire. Recovering quickly they took over bridgehead duties and later entered Grünhof.

At the end of the day the 15th held a solid bridgehead from the Elbe-Trave Canal at Basedow to Tesperhude. The battalion headed north towards the Sachsenwald, where suicide 'pockets' were still holding out, and at Bornsen there was a brisk engagement with Marine cadets manning flak guns. When things became sticky there was a flutter of white handkerchiefs from the Germans and the Scots trooped into Bornsen.

Early in May the division moved from near Hamburg to Lübeck, the 227th Brigade establishing itself around Ahrensburg. Contact had been made with the Russian Army on the Baltic and the Wehrmacht was 'kaput'. Dejected shuffling German troops milled around among thousands of homeless refugees and displaced persons fleeing before the Russian advance. No more goose-stepping – the goose was cooked!

Hostilities ceased on the morning of May 5. The German forces in North-West Europe laid down their arms in unconditional surrender. At the beginning of July the 15th (Scottish) Division handed over to the Russians and withdrew behind the demarcation line agreed at the Yalta Conference.

As in the 1914-18 conflict the great warrior traditions of the Highland clans and their septs were again nobly upheld in World War II by the twentieth century Argyll and Sutherland Highlanders. This was proven in the long list of battle honours awarded to the Regiment:

Somme 1940, ODON, Tourmauville Bridge, Caen, Esquay, Mont Pincon, Quarry Hill, Estry, Falaise, Dives Crossing, Aart, Lower Maas, Meijel, Venlo Pocket, Ourthe, Rhineland, Reichswald, RHINE, Uelzen, Artlenberg, North-West Europe 1940, '44-45, Abyssinia 1941, SIDI BARRANI, EL ALAMEIN, Medenine, AKARIT, Djebel Azzag 1942, Kef Ouiba Pass, Mine de Sedjenane, Medjez Plain, LONGSTOP HILL 1943, North Africa 1940-43, Landing in Sicily, Gerbini, Adrano, Centuripe, Sicily 1943, Termoli, Sangro, Cassino II, Liri Valley, Aquino, Monte Casalino, Monte Spaduro, Monte Grande, Senio, Santerno Crossing, Argenta Gap, ITALY 1943-45, CRETE, Heraklion, Middle East 1941, North Malaya, GRIK ROAD, Central Malaya, Ipoh,

Slim River, Singapore Island, MALAYA 1941-42. (The ten printed in capitals appear on the Queen's Colour.)

In a few months the wind of change blew strongly and there were many comings and goings. The 2nd Argylls were among the goings, leaving the 15th (Scottish) Division to join the 51st (Highland) Division. After serving a year in the Rhine Army the 2nd returned to the U.K. in December, 1946.

On the 'pruning' of all Regular Army infantry regiments (except the Guards) to one battalion strength in 1947 the 1st Argylls survived. The 2nd went into 'suspended animation' early that year and a cadre was absorbed by the 1st.

The 1st Battalion The Argyll and Sutherland Highlanders arrived in Hong Kong in June 1949. A year later the Korean War broke out and the Argylls were the first British troops to enter the combat zone where they assisted the South Koreans against invasion from the Communist-dominated North.

Landing at Pusan towards the close of August 1950, they found the Americans desperately holding the Naktong perimeter and the Scots were committed to battle in this area. With the 1st Middlesex Regiment the 1st Argylls formed the British Brigade which early distinguished itself in defensive fighting under U.S. command.

The principal engagement of the battalion came on September 23 when two companies carried out a surprise attack at dawn on a feature mapped as Hill 81. They got onto the ridge and consolidated. The North Korean guns pounded the hilltop and there were numerous casualties.

When the expected enemy counter-attack materialised in great strength artillery support was suddenly withdrawn. Enemy shelling and mortaring mounted in fury and groups of North Koreans began infiltrating. Casualties were being evacuated and ammunition was running low. The situation was becoming critical and Major Kenneth Muir began 'circulating' among his Argylls in the forward positions inspiring and encouraging them.

An air-strike was requested and recognition strips were laid out, but by a tragic error the American aircraft dropped napalm bombs on the two depleted, hard-pressed companies and raked them with their machine-guns. Fire enveloped the crest of the hill, destroyed the reserve 'ammo' and forced the Argylls temporarily below the ridge bearing their wounded.

In a courageous attempt to 'get through' to the American bombers Major Muir stood up in the midst of the inferno and frantically waved a recognition strip, but his gallantry was in vain. He immediately set about reorganising the survivors while stretcher-bearers carried away the scores of wounded. He was left with a fighting strength of less than fifty and ammunition was down to a few rounds per man.

Under fire, Major Muir led the Argylls back to the crest of the smoke-shrouded flame-enveloped hill and they held it for another half hour though their number steadily lessened. He moved about rallying the remnants of his two companies in full view of the advancing North Koreans. Major Muir then got down behind a 2-inch mortar and planted bombs among them until he was mortally wounded by bursts of automatic fire.

But a few Argylls succeeded in fighting their way out of encirclement and the story of Kenneth Muir and The Thin Khaki Line became known. A posthumous Victoria Cross was later awarded; the first V.C. bestowed for valour in Korea had been won by an Argyll. Nor was there any rancour shown towards the Americans. Theirs was the philosophy of soldiers – 'just one of those things'.

This action reduced the battalion to two rifle companies but they remained fully operational. The 1st Argylls – operating in the Commonwealth Brigade – participated in several spirited engagements during the rapid advance northwards to Taechon, within twelve miles of the Manchurian mountains.

The Korean War seemed to be drawing to a close but the entire situation changed overnight when Communist China poured masses of well-equipped seasoned troops into the conflict. Then the United Nations forces had to embark on a fighting withdrawal to the south of the peninsula.

In February 1951, when the snow had disappeared, the initiative was regained and a slow advance began through the mountains. The 1st Argylls fought their final action in this campaign on April 8 and a fortnight later, on being relieved, the battalion embarked at Inchon bound for Hong Kong. In August 1952, they sailed for home. And Pakchon, Korea 1950-51 appeared among their battle honours. They are borne on the Queen's Colour.

Between 1953 and 1959 the Argylls were employed on 'fire brigade' duties at several tension flashpoints. The battalion was rushed out to British Guiana in the late autumn of 1953 to maintain order during a period of political unrest, but as a result of firm tactful handling the situation soon improved and the Argylls sailed for home towards the close of 1954. Early in 1955 the battalion joined the Berlin garrison and returned to the U.K. in February 1956.

When President Nasser of Egypt arbitrarily seized the Suez Canal in November 1956, an Anglo-French expedition was sent to regain control of the strategic canal, the 1st Argylls forming part of the 19th Brigade. This brigade arrived at Port Said in mid-November to secure the town, but as airborne troops had already landed, completed their task and withdrawn, the Argylls experienced little action and no casualties. They were on the way home a few days before Christmas.

By the end of 1957 Cyprus was aflame with terrorism and sabotage and from early 1958 until the autumn of 1959 the Argylls were engaged on an internal security role. They operated in the towns, villages and mountains, set up road blocks, cordoned off areas for searches for wanted men and supplies of arms, and provided guards on Government buildings and escorts for convoys passing through danger zones.

They experienced 'Murder Mile' in Nicosia and throughout their service in 'Trouble Island' showed admirable tact and restraint despite great provocation. The battalion earned high praise – even from the warring Greek and Turkish Cypriots.

The Argylls were back in Scotland in mid-October 1959, and a few weeks later joined the 20th Brigade at Lemgo, Germany. The next homecoming was in the late autumn of 1962.

In mid-February 1964, the 1st Argylls were air-lifted from Turnhouse to Singapore after being expertly coached in jungle-craft by a formation of the 1/6 Queen Elizabeth's Own Gurkha Rifles. The Scottish Highlanders and Indian Highlanders played extremely rough games in the dense plantations of the Forestry Commission in Argyllshire and Stirlingshire.

It was a battle of wits and endurance in near Arctic weather conditions with the Argylls winkling out Gurkha 'terrorists' from their cunningly contrived hide-outs. And not infrequently the stalkers found themselves stalked and the ambushers ambushed!

The Argylls were apt pupils and the Gurkhas excellent instructors in the un-gentle art of jungle combat. And who better than the 1/6 with a record of 'kills' to their credit in the twelve years campaign against the Communist guerillas in Malaya.

The 'Jocks' and 'Johnnies' were the friendliest of enemies as they trooped cookhouse-wards in the evening, but the best summing-up came from the Argylls. 'It wuz wurse than a Rangers and Celtic gemme on Ne'erday, so it wuz!'

In the confrontation campaign launched by Indonesia against Malaysia, then in the birth-pangs of nationhood, the Argylls began 'driving the jungle' in North Borneo. The 1,000-mile border and much of the interior was interspersed with foul-smelling mangrove swamps, rushing torrents, treacherous, swirling winding rivers and a complex of stagnant backwaters and creeks. Such maps as existed could not be relied on and large regions were virtually unexplored.

Detachments hacked their way through the dense, green, rearing walls of foliage and clinging prickly tangled undergrowth when on patrol, in taking up ambush positions and in moving observation posts. Clothes and equipment, often sodden, from the torrential monsoon rains and immersion in water, decayed and rotted on their sweating bodies in the dry parching heat during operations in the eerie, shadowy-half-light.

Tracks were avoided as they may have been rigged with booby-traps or led to a sudden ambush. There was the squawk and flutter of birds, the whir and drone of myriads of insects and the occasional dart of a disturbed animal or reptile.

Native trackers scanned the 'floor' night and day for traces of enemy infiltrators and each soldier was tensed for instant action. An unusual sound or movement and at a signal the patrol would 'freeze' or melt quickly and silently into the jungle, weapons ready to engage.

Early in August it was announced that a band of Indonesian infiltrators had attacked a security post at Pa Lungan, a few miles from the Eastern Sarawak border, with small arms and mortar fire. The defenders drove them off and in the follow-up operation a detachment of Argylls overtook the raiding party and in a running fight killed five of them.

In May 1965, there were further clashes west of Kuching. In a pursuit the Scots sent down several Indonesian regulars and the remainder scattered over the border. The wild men of Borneo will long remember the Argylls – many have scars for souvenirs!

The battalion was flown into Glasgow Airport in mid-October 1966. On June 21, 1967, the Argylls moved from Plymouth to Gatwick where they were air-lifted out to strife-torn Aden. They were immediately deployed in an internal security role after the disastrous Arab six-day war with Israel.

Within a few days the battalion was making front-page news. At first light on July 4 the Adenis in the Crater district awoke to the skirl of pipes. This area had been in rebel hands for 13 days following a mutiny by South Arabian forces and police, and an ambush in which 12 Northumberland Fusiliers were killed.

From the rooftop of their three-storey H.Q. in the Aden Commercial Institute – dubbed 'Stirling Castle' by the Argylls – their pipers and drummers gave spirited renderings of 'Scotland The Brave' and 'The Barren Rocks o' Aden'. The three-pronged drive into the labyrinth of narrow alleys was supported by armoured cars of the 3rd Dragoon Guards and ended with the Police H.Q. being occupied. The Highlanders promptly re-named it 'Dumbarton Castle'.

In advancing into the southern part of the Crater the Argylls set up a chain of 'checks' and barbed wire and sandbagged gun positions. 'Recce' patrols had slipped in on the preceding five nights and selected these vantage points undetected by the Adenis.

This well-planned operation which ended the 'siege' was carried out quickly, effectively and without bloodshed except for the shooting of three Arab dissidents. While on duty in the Crater patrols, detachments and posts from time to time came under bazooka and grenade attacks and rifle fire, but marksmen of the battalion proved more than a match for these hit-and-run raiders. The English Bulldog had growled – but the Scottish Lion could bite!

On November 16, 1967, the Southern Yemen People's Republic was 'born' and 128 years of British rule ended. After having controlled for 145 days all movement in the Crater, cockpit of the warring factions, the 1st Argylls lowered the regimental flag and the pipe-major played 'The Barren Rocks o' Aden'.

Then the battalion marched out with its traditional elan and gallant bearing as units of the South Arabian Army took over the vacated positions. The Argylls were air-lifted to Lyneham, Wiltshire, the first groups arriving on November 27.

'The ethos of the modern army is the development of a much more high-powered soldier. You want chaps who are absolutely first-class fighting animals – self-controlled, disciplined James Bonds. They have got to be like greyhounds and they have to be as tough as nails – take anything. And one of them should be able to do the job that you now need 30 men to do.'

These were the comments of Lieutenant-Colonel Colin Campbell Mitchell, who commanded the battalion in Aden. And there is little doubt that his battling Argylls inspired them. Thus did a fighting Highland infantry colonel compliment his *saighdearan* (soldiers).

But early in July 1968, there was anti-climax. A Defence White Paper decreed that the 1st Argylls would disband by September 1972. So the 'fiery cross' in the form of a nation-wide 'Save the Argylls' campaign to obtain 1,000,000 signatures was soon under way.

With the battalion it was business as usual. In mid-September it was flown from Fairford, Gloucestershire, to Cyprus to take part in a month's troop movement exercises, including air mobility and infantry training.

The Argylls were air-lifted from Luton and Lyneham to Berlin in mid-April 1969. They patrolled round the Communist barriers encircling West Berlin and guarded Allied military trains moving through East Germany. They also provided guards for Spandau Prison where Rudolf Hess was incarcerated.

Despite the gloomy predictions of Jeremiahs and other prophets of doom, Scotland still campaigned for the retention of the Argylls and Harry Lauder's classic 'Keep Right on to the End of the Road' took on a new significance. Within a few months well over 1,000,000 names were appended to the 'Save the Argylls' petition.

It was dispatched from Stirling, 'home' of the regular battalion, to London by rail under strict security guard. On arrival the boxes containing the pages of signatures were conveyed to the House of Commons in an armoured van. The promoters may have feared the attention of hi-jackers for the boxes were whisky cartons! But the Ministry of Defence was adamant.

On June 19, 1970, the day after the General Election, there was another 'disbandment'. The electorate had 'sacked' the Labour Government, thus confounding the pollsters and Press pundits – and ruining Harold Wilson's reputation as a performer of miracles!

Powerful influences were at work on the battalion's behalf as the Conservatives were known to favour its retention. Soon speculation was rife and hope sprang anew. Advance parties of the 1st Argylls were then preparing for the return flight from Germany and the remainder was scheduled to follow, duly arriving at Lossiemouth and Glasgow in mid-July.

On returning from leave the Argylls assembled at Fort George. There, in early August, the battalion was informed that it had been 'reprieved'. Naturally this was received with mixed feelings. For the 'Thin Red Line' was to become much thinner – reduced to company strength.

There were some who considered it was a betrayal by the Whitehall warriors of the 'Chairborne Division', but most accepted the decision with a measure of relief and a degree of thankfulness. It had been a 'lang sair fecht' to save the battalion, but the Argylls were to soldier on – and that was preferable to disbandment.

At the end of October Lord Balneil, Minister of State for Defence, announced in the House of Commons that he looked forward to the day when recruitment in the Scottish Division would mean that the Argylls could once again be a full major unit.

An Opposition question about what possible role one company of the Argylls might play brought the reply from the Minister that it could be an air portable company.

In the autumn the 1st Argylls furnished the Royal Guard at Balmoral. The gleam in the eyes of the vigilant *saighdearan* matched the flash of their weapons and accoutrements. No doubt this was observed by Her Majesty The Queen, their Colonel-in-Chief, and by other members of the Royal Family. Possibly they too were 'rootin'' for the Argylls.

The Army Board in early December approved new titles for the infantry units previously faced with amalgamation or disbandment and were to soldier on as companies. The Argylls were appropriately designated the 1st Battalion The Argyll and Sutherland Highlanders (Princess Louise's) Balaclava Company.

Several days later the break-up of the battalion at Fort George was announced and it was scaled down to company strength. Drafts of soldiers left to join various Scottish regiments, with the proviso that they would be recalled to the Argylls should battalion status be authorised at some future date. Those who had completed their engagement were demobbed.

Officers posted to other corps wear the Argyll mess kit and similarly other ranks are still designated Argylls. So Argyll and Sutherland Highlanders will 'walk tall' wherever they serve.

In keeping with regimental tradition the Commanding Officer, Lieutenant-Colonel Sandy Boswell, shook hands with every departing man and, as the new establishment did not provide for an officer of his rank, he handed over command to Major Ian Purves Hume with Captain David Thomas as 2 i/c. Lieutenant-Colonel Boswell had by then been appointed to a post at Army Strategic Command, Wilton.

January 20, 1971, will go down in the saga of the regiment as a 'day of hope'. These were the inspiring words of Her Majesty The Queen when the 120 men of the Balaclava Company paraded before her on the esplanade at Stirling Castle, ancestral 'home' of the Argylls. Her words were drowned in the cheers of the resplendant *saighdearan*, former soldiers of the regiment and a large assembly of their guests.

At this, the first public appearance of the Balaclava Company, their Royal Colonel-in-Chief since 1947, emphasised that 'a new chapter is now opening in the Argylls history. Whatever regrets must still remain for those who have left the battalion let there be no doubt that this day is one of hope. The battalion lives on in the Balaclava Company.

'To those who have left, some for service in other battalions of the Scottish Division and some for civilian life, I would like to say you have served your country and your regiment with unswerving loyalty and cheerful efficiency and, wherever you go, my thanks and my best wishes for the future go with you.'

Her Majesty continued : 'To those who remain to serve in the Balaclava Company under the Colours I presented to the battalion in 1953, I say the task of preserving the high standards and honourable traditions of The Argyll and Sutherland Highlanders is now yours.

'I have been impressed by what I have seen of your smartness and steadiness and I am confident that the reputation of the regiment is safe in your hands. I wish you all possible good fortune.'

Her Majesty, her Argyll and Sutherland Highlanders brooch sparkling, passed down the ranks and had encouraging words for fresh-faced recruits and bemedalled veterans. The pipes skirled the regimental marches 'Highland Laddie' and 'The Campbells Are Coming' and these stirring airs resounded and echoed over the Castle battlements.

Her Majesty lunched at the headquarters mess in Stirling Castle before attending the parade and inspection of the formation, which was headed by the Argylls 20-year-old Shetland pony mascot, Cruachan II.

The Balaclava Company later entrained for Barnard Castle, in the Catterick Camp area. And appropriately enough the engine pulling the train was 'The Argyll and Sutherland Highlander'.

On arrival they joined 24 Airportable Brigade as part of Strategic Command, liable for service in any part of the world as 'trouble shooters'. In May 1971, The Balaclava Company received its first overseas posting; a six months tour of duty on 'The Rock', sun-drenched Gibraltar.

ACKNOWLEDGEMENTS

Public Relations, Ministry of Defence, Whitehall, London.

Imperial War Museum, Lambeth, London.

Regimental Headquarters and Museum, The Black Watch (Royal Highland Regiment), Balhousie Castle, Perth.

Regimental Headquarters, The Queen's Own Highlanders (Seaforth and Camerons), Cameron Barracks, Inverness, and Museums of The Queen's Own Highlanders, The Seaforth Highlanders (Ross-shire Buffs, Duke of Albany's), and The Queen's Own Cameron Highlanders, Fort George, Inverness-shire.

Regimental Headquarters and Museum, The Gordon Highlanders, St. Luke's, Viewfield Road, Aberdeen.

Regimental Headquarters and Museum, The Argyll and Sutherland Highlanders (Princess Louise's), The Castle, Stirling.